❧ Questioning Traditi

Language, and Myth

Michael R. Molino

❦ Questioning Tradition, Language, and Myth

The Poetry of Seamus Heaney

The Catholic University of America Press

Washington, D.C.

The paper used in this publication meets the minimum requirements of
American National Standards for Information Science—Permanence of Paper
for Printed Library materials, ANSI Z39.48-1984.
∞

Library of Congress Cataloging-in-Publication Data
Molino, Michael R., 1956-
  Questioning tradition, language, and myth : the poetry of Seamus
Heaney / by Michael R. Molino.
    p.   cm.
  Includes bibliographical references and index.
  1. Heaney, Seamus—Criticism and interpretation.   2. Ireland—In
literature.   I. Title.
  PR6058.E2Z77   1994
  821'.914—dc20
  93-42712
  ISBN 0-8132-0796-7
  ISBN 0-8132-0797-5 (pbk.)

For Mary

❧ Contents

❧ Acknowledgments

I consider literary criticism a form of interpretation that presents a particular reading of a text or series of texts and in so doing then establishes a context in which further interpretations are possible. With that view, I hope this study provides readings that expand our current understanding and appreciation of Seamus Heaney's poetry and encourages further and alternative studies in the future. So too, I owe a debt to those critics whose work precedes mine, providing critical practices and interpretations that inform my own and establishing critical contexts upon which this study depends. Many of these critics are given voice in the following pages, while others appear in notes and references. My thanks are extended to all.

There are others, though, whose presence is less obvious—teachers of mine, for instance, whose influences I alone observe and thus wish acknowledged. First and not the least of these is the late Joseph Bentley, in whose intellectual debt I and many others no doubt remain. I would also like to thank the graduate English faculty at Marquette University for their assistance and encouragement in matters scholarly and otherwise over the years—particularly Edward Duffy, Michael Patrick Gillespie, and John Boly. My family and friends should be recognized, too, because they had to listen to me discuss, and at times lament, this project over the last few years. My wife, Mary Bogumil, to whom this book is dedicated, exhorted me along the way, proofread material, and stayed with me in spirit during the long, solitary hours of writing.

Others provided assistance in various ways. The interlibrary loan department at Iowa State University deserves my sincere thanks for hunting down many sources for me, at times with limited bibliographical information, and bringing a little bit of Ireland to the middle of Iowa—no small feat. Moreover, Dale Ross,

x   Acknowledgments

chair of the English department at ISU, thank you for a teaching schedule that made this book possible, truly. Christina Hunt Mahony, Richard Peterson, Janel Mueller, Maureen Callahan, and several readers at *Modern Philology* provided valuable editorial suggestions along the way. They spoke, I listened, and sometimes I even acted. Finally, I must recognize the people at the Catholic University of America Press who assisted me with their advice, patience, and time: David McGonagle, Susan Needham, and Liliane McCarthy. Any errors that appear in these pages after such help is undoubtedly my responsibility.

Chapter 3 of this book appeared in a slightly abbreviated and modified form under the title "Flying by the Nets of Language and Nationality: Seamus Heaney, the 'English' Language, and Ulster's Troubles" in *Modern Philology* 91 (Nov. 1993), 180–201, and appears by permission of the publisher, © 1994 by the University of Chicago. All rights reserved. Reprinted by permission of Farrar, Straus & Giroux, Inc.: Excerpts from *Poems 1965–1975* by Seamus Heaney. Copyright © 1980 by Seamus Heaney. Excerpts from *Field Work* by Seamus Heaney. Copyright © 1976, 1979 by Seamus Heaney. Excerpts from *Station Island* by Seamus Heaney. Copyright © 1985 by Seamus Heaney. Excerpts from *The Haw Lantern* by Seamus Heaney. Copyright © 1987 by Seamus Heaney. Excerpts from *Seeing Things* by Seamus Heaney. Copyright © 1991 by Seamus Heaney. Excerpts from *Preoccupations* by Seamus Heaney. Copyright © 1980 by Seamus Heaney. Excerpts from *The Government of the Tongue 1978–1987* by Seamus Heaney. Copyright © 1989 by Seamus Heaney. Excerpts from *The Cure at Troy* by Seamus Heaney. Copyright © 1991 by Seamus Heaney. Excerpts reprinted by permission of Faber and Faber, Ltd.: *Death of a Naturalist* © 1966, *Door into the Dark* © 1969, *Wintering Out* © 1972, *North* © 1975, *Field Work* © 1979, *Station Island* © 1984, *The Haw Lantern* © 1987, *Seeing Things* © 1991, *Preoccupations* © 1980, *The Government of the Tongue 1978–1987* © 1988, and *The Cure at Troy* © 1990.

❦ Abbreviations for Commonly Cited Works by Heaney

Death of a Naturalist	(DN)
Door into the Dark	(DD)
Wintering Out	(WO)
North	(N)
Field Work	(FW)
"Open Letter"	(OL)
Sweeney Astray	(SA)
Station Island	(SI)
Haw Lantern	(HL)
Seeing Things	(ST)
The Cure at Troy	(CT)
Preoccupations	(P)
The Government of the Tongue	(GT)

❧ Questioning Tradition,

Language, and Myth

1 🎋 A Question of Tradition

> A writer who cares who he is and where he comes from looks
> about him and begins by examining his colleagues. In that very
> act a writer in Ireland must make a basic choice: do I include
> writers in Irish among my colleagues? Or am I to write them
> off as a minor and embattled group, keeping loyal—for the
> best of reasons—to a dead or dying language? Some of the best
> writers in Irish already believe that their language is doomed, re-
> jected by its people. They are pessimistic, but my instinct tells me
> they are right. So I turn only toward those who are writing in En-
> glish. And, to speak only of the poets, the word "colleague" fades
> on the lips before the reality: a scattering of incoherent lives. It
> will seem on a bad day that they are a few madmen and hermits,
> and nothing more. I can learn nothing from them except that I
> am isolated.
>
> So I begin again, and look for the past in myself.
>
> — *Thomas Kinsella, "The Irish Writer"*

It seems fair to conclude from the quotation above that
Thomas Kinsella is a writer in turmoil, a writer who seeks, even
longs for, a coherent tradition in which he can locate himself. The
question is one of tradition and identity. Kinsella describes the
Irish writer's challenge to find a group with whom he or she can
detect a sense of comradeship or like-mindedness. When Kinsella
cannot find such a group, he "look[s] for the past in [himself]."
For Kinsella, the past persists and finds articulation through the
individual writer while the individual writer explores the past
through his or her work. J. C. C. Mays takes Kinsella's point a step
further when he states that the Irish writer inevitably must first
stake out "critical principles" toward and establish a relationship
with "the traditions he inherits or is aware of." According to Mays,
this first step entangles the writer "in predicaments of national

and personal identity."[1] However, staking out critical principles and establishing a relationship to traditions is not an easy task for the Irish writer. Mays uses the term *traditions* because the Irish writer does not inherit a continuous and unified cultural or literary heritage—though there have been attempts in the past, by groups such as the Revivalists, to create one. Instead, the Irish writer, as Kinsella has said elsewhere, "is the inheritor of a gapped, discontinuous, polyglot tradition."[2] Along the same lines, Thomas Flanagan asks, where "could [an Irish] writer look for a tradition; what assumptions could he take to be common to his society; how, indeed, could he be sure that Ireland boasted a society in the ordinary sense of the term? For Ireland was . . . many nations, having little in common and holding but a slight discourse with each other."[3] The inheritor of such discontinuous and disparate traditions faces the problem, not only of audience (For whom does one write?), but of identity, for the writer's identity, insofar as it is influenced and molded by the inherited traditions, will be equally fragmented. It is at this point that my study begins.

My focus is Seamus Heaney's excavation of, interaction with, separation from, alteration of, and responsibility toward the complex and, at times, contradictory traditions he finds himself a part of. Key to the poetry of Heaney is the question of tradition, but that question is tied to two other questions—that of language and that of myth. Collectively, the topics of tradition, language, and

1. J. C. C. Mays, "Mythologized Presences: *Murphy* in its Time," in *Myth and Reality in Irish Literature*, ed. Joseph Ronsley (Ontario: Wilfrid Laurier UP, 1977) 202.

2. Thomas Kinsella, "The Divided Mind," in *Irish Poets in English*, ed. Sean Lucy (Cork: Mercier, 1973) 217. In this context Kinsella, discussing both the modern writer in general as well as the Irish writer, refers to "a living tradition" (213/14), which implies a sense of organic unity and continuation. In fact, he refers to English and French literature as examples of a "continuous tradition" (216). To that extent I differ with Kinsella, as will be evident later in the book. I agree more with Foucault's assessment in "Nietzsche, Genealogy, History" that history (and tradition) is a discontinuous or disjunction progression. Harry Levin charts the history of tradition, both the term and the concept. See Levin, *Contexts of Criticism* (Cambridge: Harvard UP, 1957) 55–66, as well as Eric Hobsbawm and Terence Ranger, eds. *The Invention of Tradition* (Cambridge, Mass.: Cambridge UP, 1983).

3. Thomas Flanagan, *The Irish Novelists: 1800–1850.* (New York: Columbia UP, 1959) 6.

myth recur throughout Heaney's poetry. In his early works, though, tradition, language, and myth are examined, at least to some extent, individually as Heaney sorts through his cultural and literary heritage. The fact that each of these issues is explored separately in succeeding volumes of poetry does not make them themes in the traditional sense—that is, unified, coherent, or isolated topics that, poetically rendered, either provide the writer or the reader access to the "Hidden Ireland" as Corkery envisioned it or act as the vehicle for reaching (or creating) a stable identity and origin. Rather, the questions of tradition, language, and myth, as they are explored in Heaney's poetry, lead away from the notion of a Hidden Ireland or a stable origin rooted in a Celtic past and then passed on, broken but still potent, over the centuries. While I shall discuss tradition, language, and myth separately at first, it is important to see these as interrelated elements which constitute the "gapped, discontinuous, polyglot tradition" that Kinsella identifies as the Irish writer's heritage.

In his poetry, Seamus Heaney explores the continuation of the past—manifest in the form of tradition, language, and myth—in the present and evaluates the molding effect that the past has had on himself and his culture. Heaney looks for the past in himself and in the people and places he knows best, but he does not, as Jeremy Hooker claims, wish "to remember and conserve the past."[4] Heaney's relationship with the past is more complex: he does not poetically create voices whose utterances ascribe a moment in a singular, linear progression of tradition. Moreover, Heaney does not have a narrow political agenda that he wishes voiced through his poetry, although, as Andrew Waterman points out, such an agenda has traditionally been expected of the Irish writer:

[A] writer born here [in Ulster], as elsewhere in Ireland, suffers the further constraint of being expected to define exactly where he stands in relation to some or other concept of nationalism and cultural allegiance; a con-

4. Jeremy Hooker, *Poetry of Place: Essays and Reviews 1970–1981* (Manchester: Carcanet, 1982) 11.

straint Englishmen, however sensitive to personal roots, are fortunate to be free from in this form, for it is ultimately narrowing and exclusive.[5]

Throughout his career, Heaney has resisted the call to "conserve the past" as well the call to arms. He is neither a gentle yet plaintive pastoralist nor a defiant yet articulate patriot. In his early volumes, Heaney's poetry resonates with voices that assimilate yet subvert these two, often contradictory, facets of his tradition. While tradition may provide a rich resource of experience for exploration, act as a source of continuity, or provide a sense of ready-made identity, it can also act as a deterrent to creative exploration, insist upon a singular or linear perspective on its own development, or repress the possibility of continued self-identification. Working with and through this complex web of tradition is difficult, but it is a necessary first step to understanding the question of tradition.

In "Tradition and Difference," his review article of M. H. Abrams's *Natural Supernaturalism*, J. Hillis Miller asserts that there are four possible reasons the myths Abrams so thoroughly identifies and explicates (as well as their attendant concepts, metaphors, practices, and narrative patterns) have persisted over so many years: (1) that they are "the truth," inscribed by God and indeed not fictions at all, (2) that man has been in a kind of sleep for centuries and unwilling or unable to generate any variations on the old themes, (3) that these myths are "programmed into" language and that they have imposed themselves upon human consciousness over the years, and (4) that "there are no tools or materials for their construction but language, and our language contains no terms, no concepts, and no metaphors which are not inextricably implicated in the pattern of metaphysical thinking."[6] In short, language is the means by which we perceive the past, and our perceptions of the past can only be made conscious and articulated through language. In Heaney's verse, the influences of tradition are too strong and too much a part of his personal and

5. Andrew Waterman, "Ulsterectomy," in Best Poetry of the Year Selected by Dannie Abse, *Poetry Dimension Annual 6* (London: Robson, 1979) 42.
6. J. Hillis Miller, "Tradition and Difference," *Diacritics* 2.4 (Winter 1972): 10.

cultural consciousness to be ignored. Tradition entails the beliefs and practices of the culture as well as the fact that it is not derived from a single, stable origin. Consequently, each time the speaker in one of Heaney's poems forges a new utterance that excavates tradition that speaker both regenerates and subverts tradition in a complex interplay of sameness and difference—what Derrida calls "originary repetition."[7]

In his first two volumes of poetry, Heaney stands between Hillis Miller's third and fourth alternatives—that is, between the assertion that the myths which constitute his tradition are "programmed into" his language and the assertion that these myths are always already inscribed by language. For instance, Heaney frequently probes tradition in an attempt to discern whether or how the Irish consciousness has been influenced or infected by its tradition. Other Irish writers have made their opinion on the subject clear enough. In "Valediction," his diatribe against Ireland, Louis MacNeice describes his Irish heritage as something that has had a debilitating or, to vary upon Hillis Miller's terminology, "programming" influence on his consciousness:

> I can say Ireland is hooey, Ireland is
> A gallery of fake tapestries,
> But I cannot deny my past to which my self is wed,
> The woven figure cannot undo its thread.[8]

Although the metaphor Joyce chooses suggests some hope for escape, the nets that so preoccupied young Stephen Dedalus represent both a formative and restrictive heritage: "When the soul of a man is born in this country there are nets flung at it to hold it back from flight. You talk to me of nationality, language, religion. I shall try to fly by those nets."[9] In his poem "A Farewell to English," Michael Hartnett sees British colonialism and its systematic marginalization, if not complete negation, of the Irish people

7. Jacques Derrida, *Writing and Difference* (Chicago: U of Chicago P, 1978) 202.

8. Louis MacNeice, *The Collected Poems of Louis MacNeice*, ed. E. R. Dodds (New York: Oxford UP, 1967) 52–53.

9. James Joyce, *A Portrait of the Artist as a Young Man* (New York: Viking, 1964) 203. Hereafter cited as *Portrait of the Artist*.

and the Irish language as both his legacy and his point of departure as a poet:

> All that reminds us
> we are human and therefore not a herd
> must be concealed or killed or slowly left
> to die, or microfilmed to waste no space.
> For Gaelic is our final sign that
> we are human, therefore not a herd.[10]

Heaney is certainly sensitive to such perspectives of Irish culture.
In "Poor Women in a City Church," the practice of religious devotion and adoration (its icons in the form of the statue of the timeless Virgin and the slowly burning candles on the altar) and the
"Old dough-faced" worshippers themselves melt gradually into a
single entity: "In the gloom you cannot trace / A wrinkle on their
beeswax brows" (DN 42). The worshippers' identity, even their
physical characteristics, acquiesce to the molding effects of their
religious heritage.

Heaney shows himself aware of Hillis Miller's fourth alternative as well, that the tradition he wishes to excavate is both a product of and perpetuated by language. Tradition, from this perspective, is a palimpsest of discursive surfaces, not something written
and then erased, but something written and written again, one
layer on top of the other. As each new layer of the palimpsest is
written, certain portions seep through or in some way influence
the layers that follow. Perhaps this is what Hillis Miller meant by
"programmed," a repetition that occurs enough that it "appears"
to have always been that way. As a consequence, people begin to
think it "must" be that way. Soon people organize institutions to
ensure that it stays that way. This process of assimilation and cod-
ification explains the recurring and alluring power of nationalist
and revivalist ideologies.

The postmodern writer, however, is skeptical of such linear
concepts of knowledge and seeks to disrupt the view that tradition follows a natural, even sequential order of development.

---

10. Michael Hartnett, *Collected Poems*, Vol. 1 (Dublin: Raven Arts Press, 1985) 162.

Ihab Hassan, who has spent a good portion of his career defining postmodernism, explains the postmodern perspective in the following way:

[T]he prevalence of postmodernism today, if indeed it prevails, does not suggest that ideas or institutions of the past cease to shape the present. Rather, traditions develop, and even types suffer a seachange. . . . In this perspective postmodernism may appear as a significant revision, if not an original *épistémè*, of twentieth-century Western societies. . . . Thus postmodernism, by invoking two divinities at once [Apollonian conjunctions and Dionysian disjunctions], engages a double view. Sameness and difference, unity and rupture, filiation and revolt, all must be honored if we are to attend to history, apprehend (perceive, understand) change both as a spatial, mental structure and as a temporal, physical process, both as pattern and unique event.[11]

With this definition in mind, Heaney, at least in his first two volumes of poetry, may be characterized as a postmodernist in the making, a writer inclined in the postmodern direction but still not fully immersed in a postmodern perspective of history, tradition, and the practice of writing. Heaney becomes a postmodernist of the sort described by Hassan with the publication of *Wintering Out* and *North*, when he experiments with the ways by which etymology and dialect can be used as a form of "rupture" within and "revolt" against a tradition (specifically the British cultural and linguistic influence) that seeks to marginalize and silence all others. Heaney's use in *Wintering Out* of Irish words and dialect, words with complex etymologies, and words foregrounded in such a way that they can be reinscribed acts as a form of "reterritorialization" of the dominant language and of the English tradition forced upon the Irish consciousness.[12] In his fourth volume, *North*, Heaney invokes, not the two divinities of Hassan's paradigm, but Yeats and Joyce. Yeats, rather than being an influence of Apollonian conjunction, articulates the power of myth

11. Ihab Hassan, *The Postmodern Turn: Essays in Postmodern Theory and Culture* (Columbus: Ohio State UP, 1987) 84/88.

12. The term *reterritorialization*, used by Gilles Deleuze and Félix Guatarri in relation to the discourse of "minor" literature written in a "major" language, is more thoroughly explored in chapter 3.

through an Antaeus-like connection with the earth and Ireland's mythic past. In contrast, Joyce is a force of demythification, a Hercules, who wrestles with Antaeus and strives to tear him away from attachment to a mythic past—what Heaney calls a "dream of loss and origins" which acts as "pap for the dispossessed" (N 52, 53).

In *Death of a Naturalist* and *Door into the Dark*, though, Heaney is primarily an explorer, charting his ground, then excavating and reinscribing tradition. For instance, in "Digging," the first poem in *Death of a Naturalist*, the speaker in the poem, a writer, creates an analogy between his own work with a pen and the work of his father and grandfather with a spade. The title of the poem, "Digging," is in the form of a nonfinite verbal, which has voice and tense inflection. The word *digging* appears three times in the poem: the first in the present, "My father, digging"; the second in the past, twenty years away, recalled in a memory, "he was digging"; the third in reference to the grandfather, even further in the past, but in reference to a present moment, the single word sentence, "Digging."

The poem begins as a recollection of events in tranquility—the speaker's thoughts of his father and grandfather as farmers, men of the soil. The frame of the poem is the speaker sitting at his desk, pen "snug as a gun" in his hand. The second stanza initiates a sequence that lends itself to contrasting interpretations: the speaker hears the sound of his father digging in the garden below (the son looking down upon the father); the father bends low to thrust his spade into the earth and "comes up twenty years away / Stooping in rhythm through potato drills." The father "twenty years away" could be the speaker remembering a past event that parallels or echoes the present, or the father could be digging (in an archaeological sense) to a time far "away," each spadeful apparently bringing him closer to the past, his origins.

The fact that the father has some kind of "rhythm" implies the naturalness of his actions, although it could be the speaker's perception of the father being in harmony with nature, a trait the speaker feels he does not share. Similarly, the speaker's grandfather spent his days, "going down and down / For the good turf. Digging," as if the depth of the soil holds a special secret.

The second-to-last stanza is significant because it could be either a moment of continuation or a moment of rupture in tradition: "The cold smell of potato mould, the squelch and slap / Of soggy peat, the curt cuts of an edge / Through living roots awaken in my head" (DN 14). The smells and the sounds of digging, as well as the cuts of the spade in the turf, "awaken" in the speaker's head. Are these synaesthetic sensations triggering memories that the speaker recalls in his contemplative state—that is, are the "smell," the "squelch and slap," and the "cuts" memories awakened in the speaker's mind as he looks down upon his father digging? Or, is the act of digging turf also the act of excavating the speaker's personal heritage (his lineage through his father and grandfather) or his mythic/historical heritage (a connection with a tradition of soil and land)?

Both interpretations are invited by the images of the son, the father, and the grandfather—ancestral echoes of men of the soil. With the latter interpretation, though, the words *squelch and slap* resonate not only with experiences of life on the farm, but of political and social repression. The words *smell* and *cuts* evoke not only images of cutting turf, but of battles fought and lives lost throughout a history of violence. The paradox of digging is that it is both an act that bonds the generations as well as an act that severs "living roots." Digging is, then, both a productive and a destructive act. The poem ends as the speaker chooses to continue his digging, not with a spade but with a pen.

Digging, however, does not merely uncover layers of historical violence or take someone, such as the speaker's father, back to a stable origin or past; digging itself is a form of violence, as the image of the gun implies. Digging with a spade or with a pen not only uncovers but also severs the living roots of the past. In his essay "'Pap for the Dispossessed': Seamus Heaney and the Poetics of Identity," David Lloyd argues that Heaney's search into the past is designed to retrieve a lost origin, a moment of isomorphism between individual and native soil, between present and past, between writer and source:

"Digging" holds out the prospect of a return to origins and the consolatory myth of a knowledge which is innocent and without disruptive effect. The gesture is almost entirely formal, much as the ideology of nine-teenth-century nationalists—whose concerns Heaney largely shares—was formal or aesthetic, composing the identity of the subject in the knowing of objects the very knowing of which is an act of self-production. This description holds for the writer's relation to the communal past as well as to his subjective past: in the final analysis, the two are given as identical. Knowledge can never truly be the knowledge of difference: instead, returned to that from which the subject was separated by knowledge, the subject poses his objects (perceived or produced) as synecdoches of continuity."[13]

Such an interpretation ignores the violence of digging—the "nicking," the "slicing," the "heaving," and the "curt cuts"—all of which sever "living roots." A poet who wants exclusively to "return to origins and the consolatory myth of a knowledge which is innocent and without disruptive effect" would be more inclined to write about *tracing* living roots, *nurturing* living roots, or *merging* living roots.

The act of digging into the turf—like excavating the peat bogs of Jutland and Ireland in later poems—is not merely commemorated, but performed in the poem, for the poem is a form of digging. Furthermore, digging is more than a simple analogy; it represents a process of writing that recurs throughout Heaney's poetry. Writing entails a conflation or juxtaposition of past events, memories of past events in the present, and the moment of utterance which, because it often resonates with ambivalent or contradictory impulses, can be a disruptive factor in the continuation of the speaker's tradition. The connection between digging—with all its personal, political, historical resonances—and writing is the most important aspect of Heaney's poetic imagination.

The word *digging* signifies an act that occurs always in the present, but that present moment may concern a memory of past events. Thus, in "Digging," the father and the grandfather are

13. David Lloyd, "'Pap for the Dispossessed': Seamus Heaney and the Poetics of Identity," *Boundary 2* 13 (1985): 327; rptd. in Lloyd's book *Anomalous States: Irish Writing and the post-Colonial Moment* (Durham, N.C.: Duke UP, 1993) chap. 1; and *Seamus Heaney: A Collection of Critical Essays*, ed. Elmer Andrews (New York: St. Martin's Press, 1992) chap. 5.

captured in a continually present moment as events from the past continue, or echo, in the present. The act of writing, like that of digging, is a consistently present moment that, while inhabited by echoes of the past, truncates and reinscribes those echoes as they occur. In other words, the tradition that has so influenced Heaney and of which he often writes is not evolving in any linear or teleological sense, even though some may read it as such. Each poem has the potential to contribute to that apparent evolution or progression of tradition, but it also has the potential to create a rupture in that tradition. Tradition, like the "self," is a collection of discursive surfaces inscribed by language and open to the free-play of language.[14] No single meaning is possible, and no place of origin exists outside this free-play of language. Thus, one cannot expect to arrive at a form of meaning external to language.

From a postmodern perspective, writing is neither the creation of something entirely new nor the capture of an essential meaning that springs forth from a timeless origin. The writer's text is, as Derrida defines it, "a field of forces" that vie with one another, contradict one another, and resist attempts to homogenize them into a singular meaning.[15] Each new text intrudes upon, competes with, and severs the texts that precede it, which is the violence of digging. Consequently, a poem such as "Personal Helicon"—which explores the complex interrelationship of tradition, personal experiences, and the practice of writing poetry—entails a reinscription of both the speaker's past and the speaker's self.

"Personal Helicon" begins with the past, memories of a child-hood fascination with wells:

> As a child, they could not keep me from wells
> And old pumps with buckets and windlasses.

---

14. Tradition cannot be abandoned completely, however, in favor of the unrestrained free-play of language. Frank Lentricchia has already shown how the "Yale deconstructionists" in their misreading of Derrida did so only to become preoccupied with the *mise en abyme*. To go too far in the other direction, moreover, is to lose sight of the always already textuality of tradition, and therein lies unquestioning faith or, worse, unabandoned political, religious, or mythic abstraction and propaganda. See Lentricchia, *After the New Criticism* (Chicago: U of Chicago P, 1980) 180.

15. Jacques Derrida, "But, beyond . . ." *Critical Inquiry* 13 (Autumn 1986): 168.

> I loved the dark drop, the trapped sky, the smells
> Of waterweed, fungus, and dank moss.
>
> (DN 57)

The first four stanzas recall the various wells around which the speaker played as a child. Once again the speaker is prying into roots. As in "Digging," Heaney captures the sights and sounds, the synaesthetic impressions, of this experience. Also, the "dark drop" into the well and the living weeds, fungus, and moss that live in the well recall the experience of digging turf. In the final stanza, though, the speaker distinctly shifts to the present:

> Now, to pry into roots, to finger slime,
> To stare big-eyed Narcissus, into some spring
> Is beneath all adult dignity. I rhyme
> To see myself, to set the darkness echoing.
>
> (DN 57)

These lines are tinged with irony. The act of being "big-eyed Narcissus," despite the negative implications customarily associated with narcissism, is one of self-exploration.

The poem's title refers to the Helicon, a Grecian mountain range that was the mythic home of the Muses. The word is used synonymously for artistic inspiration. A helicon is also a musical instrument, something that must be played, and whose musical qualities only exist in the present moment. Thus, a personal helicon is both the source of inspiration and the instrument for that inspiration—just as digging is the method and result of writing. The exploration of roots and slime is the act of excavating—which not only reveals but severs—those elements that constitute one's cultural unconscious—tradition, language, and myth. The speaker claims to "rhyme / To see myself." A rhyme is an echo, and rhyming is the act of poetic creation. The speaker wants "to set the darkness echoing," to create a text in which all the elements of consciousness, one's cultural consciousness in conjunction with one's personal experience, reverberate or echo, which is an act of seeing one's self, of self-creation through a process of centerless repetition.

Many critics have noted that Heaney is tentative about the

value of poetry in his early volumes, constantly needing to justify the act of writing poetry in relation to more practical pursuits, such as digging potatoes, thatching a roof, or forging a horseshoe.[16] In "Personal Helicon," that lack of assurance lingers, but the speaker realizes that the act of writing locates him within a tradition, just as the memory of his father and grandfather did. And, just as the speaker had to situate himself in relation to his ancestors in order to discern his own continually shifting identity against the discursive surfaces of his tradition, so too the speaker discovers that the poetic utterance is the point at which that tradition and his identity intersect and that the utterance recovers or discovers a discursive plurality and grasps the numerous discursive sequences that constitute his tradition. And these sequences are, to a significant extent, heterogeneous and contradictory.

Heaney stated during an interview on the BBC that the "dark centre, the blurred and irrational storehouse of insight and instincts, the hidden core of the self—this notion is the foundation of what viewpoint I might articulate for myself as a poet."[17] Heaney's words here are important because he refers to "the hidden core of the self," which seems to create and to erase the self in the same stroke. The word *core* implies some certain presence or essential being that Heaney calls "the self." On the other hand, that core, if it actually exists, is "hidden" by the "blurred and irrational storehouse of insight and instincts" that either is or surrounds the "dark centre." The words *insight and instincts* designate both learned and innate knowledge, as if the Irish writer is born into a tradition that influences him from within but also learns about that tradition from without.

Like the storehouse of experiences, tradition, and myth that influences it, the "hidden core" that Heaney identifies as the self is

16. See, e.g., Seamus Deane, *Celtic Revivals: Essays in Modern Irish Literature* (London: Faber, 1985) 174ff; James Liddy, "Ulster Poets and the Catholic Muse," *Éire-Ireland* 13.4 (1978): 136–37; Blake Morrison, *Seamus Heaney* (London: Methuen, 1982) 21–34, and "Speech and Reticence: Seamus Heaney's *North*," in *British Poetry Since 1970: A Critical Survey*, ed. Peter Jones and Michael Schmidt (Manchester: Carcanet, 1980) 103–11; and Alan Shapiro, "Crossed Pieties," rev. of *Poems: 1965–1975* and *Preoccupations: Selected Prose 1968–1978*, by Seamus Heaney, *Parnassus* 11.2 (1983/84): 338.

17. Partially reprinted under the title "King of the Dark," *The Listener* 5 Feb. 1970: 181.

always already a construct of language. To the creative imagination, this tradition, this "irrational storehouse," is both a gift and a curse. If Heaney sounds unnecessarily obtuse here, it is no wonder. The Irish writer's vision of tradition has always been a crepuscular one. As Seamus Deane points out, "So vague an idea of tradition and continuity as Ireland's needed all the dimness it could get, a fact of which the young Yeats was perhaps too keenly aware. Twilight was the proper imaginative hour [with its anticipation of a new dawn] for those vanished Celtic civilisations."[18] Consequently, the Irish writer who wishes not to repeat the mistakes of the past must be wary of too eagerly embracing tradition — from which, of course, he or she has no permanent escape — all the while seeking new avenues for exploring that tradition and creating his or her own identity. The "self," then, created in "Personal Helicon," as with the "dark centre," is not a self in any normative sense, but the self of the utterance, the self of the moment. Every utterance creates a new self — from a different perspective, in a different context, in relation to a different point in time or history, or in relation to some element of the speaker's tradition.

"Digging" and "Personal Helicon," respectively the first and last poems in *Death of a Naturalist*, establish a framework that recurs throughout Heaney's other poetry. His poetry is one in which the act of poetic creation or articulation is permeated with his personal experiences and the tradition of his country and his race. As Heaney states, "Our sense of the past, our sense of the land and perhaps our sense of identity are inextricably interwoven."[19] Even the persona or speaking voice in these two poems, as in many of Heaney's poems, is a poet or writer, a person actively engaged in excavating, examining, interpreting, and reinscribing his own experiences and tradition.

The speaker in Heaney's poems does not wish to blend with the events of the poem, to become one with the objects of his poetic vision, as Keats suggests in his "Ode to a Nightingale." Rather, it

18. Seamus Deane, "An Example of Tradition," *The Crane Bag* 3.1 (1979): 373.
19. Qtd. in Terence Brown, *Northern Voices: Poets from Ulster* (Dublin: Gill and Macmillan, 1975) 180.

is that difference between self and past, of self and tradition, that is all-important. The speaker's ironic tone of self-condemnation in "Personal Helicon," that his actions are "beneath all adult dignity," reinforces this interplay, but the playfulness of the last stanza does not diminish the importance of the present utterance. Rather, it reveals a self-conscious interplay as the speaker articulates neither the past alone nor a completely original utterance. The two are bound together. The interplay, though, is not merely an opposition or dichotomy in that the speaker cannot see himself without prying into his roots or fingering slime, and it is only through the act of reinscribing events, exposing roots, severing and awakening them in the writer's mind, that the rhyme is possible. Consequently, the act of setting the darkness echoing is not just the act of uttering new words; it is hearing the echoes of the past (of his roots), assimilating them into himself, and setting the darkness echoing with a new utterance—one which is simultaneously a continuation of the past as well as a rupture within that continuation, a "co-opted and obliterated echo" (HL 24).

Even though many of his poems, such as "Digging" and "Personal Helicon," comprise elements or memories of personal experiences in rural Ulster, the tradition of which Heaney writes is not singular. Heaney asserts in his essay "The Interesting Case of John Alphonsus Mulrennan" that Ireland is a land composed of several, often contradictory traditions that, despite their apparent exclusivity, are mutually dependent and invariably influential on all who call themselves Irish:

What each version of Irish tradition does, then, is to venerate ancestors of some kind, to posit an original place and an original language and culture and to pine for its restoration, or at least to judge present conditions in the light of this lost ideal. Whether Anglo-Irish or Catholic Gaelic or Protestant Planter, each tradition intersects with a social and political vision. Each is symptomatic of the fracture in the island's history. Each is a tradition with a small *t* pining for a more inclusive and ample possibility. Each is stay-at-home, inward looking, pious, exclusive and partial. Each of them is the invention of writers needing a structure upon which to stretch their individual sensibilities and temperaments. Each arose from a sense that that English tradition which I evoked [earlier in the article] is inadequate to the Irish experience, and each attempted consciously to fill the lack.[20]

In many of his early poems, Heaney expands his scope to include the complex interaction among these competing traditions. Heaney is wary of exalting one over the others, even if he has been most influenced by one of them, because he is aware that each is indeed "the invention of writers needing a structure upon which to stretch their individual sensibilities and temperaments." In other words, each tradition is the product of language, perpetuated by language, and, invariably, excavated by language. The words *stretch* and *structure* express an interdependence between the traditions that act as the superstructure of the individual writer's experience and the creative process of the writer, his or her "stretch." Furthermore, the awareness of such an interdependency places the onus of reflexivity on the writer—that is, the writer's "stretch" may not solely entail a repetition of his or her tradition (the "structure"), but may instead entail debunking the assumptions of exclusivity that the tradition asserts in an attempt to protect and perpetuate itself. The writer, then, must write a metatraditional poetry whose topic is the tradition itself and the means by which the writer excavates that tradition.

Thus, the question of tradition involves a complex interplay of past events, present events, language, and myth. As far as the question of language is concerned, Stephen Dedalus is the spokesperson for many Irish writers because Stephen, as a fledgling writer, perceives the nets of nationality, language, and religion as working together to hold back the soul of the Irish writer. In the case of nationality and religion, Stephen's point is not difficult to understand, as such issues recur throughout *Dubliners, A Portrait of the Artist as a Young Man*, and *Ulysses*. However, Stephen mentions a third net, language. Why would a young man striving to be a literary artist perceive the vehicle for his art as a net by which he must fly? Why is language the means by which Stephen's soul will be held back? One answer, provided by Stephen himself, is

20. Seamus Heaney, "The Interesting Case of John Alphonsus Mulrennan," *Planet* (Jan. 1978): 39.

that his "ancestors threw off their language and took another."[21] This answer, typical of Stephen's penchant for excess, registers an angry and not completely accurate response to a complex problem that as a writer Stephen himself will have to face. The language of the Irish writer who writes in English is appreciably, yet undoubtedly, the language of the "other," the oppressor, the empire, the British historical and literary tradition.

In his oft-cited conversation with the dean of studies, an Englishman, Stephen is frustrated by a breach in communication — a vernacular problematic — that occurs over the words *funnel* and *tundish*. For Stephen, the breach signifies a far greater difference, even incompatibility, between the tradition in which he finds himself and the tradition which the dean represents:

—A tundish, said the dean reflectively. That is a most interesting word. I must look that word up. Upon my word I must. . . . The little word seemed to have turned a rapier point of his sensitiveness against this courteous and vigilant foe. He felt with a smart dejection that the man to whom he was speaking was a countryman of Ben Jonson. He thought:
—The language in which we are speaking is his before it is mine. How different are the words *home, Christ, ale, master,* on his lips and on mine! I cannot speak or write these words without unrest of spirit. His language, so familiar and so foreign, will always be for me an acquired speech. I have not made or accepted its words. My voice holds them at bay. My soul frets in the shadows of his language.[22]

Heaney registers a response to the "English" language similar to Stephen's when he states that words such as *ale, manor, sheepfold, pew,* and *soldier* are "to a certain extent exclusive," that non-English speakers of the English language do not "possess" these words the way a native speaker does. Heaney concludes that "We [that is, the non-English] know the sense of [such words] but we are not intimate with the musk of their meaning."[23]

The net of language that Stephen identifies is, then, also the net

21. *Portrait of the Artist,* 203.
22. *Portrait of the Artist,* 188–89. Hugh Kenner provides a valuable explication of this passage, analyzing each of the words that separates Stephen and the dean. See Kenner, *A Colder Eye* (New York: Knopf, 1983) 49–50.
23. "The Interesting Case of John Alphonsus Mulrennan," *Planet* (Jan. 1978): 35.

of nationality, of history and politics. The two for Joyce, as for Heaney, cannot be distinguished. Also, as the conflicts of nationality and language that constitute Irish history and politics are often linked to the Protestant/Catholic conflict, all three nets, to some extent, work in combination to hold back the Irish soul. Stephen's solution to this problem is to leave Ireland, which he plans to do at the end of *Portrait of the Artist*, and which Joyce actually did in 1904. However, this course of action does not guarantee flying by those nets. Stephen returns to Ireland at the beginning of *Ulysses*, and Joyce spent all his artistic energy writing about Ireland. Another solution is to write in another language, as did Samuel Beckett, who adopted French as his literary language. But the choice of another language did not make Beckett any less an Irish writer. None of these solutions completely alleviate the question of language for the Irish writer. Heaney and a new generation of Irish writers had to develop a way of addressing this old problem in a new way.

Clearly, any discussion of Irish history and politics concerns language, and conversely any discussion of language necessarily involves a multitude of topics, including historical considerations. Heaney does not ignore or remain silent about these factors in his poetry: the question of language, for instance, is paramount to the poems of *Wintering Out*. Heaney is not alone, though, in his concern over the question of language. The playwright Brian Friel in his play *Translations* links the question of language to the Irish heritage of dispossession and loss.

Friel is one of the founders of the Field Day Theatre Company, a group dedicated to excavating Ireland's tradition(s). In his play *Translations*, Friel dramatizes the dispossession of the Irish people from their land and their language—that is, the marginalization of the Irish language by the imperialism of the British empire. For Friel, Stephen Dedalus's well-known encounter with the dean of studies and Stephen's subsequent realization that the "language in which we are speaking is his before it is mine" is an outgrowth of the events portrayed in *Translations*.

Set in County Donegal in 1833 during the Ordnance Survey of Ireland by the British Corps of Royal Engineers, *Translations* envisions a transition in Irish history and consciousness when the British, under the auspices of creating accurate maps of Ireland, transcribed, Anglicized, or changed outright Irish place names in favor of names more conducive to the English tongue. The implication of the play's historical setting and action is that the Irish, through their contact with the British, began to lose, not only their native tongue, but their sense of place, belonging, and tradition as a result of a linguistic invasion during the Ordnance Survey.

Perhaps one example will suffice. The character of Sarah is described in the stage directions as having a "speech defect so bad that all her life she has been considered locally to be dumb and she has accepted this: when she wishes to communicate, she grunts and makes unintelligible nasal sounds. She has a waiflike appearance and could be any age from seventeen to thirty-five."[24] The range of ages for Sarah is intriguing: if she is thirty-five, then she was born in 1798, the year of the United Irishmen Rebellion; if she is younger, then she was born after the Act of Union with England and thus during the time of British hegemony. At the beginning of the play, Sarah struggles just to say her name. When she is successful, Manus claims, "Nothing can stop us now."[25] By the end of the play, however, when the British commander, Captain Lancey, questions her, Sarah can only helplessly stammer.

Though not a member of Field Day, John Montague also focuses upon the lost heritage of those whose language is marginalized to the point of near extinction. In his poem the *Rough Field*, which predated Friel's play and Field Day by several years, Montague refers to Northern Ireland as "A severed head speaking with a grafted tongue," a reference to Ulster's history of invaders and colonialism as well as to the loss of the Irish language.[26] Montague's poem is a mosaic of time that distinctively assembles woodcuts from Derricke's *Image of Ireland* (1581), personal experience, local stories, extracts from anti-Catholic pamphlets, ex-

---

24. Brian Friel, *Selected Plays* (London: Faber, 1984) 383.
25. Friel, *Selected Plays* 385.
26. John Montague, *The Rough Field* (Dublin: Dolmen Press, 1972) 26.

cerpts of a letter from a Jesuit uncle decrying the decline of religious faith among Catholics, prophetic utterances, as well as various anthropological, sociological, historical, political, and geographical topics. In section 4 of the poem, for instance, Montague, like Friel, refers to the dispossession of land and tradition that accompanies the loss of one's native language: "The whole landscape a manuscript / We had lost the skill to read, / A part of our past disinherited."[27] Later in this section, Montague describes a child who "stumbles over lost / syllables of an old order" as the child tries to learn a second language that used to be the primary language of his people.

What is one to make of Friel's play or Montague's poem? Are they threnodies of a lost tradition that the two authors in a form of reactionary longing wish to reestablish? Edna Longley believes so when she contends that Friel's "play does not so much examine myths of dispossession and oppression as repeat them."[28] John Wilson Foster in an essay on Montague makes a similar point: "The Ulster Catholic writer has lived for so long with the imagery of land-decay and land-loss that he has become addicted to it. . . . What he wants is . . . a mythic landscape of beauty and plenitude that is pre-Partition, pre-Civil War, pre-Famine, pre-Plantation and pre-Tudor."[29] Both Longley's and Foster's positions assume that what is often called "the Irish thing" is necessarily a dichotomous matter, that it is exclusively a matter of "us" versus "them." Also, Longley and Foster accuse some Irish writers of envisioning a tradition that has since passed away, making a fetish of that tradition, and longing for its total restoration. However, such a description of tradition is debatable.

Gerald Bruns maintains that tradition is "not a structure of any sort but is just the historicality of open-ended, intersecting, competing narratives that cannot be mastered by any Great Code."[30] In a comparison of the Judaic and Christian traditions, Bruns ar-

27. Montague, *The Rough Field* 30.
28. Edna Longley, "Poetry and Politics," *The Crane Bag* 9.1 (1985): 28.
29. John Wilson Foster, "Landscape of the Planter and the Gael in the Poetry of John Hewitt and John Montague," *Canadian Journal of Irish Studies* 1.2 (1975): 21.
30. Gerald Bruns, "What is Tradition?" *New Literary History* 22 (Winter 1991): 11.

gues that the Christian tradition assumes itself as the correct if not foreordained successor of the Judaic tradition—that is, the old dispensation has ended and been replaced in its entirety by the new dispensation. Bruns points out that the continued existence of Judaism—not to mention Islam, which only compounds the problems of exclusivity—belies the plenitude of the Christian tradition. The hyphen in Judeo-Christian, then, is not a designation of time or old *versus* new, but of the inescapable interconnection between the two narratives, the suture that binds the two while exposing a lack as well. The conclusion that Bruns draws from this analysis is that "time is split lengthwise as a rift among adjacent histories, not hierarchically as a progression of epochs."[31] A critical approach such as Bruns's that understands tradition as mutually interdependent narratives, linked but not indiscernibly isomorphic, resembles Michel Foucault's analysis of his own critical and genealogical process in his essay "The Order of Discourse":

Of course, history has for a long time no longer sought to understand events by the action of causes and effects in the formless unity of a great becoming, vaguely homogeneous or ruthlessly hierarchised; but this change was not made in order to rediscover prior structures, alien and hostile to the event. It was made in order to establish diverse series, intertwined and often divergent but not autonomous, which enable us to circumscribe the "place" of the event, the margins of its chance variability, and the conditions of its appearance.[32]

Bruns's and Foucault's perspectives are invaluable in explaining the coexisting—or cohabiting—traditions of Ireland.[33]

Longley and Foster assume that some Irish writers long for the renewal of that old dispensation, a renaissance of the old ways and the old tongue. While such may have been the case in the past with Douglas Hyde and the Gaelic League, in the nationalist movements of the nineteenth century, or among Yeats, Synge,

31. Bruns, "What is Tradition?" 15.

32. Michel Foucault, "The Order of Discourse," in *Untying the Text: A Post-Structuralist Reader*, ed. Robert Young (Boston: Routledge and Kegan Paul, 1981) 68.

33. For other valuable discussions of the complexities of Irish traditions, see Seamus Deane's *Celtic Revivals*, particularly chapters 1–3 and 7, and Norman Vance, *Irish Literature: A Social History* (Oxford: Blackwell, 1990), chap. 1.

and Lady Gregory, many contemporary Irish writers and critics envision their tradition as an ongoing fracture or wound that has been sutured and scarred but not healed. Put another way, tradition is a collocation of competing narratives that cannot view itself without also viewing the other. In fact, the poet and critic Seamus Deane cautions against exclusive views of tradition, warning that "insurgent nationalisms attempt to create a version of history for themselves in which their intrinsic essence has always manifested itself, thereby producing readings of the past that are as monolithic as that which they are trying to supplant."[34] Heaney poses a similar point:

And if Joyce is exemplary in revealing that the conceptions, loyalties and ideals of cross-channel culture are not necessarily to be shared by our insular imagination, he is also exemplary in refusing to replace that myth of alien superiority by the myth of native superiority. If the coherence of English culture is a fruitless aspiration, equally fruitless is the dream of a Gaelic order restored . . . [because it] can, on the one hand, be a holding, grounding, utterly necessary exercise in self-definition and self-respect, an insistence on dwelling within conceptions and ideals which animate a certain community and the individuals within that community. It can say, we prefer the dream of a mainland home, we shall remember ancestry and maintain solidarity with our traditional values. . . . But the very strenuousness of this maintained effort constitutes its negative aspect.[35]

Like Heaney and Deane, Hugh, the hedge-school master in Friel's *Translations*, warns against the sort of reactionary thinking described by Longley and Foster. Hugh tells his Irish students that "we must learn those new names. . . . We must learn where we live . . . [and] that it is not the literal past . . . that shapes us, but images of the past embodied in language . . . [and] we must never cease renewing those images; because once we do, we fossilize."[36]

From this perspective, the image of the Irish past must be continually reinscribed to avoid fossilization. As Hugh points out,

34. Terry Eagleton et al., *Nationalism, Colonialism, and Literature*, intro. by Seamus Deane (Minneapolis: U of Minnesota P, 1990) 9.
35. Seamus Heaney, "Forked Tongues, Ceilís and Incubators," *Fortnight* 197 (1983): 20–21.
36. Friel, *Selected Plays* 444–45.

learning the names is tantamount to learning where we live, or as Deane explains, "The naming or renaming of a place, the naming or renaming of a race, a region, a person, is, like all acts of primordial nomination, an act of possession."[37] But the place where many Irish citizens live has a double inscription, a suture where the wound of colonialism and the loss of a former national identity has begun to scar over.

So a paradox exists for many Irish writers, the paradox that the past that shapes them is an image of the past embodied in language, but that language is a constant reminder of a loss and of a name given by another. Both Friel and Montague know that they are writing in English, though they do not consider abandoning the English language entirely, as Michael Hartnett does in "A Farewell to English," or as have other writers who now write in Irish. Also, Friel's play is written and performed in English even though the audience imagines the Irish characters speaking to one another in Irish. Michael Toolan believes, and he echoes the sentiments of Edna Longley, that this fact makes much of *Translations* satiric if not ridiculous.[38] However, despite the practical fact that a bilingual play would for the most part not be understood by many members of the audience, writing in Irish does not preclude the grafted tongue, nor does it transport the writer back to the time when he or she was able, as Montague claims, to read the "whole landscape [as] a manuscript." In contrast, writing in English can be a form of revolt, what Deane calls the Irish speaker's "almost vengeful virtuosity in the English language," which is "an attempt to make Irish English a language in its own right."[39]

Montague's image of the severed head speaking with a grafted tongue powerfully articulates the questions of tradition and language facing many Irish writers. The severed head is undoubtedly a sign of military and political victory—metaphorically severing the head from the body politic or literally the practice of carrying

37. Eagleton et al., *Nationalism, Colonialism, and Literature* 18.
38. Michael Toolan, "Language and Affective Communication in Some Contemporary Irish Writers," in *Cultural Contexts and Literary Idioms in Contemporary Irish Literature* by Michael Kenneally (Gerrards Cross: Colin Smythe, 1988) 143–44.
39. Eagleton et al., *Nationalism, Colonialism, and Literature* 10.

the head of one's defeated foe on the tip of a spear or sword. Montague incorporates into his text the words of Sir John Davies and Sir Arthur Chichester, both of whom after the Act of Union translated military superiority into significant—if not total—political control. Montague also incorporates an account of the Flight of the Earls in the early seventeenth century, which corresponded with the English plantation—or colonization—period in Irish history and the loss of Ireland's Celtic chieftains.

These voices and events signify the severing of the Irish head. However, while the head may be totally severed, the tongue is not. To graft in a surgical or botanical sense means to join—though portions of the original shoot and graft persist after the grafting. One does not uproot a tree or cut it down in order to graft it. Rather, the old and the new are linked, eventually to grow together, distinct, but interrelated. The word *graft* can also mean stolen or embezzled money, as in the sense of a politician taking a bribe. Montague's grafted tongue may be fused with the English tongue, but that tongue, while having had something taken from it, is also capable of taking something itself. Thus, the graft joining the English tongue with the Irish tongue resembles the hyphen Gerald Bruns identifies as inextricably joining Judaism and Christianity. The Irish writer, then, is not entirely assimilated by the English language, and the intrusion of the Irish into the English community has created a new language, the Irish-English, which acts, to use Derrida's terminology, as a supplement that contradicts the plenitude of the English language, the failure of British imperialism to define everything as itself.[40]

40. Seamus Deane and other Field Day writers have addressed this topic. For instance, Deane states that "it was only when the Celt was seen by the English as a necessary supplement to their national character that the Irish were able to extend the idea of supplementarity to that of racial difference. This is a classic case of how nationalism can be produced by the forces that suppress it and can, at that juncture, mobilize itself into a form of liberation" (see Eagleton et al., *Nationalism, Colonialism, and Literature* 12/13). One of those points of juncture, according to my argument, is dialect and variations of speech and meaning that allow what was once taken away, language, to be used to create something new, a form of expression that does not long for the old days, but does not ignore them either, and sees the Irish character and history as ineluctably interconnected with the English, the Vikings, and all others with whom it has had contact over the past eight hundred years.

The focus of this study is Seamus Heaney's struggle with and celebration of the diverse tradition that constitutes his consciousness as a poet in particular and Irish society in general. At times, tradition can be oppressive—in the form of religious structures that mold or mar the individual consciousness in one stroke, in the form of a relentless longing for a lost past that forms itself into a myth of origin and descent, or in the form of recalcitrant and competing discourses that recur with such frequency that they fail to do anything but articulate old prejudices and hatreds. At other times, though, tradition can be a rich resource of texts that resonate through and contrast with the writer's text. Heaney finds, for instance, a fecund literary tradition that includes British, Gaelic, and, in later volumes, international strains. He also explores languages and dialects that vary from local and idiosyncratic speech to monologic discourses—all the while, of course, never forgetting his place and heritage as an Irish writer.

Excavating tradition is both an act of discovery as well as an act of violence. So too is the act of inscription and reinscription. Through a new text, tradition can be perpetuated, truncated, interrogated, or reinscribed. As the poet Brendan Kennelly stresses, writing is a form of violence: "The ink from my pen is violating the whiteness of the paper."[41] And that violence branches out in fractures and fissures throughout the tradition. The marks on an individual page impose themselves upon all the texts that precede them as well as upon those that follow. While avoiding the traps of tradition, a writer can work with its diversity and speak with many voices in order to inscribe a "new history," as the speaker in "Tinder" calls it, a "re-read" and "re-written" tradition that is simultaneously new but also distinctively Irish.

Such re-reading and re-writing—what in this study I shall call questioning and reinscribing tradition—recurs throughout the poetry of Seamus Heaney. *Death of a Naturalist* and *Door into the Dark* begin this questioning and reinscription, particularly in regard to the speaker's personal and past experiences. In the con-

41. Brendan Kennelly, "Poetry and Violence" in *History and Violence in Anglo-Irish Literature*, ed. Joris Duytschaever and Geert Lernout (Amsterdam: Rodopi, 1988) 18.

cluding poems of *Door into the Dark*, the questioning extends to the inscription of the political, archaeological, and historical past on the Irish landscape. The speaker in these poems often reads and reinscribes the landscape in a nonexclusive manner that underscores the multiplicity of tradition. *Wintering Out* continues this process by focusing upon the question of language and the Irish writer's role in a language that is another's before it is his or hers. Various dialect words, word-play, and words with complex etymologies abound in many poems as the speaker attempts to find and use a form of the "English" language that unleashes his particular Irish heritage.

The question of language raised in *Wintering Out* recurs as a topic and focus for Heaney throughout his career. In *North*, the perpetuation of myth through the poetic utterance is questioned, resulting in a complex series of texts that both allege and challenge the connection between Ulster's violent past and the writer's mythification of that past. *North* asks whether the "Irish thing," while certainly a conflict between British imperialism and Irish nationalism, could not be a particularly Irish conflict as well — that is, between the tendency toward mythification and the conflicting need for de-mythification.

Heaney's contribution to the Field Day series of pamphlets is a poem that presents a sophisticated yet forceful challenge to the colonial discourse which ignores differences in order to define all things as itself. In the "Open Letter," competing discourses, whose competition is both the process and the product of artistic expression, inseparably and inescapably coexist for the Irish writer. *Field Work* and *Station Island*, in turn, scrutinize the poet, who must realize that to be alive is often also to be violated, and whose work must acknowledge both song and suffering. The most recent volumes of poetry, *The Haw Lantern* and *Seeing Things*, represent Heaney's most mature work in that he abandons the self-doubt and often dire demeanor found in his early poems in favor of a more confident, assertive, and occasionally playful poetry that explores the very serious interrelationships of perception, thought, imagination, and language.

Heaney is more than a pastoralist poet writing descriptive

pieces on rural Irish life; moreover, he is no less an Irish writer just because he refuses to take up the "cause" of Irish nationalism and revolt. The competing discourses that constitute Irish history, Irish tradition(s), Irish religion(s), and Irish literature(s) find voices in Heaney's texts. And while Heaney and other Irish writers may know that they do not have a unified tradition, they are nonetheless faithful in their exploration of the tradition they do have. And it is in this way that the Irish writer questions and reinscribes his or her tradition, language, and myth.

2 ❧ Excavating and (Re)inscribing Tradition

A sense of ambivalence pervades many of the poems in *Death of a Naturalist* and *Door into the Dark* as Heaney excavates and reinscribes his tradition. The recurrence of an event or sensation from the past and the recollection of a memory or historical event certainly play an important yet varying role in Heaney's early verse: they may be the past impinging on the present; a repetition or variation of an originary utterance in the present; or a new utterance in the present that exposes, varies upon, commemorates, or contradicts an originary utterance. Recurrences or memories of the past that interact or conflict with the present occur, for example, in "Follower," when the roles of worker and helper are reversed: "But today / It is my father who keeps stumbling / Behind me, and will not go away" (DN 25). The shift in time from past to present in these words recalls a similar shift in "Digging" and "Personal Helicon." That is to say, the father in "Follower," beyond being a reference to the speaker's actual father, could also be the speaker's heritage, which lingers on "and will not go away." In "Ancestral Photograph," the photograph of the father's uncle is taken down and put away, but "Now on the bedroom wall / There is a faded patch where he has been— / As if a bandage had been ripped from skin . . ." (DN 26). In "Requiem for the Croppies," the renascent memory of the massacre at Vinegar Hill is recalled each year by the barley, which "grew up out of the grave" (DD 24). The speaker in "In Gallarus Oratory" claims that "You can still feel the community pack / This place" (DD 22). And in "Girls Bathing, Galway 1965," the "breakers pour / Themselves into themselves, the years / Shuttle through space invisibly" (DD 23). In these poems and others, the past impinges itself upon the present, or the present carries traces of the past.

Specifically, though not exclusively, in *Death of a Naturalist* and *Door into the Dark*, Heaney uses the word "now" as a transition from the past to the present, as a shift from memory to present utterance, in order to reinforce the immediacy of a present moment or to create a space for the present utterance.[1] This technique emphasizes the recurrence or memory of the past, as the events in the present stand in contrast to or in comparison with those of the past. Often, the speaker either contemplates the perpetuation of the past in the present moment or examines both past and present at once. At other times, the speaker interprets texts from the past and then creates a new text in the present moment that both resembles and dissembles the texts it echoes.

The power of tradition to influence or control the individual is the topic of "Gravities." Reminiscent of "Digging" in which tradition, in the form of "living roots," is excavated through the downward strokes of the spade/pen into the turf, "Gravities" depicts tradition as a powerful force that draws everything to itself. The initial image is of kites that only "appear" to fly freely. In actuality, though, these kites are attached to "strings, strict and invisible." And the word *reined* reinforces the sense that these strings control the kites' behavior. The rest of the poem observes the influence

1. See the following: "Ancestral Photograph" (DN 26), "Turkeys Observed" (DN 37), "Personal Helicon" (DN 57), "The Peninsula" (DD 21), "A New Song" (WO 33), "The Other Side" (WO 36), "Tinder" (WO 44), "Cairn-Maker" (WO 50), "A Winter's Tale" (WO 64), "Maighdean Mara" (WO 68), "Limbo" (WO 70), "Bye-Child" (WO 72), "Sunlight" (N 8), "Funeral Rites" (N 16), "The Grauballe Man" (N 38), "Kinship" (N 42), "Freedman" (N 60), "The Strand at Lough Beg" (FW 18), "A Postcard from North Antrim" (FW 20), "Elegy" (FW 32), "Glanmore Sonnets" (FW 33), "An Ulster Twilight" (SI 38, 39), "A Kite for Michael and Christopher" (SI 44), "Station Island" (SI 82, 89), "Holly" (SI 115), "In Illo Tempore" (SI 118), "A Daylight Art" (HL 9), "Parable Island" (HL 10), "Hailstones" (HL 14), "The Song of the Bullets" (HL 42). Heaney also uses "But today" in "Follower" (DN 25); "still" in "At a Potato Digging" (DN 33), "In Gallarus Oratory" (DD 22), "Act of Union" (N 49), "The Betrothal of Cavehill" (N 51), "Away from It All" (SI 17), "The First Kingdom" (SI 101). At times, he uses the imperative mood or a dim perception as a link to the past: "Listen" in "Shoreline" (DD 51), "Perhaps I just make out / Edmund Spenser" in "Bog Oak" (WO 14), and "Come back" in "Bone Dreams" (N 29).

of gravities, the tug and control of those invisible strings, on other things and individuals.

The first example is a pigeon that seems to "desert you suddenly." The pigeon responds to a natural force that calls it home. So too with lovers who quarrel and "endure a hopeless day" apart but, in the end, return to their "native port." The power of their love overcomes the anger that separated them. The words *home* and *native port* in these two examples signify a place of belonging, but they also anticipate the final stanza and the reference to the exiled Joyce and the wandering St. Colmcille (a.k.a. St. Columba, Colm, and Colum), both of whom entered into a form of self-imposed exile, banishing themselves from their native port of Ireland.

The speaker in "Gravities" thus perceives Ireland and its tradition as a deterministic influence that seeks control over all those who fall within its ken. Certainly, it is difficult to interpret strings that rein in the movement of kites, like Stephen Dedalus's nets, as anything but a negative force. Even the title, "Gravities," implies a natural force that may be defied for a short time but will eventually exert its power over everything. However, such an interpretation ignores the fact that the kites do fly: they are not completely and eternally grounded by gravity. The pigeon does not roost exclusively at home, and the lovers do experience a sense of separation. When the lovers return to each other, they experience a sense of renewal from being in their "native port." But, for the lovers, the memory of the separation lingers. They can remember the "hopeless day" of being apart, which gives them a choice. Unlike the pigeon that responds by instinct, the lovers have the choice of being together or being apart. If the speaker has a choice to resist as well as to succumb to the gravities, then these gravities are not deterministic influences, despite their apparent "rein," and St. Columba and James Joyce are examples of two who resisted the influence of the gravities.

Legend has it that St. Columba, well known as the saint who founded the monastery at Iona, left Ireland as a conscious act (*consuetudo peregrinandi*), in penance or obedience to God.[2] He certainly felt the sense of loss or separation from his native port. The fact that Columba went on to establish a powerful and far-reaching ministry does not prove that leaving Ireland was a form of liberation, but that the pain of separation, like that of the lovers in the second stanza, in part spurred Columba to great deeds. The reference to the word "mould" that St. Columba wears "next to his feet" in one sense signifies surface or garden soil, referring to St. Columba's well-known ascetic lifestyle or to the fact that he found comfort from the feel of his native soil under his feet. The word *mould* connotes the earth of the grave, the earth that is the material of the human body, as well as the world as a whole, the Earth. The soil on Columba's feet, therefore, extends beyond that of native soil to represent Columba's macrocosmic mission, beyond the scope of the gravities' rein, which linked him with all people, regardless of race.

Joyce is a different case, indeed, in that he left Ireland to escape the nets that haunted Stephen Dedalus. Because Joyce believed he could not pursue his art in his native land, he entered a state of perpetual exile through which he could break free of the forces, what he called "trolls," that threatened his integrity as a writer. Yet, like St. Columba, Joyce could not truly leave Ireland. While living in Trieste, Zurich, and, as described in Heaney's poem,

2. There is much conjecture about the legitimacy of the stories about St. Columba. For instance, Arthur Ua Clerigh insists that "it is quite a mistake to represent this mission [Columba's mission to Iona] as a penance and an exile. It was neither. Iona was regarded by Ptolemy and Bede as part of Erin. In going to Iona he was going to his own people." See Ua Clerigh, *The History of Ireland To the Coming of Henry II* (Port Washington, N.Y.: Kennikat, 1970) 349. Butler's account of St. Columba's life is part history and part legend: "St. Columba's manner of living was always most austere. He lay on the bare floor with a stone for his pillow, and never interrupted his fast. Yet his devotion was neither morose nor severe. His countenance always appeared wonderfully cheerful, and bespoke to all that beheld him the constant interior serenity of his holy soul, and the unspeakable joy with which it overflowed from the presence of the Holy Ghost." See Alban Butler, Rev., *The Lives of the Saints* vol. 1 (Baltimore: John Murphy, 1884) 361–63. Robin Flower points out that religious devotion compelled "many Irishmen in that day [to leave] their home and country. To die in exile with a stranger soil for a grave was to the Irish the extreme abnegation and the crown of the religious life." See Flower, *The Irish Tradition* (London: Clarendon, 1947) 57.

"Blinding in Paris," Joyce wrote exclusively about Ireland. In his biography of Joyce, Richard Ellmann states that "Joyce held tenaciously to the character of the exile, punishing himself and his country, full of distrust and nostalgia for her."[3] The lines about Joyce in Heaney's poem are in part derived from Ellmann: "Joyce always received Irish visitors cordially, and delighted in the testing of his memory, and theirs, by naming all the shops in order along O'Connell Street, or by questioning them about other people and places he had known."[4]

Throughout the biography, Ellmann documents Joyce's ambivalence toward Ireland. At times, Joyce was affectionate, even sentimental, about Ireland, at other times extremely caustic. Out of this ambivalence, Joyce's genius flourished. As a result of his separation from Ireland, he was able through his art to curtail both his anger over and his nostalgia for Ireland, although the former may be seen in the Citizen's diatribe in "Cyclops" and the latter in Simon Dedalus's patriotic songs in "Sirens." Both St. Columba and Joyce undoubtedly were pulled by the gravities of Ireland, but not inexorably so, and in the tension that resulted, their lives and works would have an impact far beyond the boundaries of Ireland, a point made evident in "Station Island," in which Joyce's voice is described as "eddying with the vowels of all rivers" (SI 92).[5]

The paradox of both St. Columba and Joyce is that their separation from their native port, and in the case of Joyce his isolation from others as well, was the impetus to a life that would effect all of humankind. At this stage in his career, however, Heaney was not ready, as Ellmann remarks of Joyce, to write "about nothing but man." Heaney still had to grapple with the gravities himself,

---

3. Richard Ellmann, *James Joyce* (Oxford: Oxford UP, 1983) 258.

4. Ellmann, *James Joyce* 579.

5. Ellmann makes a similar, though more poignant, observation: "Through blear eyes he guessed at what he had written on paper, and with obstinate passion filled the margins and the space between the lines with fresh thoughts. His genius was a trap from which he did not desire to extricate himself, and his life seemed to withdraw inside him so that Henri Michaux and others who met him then thought him the most *fermé*, disconnected from humanity, of men. Joyce, who knew he was writing about nothing but man, was in too great discomfort to attempt the correction of this impression" (*James Joyce* 574).

which he does in "The Plantation," a poem about a wood near a road that invites "all comers / To the hush and the mush / Of its whispering treadmill" (DD 50). The word *treadmill* in this line connotes an unrelenting repetition, indifferent to variation and change. Thus, the notion of tradition grinding along or the past "whispering" recalls the restricting power of tradition in "Gravities."

As the speaker moves into the wood, he senses himself in an ever-changing center or *locus* of perception encircled by the inhabitants of the wood:

> Any point in that wood
> Was a centre, birch trunks
> Ghosting your bearings,
> Improvising charmed rings
>
> ....
> Always repeating themselves.
>
> (DD 49)

The charmed rings are composed of both the recurrent vegetation in the wood as well as the hauntings of the past. The words "Ghosting," "charmed," and "Always repeating themselves" connote a type of magical existence that facilitates the recurrence of the past. The speaker senses this recurrence when he says, "Someone had always been there / Though always you were alone." Furthermore, the title of the poem adds a political, geographical, and historical dimension, evoking memories of the seventeenth century, when King James intervened in the affairs of Northern Ireland and sent Scottish settlers to Ireland.

While the first four stanzas of the poem exhibit the speaker's sense of the past in the present, the following four stanzas list various people who recently and temporarily inhabited the wood, all of whom left their mark on the place. The speaker claims that these people—"Lovers, birdwatchers, / Campers, gipsies and tramps"—entered the wood for a brief respite from the outside world. However, thinking "Its limits defined," they were disturbed to find the place more primitive, perhaps more inhabited, than they expected.

The final stanza links the two previous sections: "You had to come back / To learn how to lose yourself . . . " (DD 50). The second person here, as in previous stanzas, poses an ambiguity of referent—"You" as self-reference in the speaker's interior monologue, or "You" in a more general sense referring to anyone, as in "Each of you had to come back." In either case, being lost in the inhabited wood, which recalls the "blurred and irrational storehouse of instinct and insight" Heaney discusses in "King of the Dark," is the first step in self-discovery. The speaker implies that the inhabited wood has undefined limits. Being lost in the undefined limits of the wood is to discover, even to be subsumed by, the echoes of the past that exist there. If the wood is inhabited by the past, however, the contrary is more likely true in that the wood is or has been defined by the past and the ghosts of the past that inhabit it still, all of which occurs by means of an ever-changing center or *locus* of perception. The wood's definition, then, exists in the forms of differences, of the various and competing voices and memories that constitute Ireland's history and tradition, rather than a specified, "defined," voice and memory of a single, exclusive tradition.

The speaker of the poem finds his excursion into the wood rejuvenating, an act that recalls certain literary and fairy tale pretexts, even though he discovers he cannot escape history and tradition. The speaker in "The Plantation," in the end, does not search for a point outside tradition, a point from which he can find rejuvenation from an extratextual experience. Quite the contrary, he discovers a place in which the differences that constitute his culture resonate most freely, without the "limits defined" by any one tradition or perspective.

In his reading of the poem, David Lloyd interprets the speaker's attempts to lose himself as a sign, both on the part of Heaney and the speaker, of longing for a union with a lost origin:

[Heaney in] his work relocates an individual and racial identity through the reterritorialization of language and culture. Heaney's rhetoric of compensation—"You had to come back / To learn how to lose yourself, / To be pilot and stray" (DD p. 50)—uncritically replays the Romantic schema

of a return to origins which restores continuity through fuller self-posses-
sion, and accordingly rehearses the compensations conducted by Irish
Romantic nationalism.[6]

Such an interpretation is certainly plausible, especially if the
speaker—if not Heaney himself—is pulled inexorably by the
gravities of Irish nationalism and the myth of a lost unity or origin. The use of the second person in the final stanza, though, is
troubling. Since this voice is not clearly either the speaker's interior monologue or the speaker's direct address to an audience, the
voice might be heard as censorious, accusatory, or even satiric—
in other words, an indictment of the very tendencies that Lloyd
identifies (i.e., "you *had* to go back," you couldn't resist, you
know better, I've told you about this before).[7] In which case, the
speaker of the poem becomes an internalized other imagined as
a voice that judges, admonishes, or even chides. Consequently,
the poem leads in one direction, showing the powerful need or
wish for a place of origin and identity, only to turn the tables at
the end and chastise the speaker, even the reader, for such Romantic longings.

The practice of trying to lose oneself in order to find oneself, or
to gain a new perspective, which facilitates the poetic utterance,
recurs in "The Peninsula," a poem, like "The Plantation," written
in the second person: "When you have nothing more to say, just
drive / For a day all around the peninsula" (DD 21). It is not the
drive itself nor the experiences *per se* during the drive that possess
any rejuvenating power. Rather, the impressions that the drive
leaves in the speaker's memory will one day be the impetus to a
new poetic utterance.

6. Lloyd, "'Pap for the Dispossessed': Seamus Heaney and the Poetics of Identity,"
Boundary 2 13 (1985): 325. Lloyd notes that his use of the word *reterritorialization* differs
from that of Deleuze and Guatarri.

7. Paul de Man identifies "at least four possible and distinct types of self: "the self that
judges, the self that reads, the self that writes, and the self that reads itself." *Blindness and
Insight: Essays in the Rhetoric of Contemporary Criticism* (New York: Oxford UP, 1971) 39.
Each of these selves are evident in Heaney's poems about writing, and these various functions and identities of the self are key to what I have identified as the questioning and
reinscribing of tradition.

The transition between the first two stanzas and the last two stanzas in "The Peninsula" captures the moment when these impressions are recalled:

> Now recall
>
> The glazed foreshore and silhouetted log,
> That rock where breakers shredded into rags,
> The leggy birds stilted on their own legs,
> Islands riding themselves out into the fog
>
> And drive back home, still with nothing to say
> Except that now you will uncode all landscapes
> By this: things founded clean on their own shapes,
> Water and ground in their extremity.
>
> (DD 21)

While this experience seems to be the consequence of the speaker's communion with the *genius loci*, afterwards the speaker "still will have nothing to say." In other words, this communion, if indeed it is a communion, allows the speaker to lose himself for a brief time, but it does not necessarily result in a restored origin or a poetic utterance.

Thus, Heaney's *poiesis* differs from that of the Romantics. In some Romantic poetry, the poem enshrines the record of its inception and entails an account of both the experience itself and the creation of the poem that is its consequence and emblem. In Shelley's "Ode to the West Wind," for instance, the wind symbolizes both the poet's vision and the moment of poetic utterance, the result of which has the power to reunite the individual with the divine and renew the life of a dying world. The resulting poem, then, is both an experiential and metaphysical plenitude as well as a moment in tune with an undivided origin.

Such is not the case with Heaney's poetry. Although the speaker may be prepared now to "uncode all landscapes," he is not prepared to escape the textuality of those landscapes. In fact, his ability to "uncode" these landscapes reinforces his awareness that they are indeed always already textual. To uncode does not, moreover, necessitate an escape from textuality to the rapture of a *hors-*

texte. The sequence of events in Heaney's *poiesis* begins with experiences, the memory of those experiences (whether personal or cultural), and the assimilation of these in the mind of the poet in preparation for the poetic utterance, as occurs in "The Plantation" or the opening stanzas of "The Peninsula." The next step is the "now" of the *inaugural* moment of the poetic utterance, as occurs in the final stanza of "Personal Helicon." The result is an utterance that, far from being the remembrance of some extratextual union with a stable meaning or origin, constitutes a space for the free-play of meaning that defers the possibility of a "correct" or univocal interpretation. This creative process occurs, to varying degrees of self-consciousness, in many of the poems in *Door into the Dark*.

"Relic of Memory," for example, is a poem comprised of four stanzas, six lines each, in which the first and second stanzas, and the initial line of the third stanza occur in the present moment but demonstrate how the present becomes inhabited by the past. The lough waters that constantly lap against old oars and posts, hardening them, "Incarcerate ghosts / Of sap and season" (DD 37).

Stanza 3 recounts moments of or moments directly following creation. The lava, the star, the coal and diamond, and the meteor are prehistoric and thus apparently refer to a time free from history and tradition. However, the speaker disrupts such an interpretation when he states that all these moments or images of creation "Are too simple, / Without the lure / That relic stored." The word *lure* implies something that is both attractive and dangerous, a trap, so too something about the "Incarcerate[d] ghosts" of the relic is more alluring than moments of apparent freedom from history and tradition. It is as if the history and tradition that abide in the relic energize it, even though words of horror such as *petrify*, *ghosts*, and *drowning* are used to describe the hardened wood in the first and second stanzas.

The poem ends with the image of "A piece of stone / On the shelf at school, / Oatmeal coloured," which represents both the speaker's realization that history and tradition abide in all things, even the smallest, and a deflation of the poem's pan-historical perspective. After all, this is just a brown stone on a shelf in a school. The final image, however, is actually the initiator of the poem, and the preceding portions of the poem are both memories of the past and the poetic utterance in the present. In this way, the speaker creates a mosaic of time, a collocation of images, not a linear, cause-and-effect sequence of events. Stanzas 1 and 2 and the first line of stanza 3 are progressive, an action that occurred in the past but continues in the present. The remainder of stanza 3 is a series of images of a prehistorical past, moments or events that undoubtedly occurred because the results are readily apparent, but whose original existence remains a matter of conjecture: the "dead lava" and the "cooling star" will eventually sustain life or make themselves known as a body in the heavens or an island in the ocean; "coal and diamond," which themselves capture this passage of time in that the former is transformed into the latter, will one day be unearthed and used; and the "sudden birth" of the meteor will ultimately be seen light years away. The speaker's observations about the allure of the relic in relation to these pre-historical events occur in the first three lines of the fourth stanza at the present moment. And, finally, the perception of the stone in the classroom could either be occurring in the present or lin-gering as a memory.

The title of the poem is an apparent redundancy: a "relic" is a memory or an artifact of a past time. The word also carries reli-gious or reverential connotations, signifying an object from the past that is esteemed in the present because it commemorates something or someone from the past. However, the poem itself may be the relic of memory—both the speaker's personal mem-ory of the lough and the oatmeal colored stone as well as the memory conveyed through "Incarcerate[d] ghosts" that extend back to moments of turbulent or nascent creation. The poem, fi-nally, turns back upon itself to examine both the elements of its own creation, the recurring memory of past events that are the subject matter of poetry for the speaker, and the importance of those memories. "Relic of Memory" is not so overtly self-reflexive as some of Heaney's later poems, but it does indicate Heaney's continued fascination with the influence upon and conflict between the past and the present, particularly in relation to poetic expression.

Like "The Plantation" and other early poems, "At a Potato Digging," from *Death of a Naturalist*, exemplifies Heaney's preoccupation with the tradition of rural Irish farmers. The poem is divided into four parts with sections 1, 2, and 4 occurring in the present, or at least a memory in the present, and section 3 occurring in the past, during the Great Hunger of 1845.[8] The workers in the poem, both past and present, labor in the potato fields. The process has changed little over the years, except now a "mechanical digger wrecks the drill," and the laborers follow behind. The poem does not progress chronologically, but moves backward in time in the third section. Thus, the poem is structured in contrapuntal fashion in which the images of the diggers in the present are recalled by the images from the past. The reader in this way unearths the past in the act of reading the poem, much as the speaker unearths "living roots" in "Digging."

In section 3, the people are described as "higgledy skeletons," "faces chilled," who live in "wicker huts," while "beaks of famine snipped at guts" (DN 32). In the first section, the potatoes have "Good smells," whereas in 1845 "Stinking potatoes fouled the land." In the present, the healthy potatoes are "piled in pits," whereas during the famine the "new potato . . . / putrefied . . . / in the long clay pit. / Millions rotted along with it." The higgledy furrows of the field in the present turn into higgledy skeletons of the past. Moreover, the people are described in section one as crows that descend upon a fertile field, but in section 3, the guts of the higgledy skeletons are "sniped" by "beaks of famine."

The transition to the third section is itself a near repetition of the concluding line of section 2:

> The rough bark of humus erupts
> knots of potatoes (a clean birth)
> whose solid feel, whose wet inside

8. See Thomas B. O'Grady, "'At a Potato Digging': Seamus Heaney's Great Hunger," *Canadian Journal of Irish Studies* 16 (1990): 48–58. O'Grady makes a careful examination of Heaney's debt to Cecil Woodham-Smith's book *The Great Hunger* as well as a contrast of Heaney's "epical" portrait of the Famine with Patrick Kavanagh's "lyrical" portrait.

promises taste of ground and root.
To be piled in pits; live skulls, blind eyes.

III
Live skulls, blind-eyed, balanced on
wild higgledy skeleton. . . .

(DN 32)

The transition is also a shift from metaphor to description. The healthy potatoes from the present are described as "live skulls," with the pun on "blind-eyed," followed by the description of the famine victims' heads as "Live skulls." The transition involves a conscious reversal of the pastoral images in sections 1 and 2 to the naturalistic images in section 3. The poem not only recalls events of the past, but the imagery itself turns back upon itself. This form of self-reflexiveness does not result in reconciliation, but discloses a cultural memory that has not or will not heal: "where diggers are / you still smell the running sore" (DN 33).

The workers in "At a Potato Digging," despite their hard work and effort, still experience famine. Even their acts of religious devotion to the Earth Goddess do not necessarily result in reconciliation:

Heads bow, trunks bend, hands fumble towards the black
Mother. Processional stooping through the turf

Recurs mindlessly as autumn. Centuries
Of fear and homage to the famine god
Toughen the muscles behind their humbled knees,
Make a seasonal altar of the sod.

(DN 31)

As Henry Hart explains, "Nearly all of Heaney's pastorals juxtapose the nostalgic hope for an Eden of permanent fruitfulness, where ripeness is all, against the anti-pastoral recognition of the laborer's toil and failure."[9] Likewise, the memories of the past that occur in Heaney's poetry are not mere nostalgia, a plangent note

9. Henry Hart, *Seamus Heaney: Poet of Contrary Progressions* (Syracuse, N.Y.: Syracuse UP, 1992) 26.

of longing for bygone days. They create, instead, the space in which the speaker's words exist. In the final section of "At a Potato Digging," the speaker sees the workers "breaking timeless fasts," and "stretched on the faithless ground, spill / Libations of cold tea, scatter crusts" (DN 33). The speaker perceives both the myth of the Earth Goddess that dominates his culture as well as the fact that it is indeed just a myth. He sees the workers in the present participating in an inveterate act. Though he is not directly party to this act, it is endemic and thus part of his cultural consciousness. Consequently, there is no reconciliation for the speaker, nothing to restore or recuperate, just the alternating perceptions of past and present and the speaker's utterance that calls attention to the influential or controlling myths of his tradition.

The first poem in "A Lough Neagh Sequence" occurs in the present and explores how a discourse, privileged over many centuries, like the myth of the Earth Goddess, reaches a point of condensation that circumvents the possible meanings of tradition in favor of a solidified, universal tradition. "Up the Shore" begins with a series of myths or folkloric beliefs about the lough that have been passed down over the years and are still believed, or at least perpetuated, today:

> The lough will claim a victim every year.
> It has virtue that hardens wood to stone.
> There is a town sunk beneath its water.
> It is the scar left by the Isle of Man.
>
> (DD 38)

The first two legends render images of a deity's influence—benevolent at times, referring to the lough's "virtue," violent at others, referring to its claim of a sacrificial victim every year. The idea of a town "sunk beneath its waters" could also be the result of a disaster, similar to Pompeii's destruction, or it could be magical as in the lost city of Atlantis. The final legend, that the lough was made by a break with the Isle of Man, returns to a prehistoric time, a time before man and therefore somehow pure or sacred. In contrast, the "scar" evokes the idea of a divided country that still bears the marks of its original division—as if Ireland were divided from its inception, ripped in pieces both by invasions and British colonialism as well as by prehistoric shifts of tectonic plates. Collectively these legends create and perpetuate a relationship between the fishermen and the lough itself.

The second stanza in "Up the Shore" shifts to the technological progress that has begun on the lough. Modern fishermen have created gates and tanks to catch the eels in huge quantities: "From time to time they break the eels' journey / And lift five hundred stone in one go" (DD 38). These modern fishermen are contrasted with the older fishermen who "confront them [the eels] one by one." These older fishermen are outlaws in their own country because they violate a law every time they fish the lough. During the Plantation period, a monopoly regarding harvesting the eels was granted to the patentees of the plantations. Only since the recent Troubles and after a lengthy and embittered legal battle have the Catholic fishermen gained the right to fish Lough Neagh.

The older fishermen have also never learned to swim, even though they spend almost every day on the lough's waters. The speaker of the poem has obviously argued with these fishermen about the logic of learning how to swim, a skill that could someday save their lives. The fishermen claim quite complacently that "'We'll be quicker going down'" and that "'The lough will claim a victim every year.'" The first line of the poem is directly echoed here in the last line of the poem, and the quotation marks in the latter designate it as a specific remark by a specific fisherman. Thereby, the belief that the lough will claim a victim every year is perpetuated, told to the speaker as it was told at one time to the fisherman, and before him to someone else.

While the rest of the world may be moving into the future, these fishermen look always to the past and persist in their mythical beliefs and in their antiquated practices. The speaker in "Up the Shore" is thus in the same position as the speaker in "Digging," watching members of an older generation continue a practice in which he cannot, or will not, participate. It is not that the speaker is contemptuous of the fishermen, for he says that "There is a sense of fair play" in their fishing practices. Rather, the speaker perceives a tradition in which he is both participant and arbiter, a position the speaker in many of Heaney's poems finds himself.

Like "Up the Shore," many of the poems in *Door into the Dark* are personal and intimate looks at the Irish countryside, but not always the most attractive or most traveled parts. The speaker in these poems, like the speaker in "A Lough Neagh Sequence," is very familiar with local customs and beliefs, but also has a historical perspective. He is rooted in these places and customs, but also separate from them. Whereas the people who populate this world may be taciturn and matter-of-fact, the speaker is descriptive and eager to tell the story of a place or event.[10]

In "Whinlands," for instance, the speaker carefully paints a picture celebrating the whin, a low, spiny evergreen shrub with yellow flowers that often populates wastelands in Europe. The speaker even lights a twig to demonstrate how the thorns burn but the sticks do not:

> The tough sticks don't burn,
> Remain like bone, charred horn.
>
> Gilt, jaggy, springy, frilled
> This stunted, dry richness
> Persists on hills, near stone ditches,
> Over flintbed and battlefield.
>
> (DD 47–48)

The sticks acquire a historical dimension as the speaker's description unleashes echoes of the past. The speaker takes pride in this rugged, indestructible plant that can withstand trial by fire. Like a skeleton that cannot be completely incinerated, the whin survives, "persists," despite its environment. In addition, the speaker's tale varies upon the parable of the sower and the seeds, but in this case the seed that falls upon rock refuses to die.

The reference to "flintbed" evokes a prehistoric time, like the legend about Lough Neagh and the Isle of Man. Also, as in "Re-

---

10. Blake Morrison makes a lengthy investigation into the taciturn nature of characters in Heaney's poetry and its cultural implications. Morrison, *Seamus Heaney* (London: Methuen, 1982) 20–28.

quiem for the Croppies," Ireland's history of battles is commemorated by its plant life. The political aspect is unmistakable here as
the speaker transforms the description of the whin and its bloom
into images of death that signify a refusal to die. Growing in an
Irish countryside that has befallen many battles, the whin nonetheless persists and therby retells the story of flintbeds and battlefields.

The speaker continues his tour in "Shoreline," which entails a
broader tour of Ireland. As in "Whinlands," the speaker addresses
the reader/listener directly:

> Take any minute. A tide
> Is rummaging in
> At the foot of all fields,
> All cliffs and shingles.
>
> Listen. Is it the Danes,
> A black hawk bent on the sail?
> Or the chinking Normans?
>
> (DD 51)

The use of second person in both "Whinlands" and "Shoreline"
is an invocation to the listener—not just to listen to the speaker—
but to hear, contemplate, and respond to the persistent echoes in
these settings. Just as the past echoes in the words and deeds of
members of the older generation, so too can it be heard in isolated
places in the Irish countryside and along the shoreline that has,
like the whin, seen many ages and many battles.

The tide is a constant, but a constant of repetition and variation. It brought the invaders of the past just as it now at "any minute" makes its way into the crevices and interior places of the
island. The image of the tide "rummaging," a word that connotes
altering a place, not just investigating it, recalls other images of
constant repetition: the run of the eels up the river to Lough
Neagh; the annual ritual of digging potatoes; the act of digging,
uncovering, and severing living roots; and many other quotidian
activities. However, these activities are not truly quotidian, for
they resonate with cultural memories and tradition.

As the speaker encourages the listener/reader to "Take any minute" and "Listen," he knows that the events of times past abide in the events of the present, like the "Incarcerate[d] ghosts" of "Relic of Memory." And these ghosts are legion. Heaney has made this very point about the bogs of Ireland: "So I began to get an idea of bog as the memory of the landscape, or as a landscape that remembered everything that happened in and to it" (P 54). Along the same lines, the historian A. T. Q. Stewart attests that Ireland has endured repeated invasions which have left their mark:

By 1603, at least the eastern seaboard, and probably a great deal more of the eastern half of the province, had undergone a long history of colonization, of which only the barest written record survives. Its existence is much more obvious to the archaeologist than to the historian, and is indeed still apparent to the eye of any interested observer of the countryside. . . . The already thoroughly mixed population which existed at the beginning of historic times had to absorb wave after wave of new invaders. To it we must add the Vikings, who in the ninth century established a great many colonies in eastern Ireland and gave Ireland its first towns. The placenames of eastern Ulster provide plenty of evidence of their settlements and influences — Strangford and Carlingford loughs, islands and reefs with names like the Skerries or Skullmartin (from *skyr* meaning reef).[11]

After the Vikings came the Normans, who built imposing stone fortifications that still command a place on the Irish landscape, such as the castle at Carrickfergus on Belfast Lough. Beyond their place on the Irish landscape, these sites command a place in Ireland's tradition — its cultural psyche — as they "Stay, forgotten like sentries." This line, the last from "Shoreline," is an apparent oxymoron because it seems impossible for something to both "Stay" and be "forgotten." However, the line reads "forgotten like sentries." Ordinarily, a sentry is placed on guard not to be forgotten, but to be relieved at specified intervals to ensure alertness. These sentries, though they remain in place, are forgotten because they provide no protection. In fact, they are emblems of Ireland's unprotectable shoreline.

11. Stewart, A. T. Q., *The Narrow Ground: Aspects of Ulster, 1609–1969* (London: Faber, 1977) 31–32.

They are also emblems of Ireland's political history, what Stewart refers to as Ireland's "lamination of cultures," a palimpsest of traditions that, despite their attempts at exclusivity, are ineluctably bound together.[12] For instance, in A.D. 836 the Vikings established a base at Arklow after their initial arrival in Ireland around A.D. 795. Four centuries later, the Normans arrived and established themselves firmly in old Norse centers, including Arklow. The town was then given to Theobald Butler by Prince John, and the ruins of his castle remain. The town was allied with Kildare in the fourteenth century as part of the "land of peace." Despite all attempts to stabilize the nine counties on the eastern coast around Dublin under the Statutes of Kilkenny in 1366, the region was never completely conquered nor ever completely peaceful—as when the Irish raided Tallaght, County Wexford, and Arklow in 1331. Wexford insurgents were later repulsed at Arklow during the 1798 uprising as they were advancing on Dublin.

Carrickfergus also has a history that documents the hegemonic changes in Ireland. The castle at Carrickfergus was built by one group of invaders, the Normans. In 1316, after a year's siege during which time the inhabitants were said to have resorted to cannibalism, Carrickfergus fell to the invading forces of Edward Bruce. Later, during the Plantation period of the seventeenth century, the town was used as the site of a presbytery and a garrison town by Scottish settlers.

Carrickfergus, Arklow, and the other towns mentioned in "Shoreline" perform a double duty. In one sense, they represent the invaders who, throughout the centuries, uninvited and unwanted, have come to the Irish shoreline, a situation that many an Irish citizen believes still occurs today. On the other hand, these fortresses and towns attest to the fact that Ireland cannot be distinguished from the history of invasion and conquest that has defined it.

The speaker in "Bann Clay," for example, begins by pointing out that the stain from the clay can be seen everywhere on the boots and pants of laborers. The speaker begins with the specific

12. Stewart, *The Narrow Ground* 34.

and descriptive image of the clay and then extrapolates that image into a historical context:

> For centuries under the grass
> It baked white in the sun,
> Relieved its hoarded waters
> And began to ripen.
>
> (DD 53)

The reference to "hoarded waters" anticipates passages from other poems: the River Moyola as "hoarder of common ground" in "Gifts of Rain," the "word-hoard" of "North," into which the speaker "burrow[s]" or digs, and the poem sequence "A Northern Hoard." In "Bann Clay," the water that seeps into the earth traces back to the distant past, and "Above it, the webbed march is new, / Even the clutch of Mesolithic / Flints" do not predate it.

The idea of water imbued with the past is also the subject of "Bogland," the final poem in *Door into the Dark*. The speaker contrasts the connection between the Irish and their land with the sense of Manifest Destiny and the American West:

> We have no prairies
> To slice a big sun at evening—
> Everywhere the eye concedes to
> Encroaching horizon. . . .
>
> (DD–55)

The speaker here contemplates the "Inwards and downwards" movement of the Irish consciousness, itself rooted deeply in its native soil. He notes that archaeologists, having excavated the bogs, only find "waterlogged trunks." Like the waters of the River Bann that seep into the land or like the tide of "Shoreline" that "Is rummaging in / At the foot of all fields, / All cliffs and shingles," the Irish ground is "Melting and opening underfoot, / Missing its last definition / By millions of years" (DD 55).

The fact that the land is "Missing its last definition" implies an endless deferral or lack of closure. The land is in a perpetual state of transformation or definition, never reaching its ultimate or absolute state. Moreover, the land constantly defines and redefines itself, in contrast to the American West—mistaken as the belief may have been—which was virgin territory awaiting its original definition. A similar point is made in "Lovers on Aran" when the speaker asks, "Did sea define the land or land the sea? / Each drew new meaning from the waves' collision. / Sea broke on land to full identity" (DN 47). Heaney uses the words *define* and *definition* in these two poems, as he used *defined* in "The Plantation," to describe the land. This choice of words—beyond maintaining that Ireland defies a simple, stable identity or "definition"—connects the tradition of Ireland and its continually developing identity with language. This connection is further explored in "Lovers on Aran." As the land defines itself from the sea, or is defined by the sea, it draws "new meaning from the waves' collision." Those same waves brought the invaders of "Shoreline." Thus, the land itself, its tradition, as well as its identity, come into being through a continual process of articulation that defines and redefines the country.

In regard to the land, no permanent settlement exists, no apparent place of absolute origin. The speaker in "Bogland" proffers a connection between Irish archaeology and Irish identity: "Every layer they strip / Seems camped on before. // The wet centre is bottomless" (DD 56). The word *camped* is used to describe the various cultures laminated on top of one another that constitute the archaeology and history of Ireland. The word also means to stay for a short time in a relatively uninhabited place, a friendly foray into the wood, the way the campers and other visitors did in "The Plantation." The word also has a military connotation, the camps of invaders who have crossed the Irish shorelines over the centuries. These invaders, of course, did not remain for just a short time but stayed long enough that their arrival and their occupation blend into the tradition of the country.

The bottomless center of "Bogland" and the darkness of "Personal Helicon" complement each other, the former referring to the seemingly endless levels of history and tradition that constitute the Irish consciousness and the latter referring to the space in which the utterances of the poet exist. However, the bottomless center of "Bogland" is always already language in the form of history, myth, cultural artifacts, and folklore—repetitions or recurrences of the past that have been excavated, perpetuated, and interpreted.

Correspondingly, the poet who sets "the darkness echoing" does so only by creating a new version of those recurrences—the continuous deferral of the interpretations and meanings of the bottomless center. It is in this connection that Heaney's poetic practice becomes clear. He must plumb the depths of his native land and resound his personal and cultural past in the *inaugural* act of writing.[13] Such an act of writing is not an act of closure, of capturing the essential Ireland in a poem, because no such essential or original Ireland exists, only a bottomless center. A. T. Q. Stewart specifically illustrates the problematical nature of Irish origins:

The first inhabitants of Ulster, whoever they were, were not the Gaels. Nor were they the Uliad, who gave the region its name. The earliest recognizable concept of Ulster is the *cóiced n Uliad*, literally the province of the Uliad. It goes back to the first centuries A.D. and perhaps earlier. The capital of the Uliad is traditionally supposed to be Emain Macha, close to the city of Armagh. The great mound there has been very carefully excavated by archaeologists in recent years. It did not yield any dramatic evidence to confirm or refute this assumption, but proved beyond doubt that beneath it lay a settlement two thousand years older. In the same way, at the hill of Tara, in the Boyne valley, archaeologists have been able to show that the site had been sacred to the natives for two thousand years before the Celtic fortress was built upon it. Queen Macha was almost certainly not a Celtic queen but a much older goddess.[14]

This is not to say that history is unimportant because it cannot be specifically delineated or traced back to a specific origin.

---

13. Derrida refers to writing as *inaugural* because "it does not know where it is going, no knowledge can keep it from the essential precipitation toward the meaning that it constitutes and that is, primarily, its future," and "meaning present[s] itself as such at the point at which the other is found, the other who maintains both the vigil and the back-and-forth motion, the work, that comes between writing and reading. . . . Meaning is neither before nor after the act." See Derrida, *Writing and Difference* (Chicago: U of Chicago P, 1978) 11.

14. Stewart, *The Narrow Ground* 30.

Rather, the speaker in these poems practices what Derrida describes as "originary repetition" — that is, recurrences without origin, or centerless repetitions. The speaker intentionally avoids positing a definitive origin, whether in time or location. The fact that so many echoes of the past reverberate from prehistoric times subverts the possibility of a stable *locus* of inception. Political associations in words are just that — meanings that have been acquired over the course of time. There is no essential Ireland in which one true tradition exists that is the progeny of the one true source, in contrast to the false traditions that are perversions caused by outside influences. The influences of historical events and invaders are like the tide in "Shoreline" rummaging and seeping into the land — altering and coupling with the land, continually defining the culture and its people.

In his early poems, Heaney comprehends the complexity of his cultural heritage and avoids or subverts attempts to create a sequential or unified perspective. This is one of the fascinating aspects of Heaney's poetry because so many of the poems in *Door into the Dark* seem to invite an interpretation based on the fundamental elements of earth, air, fire, and water that bear mythic qualities. For example, water is the dominant element in "The Salmon Fisher to the Salmon," "Girls Bathing, Galway 1965," "Undine," "Cana Revisited," "Relic of Memory," "A Lough Neagh Sequence," and "Shoreline." Fire is the element in "The Forge," and "Whinlands." In "In Gallarus Oratory," "Requiem for the Croppies," "Bann Clay," and "Bogland," the dominant element is earth, and it is air in "The Given Note."

A number of poems even entail a mixture of elements under the auspices of one dominant element, such as earth and water in "Bann Clay." These elements only have mythic qualities insofar as they act as constructs of meanings that recur throughout history. The fact that they recur does not necessitate their original or essential nature. They are, instead, vehicles for creating meaning that resonate strongly in the myths and literature of various cultures because they signify and symbolize elements common to the human experience. Heaney excavates such resonances in his early poetry without falling into the trap of codifying them into a stable meaning or connecting them with an original utterance.

The image of a wood inhabited by ghosts of the past in "The Plantation" and the description of history as ages and cultures laminated on top of one another in "Shoreline" capture Heaney's vision of his country. Everywhere he looks and listens he sees and hears the past. At times it seems to haunt him; at other times it looks more like an overlapping mosaic than a linear progression of events, as if each layer of culture allows or cannot prevent parts of the layer below from showing through. In either case, the speaker is less concerned with finding a preconceived notion of Ireland than he is with finding the many facets of tradition that constitute his cultural identity.

Heaney's poetic utterances do not result in redrawing factional lines; rather, they result in a darkness that resounds with many sounds from many ages and from many perspectives. If, as Andrew Waterman insists, the Irish writer is "expected to define exactly where he stands in relation to some or other concept of nationalism and cultural allegiance," Heaney does so without falling into the obvious traps.[15] He does not forsake his heritage: many of his poems commemorate the people, places, and practices of Irish Catholics living in rural Ulster. He also writes of highly personal topics, such as his brother's death and his love for and relationship with his wife. Furthermore, a poem such as "Docker" overtly examines factional hatred in Ulster. Heaney is blind to none of these. His historical sense is neither dogmatic nor confrontational. Rather, it entails a careful and sensitive exploration of the country that is very dear to him—a country that, like language itself, is composed of differences, despite the efforts of tradition(s) to reduce all to an exclusive sameness. Perhaps this is what Heaney meant in an interview when, discussing what it was like to grow up and live in the North, he refers to both "the silent awarenesses of the division" and "the music of division."[16]

15. Waterman, "Ulsterectomy," in Best Poetry of the Year Selected by Dannie Abse, *Poetry Dimension Annual 6* (London: Robson, 1979) 42.

16. Monie Begley, *Rambles in Ireland* (New York: Methuen, 1977) 161–63.

Door into the Dark appeared in 1969, a time of great change and turmoil in Northern Ireland. Historical and political events were occurring that required a more specific and aggressive response to the "concept of nationalism and cultural allegiance." An adequate response to this crisis required a modification to Heaney's poetic practices, but that modification would not come easily.

3 ❦ Flying by the Nets of Language and Nationality

How does a writer poetically address the problems of a country whose political and cultural fissures have resulted in an apparently endless cycle of distrust, oppression, and violence? Seamus Heaney had to answer this question for himself in the late 1960s, when the "Troubles" took a decidedly violent turn and forced the civil rights movement in Northern Ireland to a moment of crisis.[1]

Creating a form of poetry commensurate with times of strident political turmoil is perhaps the greatest challenge a poet can face: "On the one hand, poetry is secret and natural, on the other hand it must make its way in a world that is public and brutal. . . . At one minute you are drawn towards the old vortex of racial and religious instinct, at another time you seek the mean of humane love and reason" (P 34). A mind pulled between two poles, so clearly evident in this quotation, can be seen throughout Heaney's work in the late 1960s and early 1970s. As a citizen and a poet, Heaney wanted to address the schism in Ulster society and the continuing problem of violence and repression, both of which had created and perpetuated an underclass of Catholic citi-

---

1. Numerous studies are available on the Troubles. The following sources provide a varied look at the violence and political unrest that have plagued Northern Ireland over the past twenty-five years or so: Paul Arthur and Keith Jeffery, *Northern Ireland Since 1968* (London: Blackwell, 1988); J. Bowyer Bell, *The Irish Troubles: A Generation of Violence 1967–1992* (New York: St. Martin's Press, 1993); John Conroy, *Belfast Diary: War as a Way of Life* (Boston: Beacon, 1987); Tim Pat Coogan, *Disillusioned Decades: Ireland 1966–87* (Dublin: Gill and Macmillan, 1987); Michael Farrell, *Northern Ireland: The Orange State* (London: Pluto, 1976); R. F. Foster, *Modern Ireland: 1600–1972* (New York: Penguin, 1988); Russell Stetler, *The Battle of Bogside* (London: Sheed and Ward, 1970); Michael Watson, ed., *Contemporary Minority Nationalism* (London: Routledge, 1990) chaps. 3 and 4.

zens, though he did not want to advocate the violent retaliation practiced by the Provisional wing of the Irish Republican Army.

In his first two volumes of poetry, Heaney's pan-historical approach—one which had made him wary of political, religious, and nationalistic dogmatisms—allowed him to explore Ireland's various traditions. But now those traditions, in the form of exclusive political and ideological factions, violently clashed in the streets of Belfast and Derry. Reflecting upon the Troubles and their impact upon the writer, Heaney writes:

> We live here in critical times ourselves, when the idea of poetry as an art is in danger of being overshadowed by a quest for poetry as a diagram of political attitudes. Some commentators have all the fussy literalism of an official from the ministry of truth . . . if a poet must turn his resistance into an offensive, he should go for a kill and be prepared, in his life and with his work, for the consequences. (P 219–20).

Heaney was not prepared to turn his poetry into "an offensive," and he certainly did not want to "go for a kill." Nonetheless, he needed to explore a form of poetic "resistance" that voiced both halves of that divided mind while avoiding the extremes of political activism and political escapism. Heaney needed to find a form of creative dialogue, an emancipating discourse that would face the realities of the ideologically motivated, violent, pragmatic political arena but would also circumvent the monologic, exclusionary, and restrictive discourses so often used by those who function in that arena.

Between 1968 and 1972 Heaney developed a polyphonic voice that displaced the political and cultural antagonisms endemic to his country and relocated them in a realm of reflexive, historical linguistics. That is, the emancipating discourse that Heaney developed to circumvent Ireland's centuries-old and mutually exclusive political monologues entailed a confrontation of historically diverse discourses within a single poem. Heaney chose to address the political /poetic dilemma that he and other Irish writers faced by making the language of Irish writers (as well as the language of the Irish people in general) the focus of—or at least a significant factor in—his poetry. Heaney thereby, at least to some extent, circumvented the political/poetic dilemma with a poetry whose vernacular problematic addressed old antagonisms in an innovative way. This move did not make Heaney's poetry apolitical; rather, it redirected the political aspects already inscribed in his language, what Deleuze and Guattari call a "reterritorialization" (or recodification) of language.[2] To map this transition in Heaney's poetic practices, I shall assess some of the overtly political poems that Heaney chose to exclude from *Wintering Out*, then examine those poems that were revised before their inclusion in *Wintering Out*, and finally place Heaney's "language poems" within the complex, and often contradictory, realm of Irish history and politics.

While Heaney was developing his polyphonic voice, many people called upon him to take sides in the antagonistic political arena, which at times he did. Many of the poems written during this transitional period reveal Heaney's struggle to find "images and symbols adequate to our predicament" (P 56). In his review of Heaney's *Wintering Out*, John Boland objects that Heaney omitted a number of poems on the Troubles that he had previously published in journals and magazines. Declaring that Irish poetry is at an "unsure point" and that Irish poets themselves seem unsure as to which direction they should go, Boland recognizes Heaney as Ireland's leading poet who will soon publish some poetry with "renewed mastery and passion."[3]

However, Boland perceives a distinct shift in some of Heaney's uncollected poems as well as those in *Wintering Out*, especially among the poems written during the period of acute political tur-

---

2. Gilles Deleuze and Félix Guattari, "What Is a Minor Literature?" *Mississippi Review* 11 (1983): 13–33. Deleuze and Guattari identify the characteristics of "minor" literature that exists in a "major" language: (1) There is a recurrent need to "deterritorialize" the dominant language; (2) experience and language are necessarily political; and (3) consciousness is collective rather than individualized. Abdul JanMohamed suggests a further quality, (4) marginality itself as a defining characteristic. See "Humanism and Minority Literature," *Boundary 2* 12/13 (1984): 295–98. While characteristics 1, 2, and 4 apply to Heaney's poetry, characteristic 3, articulating a collective consciousness, definitely does not.

3. John Boland, "Winter of Discontent," rev. of *Wintering Out*, by Seamus Heaney, *Hibernia* 1 Dec. 1972: 11.

moil in the North. Critics and reviewers alike accused Heaney of ignoring or failing to take a stance in his poetry on the violent Troubles facing Ulster.[4] Boland's main grievance is that "Whatever You Say, Say Nothing," which was published in *The Listener* in October of 1971, was not printed in its entirety in *Wintering Out*. Instead, section 4 appeared as an untitled prefatory poem dedicated to David Hammond and Michael Longley. The complete poem was not published until *North* in 1975.

With a title that seems to encourage recalcitrance and political skepticism, "Whatever You Say, Say Nothing" contraposes the very serious political problems facing Ulster—"The times are out of joint,"—with the catchwords, slogans, clichés, and platitudes that constitute the dominant discourse on "the Irish thing." The allusion to *Hamlet* is particularly interesting because the line occurs when Hamlet understands for the first time that he is bound to avenge his father's murder and set things right: "The time is out of joint; O cursed spite / That ever I was born to set it right" (I. v. 189–90). The speaker in "Whatever You Say, Say Nothing" is an unwilling Hamlet trapped by a multitude of Poloniuses—both beleaguered citizens and dispassionate journalists—who keep the violence and trouble at bay with words hollowed of meaning through relentless, unreflective use. The speaker reflects that it is

> . . . near time some small leak was sprung
>
> In the great dykes the Dutchman made
> To dam the dangerous tide that followed Seamus.
> Yet for all this art and sedentary trade
> I am incapable.
>
> (N 59)

The poem ends with the image of Long Kesh, known as the Maze, a prison used for interning without trial those who dare disrupt the *status quo*. Heaney uses this section in *Wintering Out*. The speaker describes the prison, a "real stockade," in film terms:

4. Henry Hart summarizes many of these responses to *Wintering Out* in chapter 4, "Poetymologies," *Seamus Heaney: Poet of Contrary Progressions* (Syracuse, N.Y.: Syracuse UP, 1992) 49–73.

"And it was déjà-vu, some film made / Of Stalag 17" (N 60). The analogy with the celluloid prison, beyond linking England with Nazi Germany, implies that the constant mass media coverage has familiarized violence and martial law to the point that they lose their horror.

Why would Heaney choose not to include the entire poem in *Wintering Out*? Thematically, "Whatever You Say, Say Nothing," by identifying the lack of coherent or vitalized discourse on the Troubles, could have been a valuable addition to the volume. By including just the final section of the poem, which focuses on the image of the prison, Heaney creates a context in which all the other poems in the volume must be read. The poems of *Wintering Out* must be read in the shadow of Long Kesh Prison, in conjunction or contrast with the celluloid version of the prison as well, for these poems exist within the cultural context of a military state and its constituent violence. Heaney may want to challenge the way people perceive and discuss the Troubles, but he does not want them to forget its horrors.

Although any number of reasons might move a writer to omit certain poems from a volume of poetry, the choices Heaney made when selecting the poems for *Wintering Out* are revealing. Between June 1969, the date Heaney published *Door into the Dark*, and January 1972—a period of time that corresponds with the beginning of the current Troubles—Heaney published at least forty poems in journals or magazines, only about fourteen of which were included in *Wintering Out*, published in November of 1972.[5] Among the poems published between mid-1969 and early 1972 Heaney choose to exclude two out of every three poems from *Wintering Out*. This represents an unprecedented selectivity: even in his early days of writing, Heaney was less selective. Between 1959 and May of 1966, the date his collection *Death of a Naturalist* appeared, Heaney published approximately fifty poems, includ-

5. Poems include "Serenades," "Midnight," "Navvy," "High Street 1786" (under the title "Linen Town"), "Tweed" (under the title "The Wool Trade"), "Limbo," "The Last Mummer," "Tinder," "The Tollund Man," "Home" (under the title "Summer Home"), "Mother of the Groom," "Whatever You Say, Say Nothing," "Servant Boy," and "A Northern Hoard."

ing his juvenilia published in the Queen's University literary magazines, and about half of these were reprinted in *Death of a Naturalist*.[6]

Since the publication of *Door into the Dark* in 1969, Heaney had written some overtly political poems that merely recapitulated well-established political agendas and therefore rightfully did not belong in *Wintering Out*. One such poem, the polemical "Craig's Dragoons," is a caustic political ballad designed solely to stir Catholic emotions and promote solidarity. The poem was not, in fact, published independently but was presented in an opinion piece written by Karl Miller. The poem as it appears in Miller's article reads:

Craig's Dragoons (Air: "Dolly's Brae")

Come all ye Ulster loyalists and in full chorus join,
Think on the deeds of Craig's Dragoons who strike below the
    groin,

And drink a toast to the truncheon and the armoured water-hose
That mowed a swathe through Civil Rights and spat on Papish
    clothes.

We've gerrymandered Derry but Croppy won't lie down,
He calls himself a citizen and wants votes in the town.
But that Saturday in Duke Street we slipped the velvet glove—
The iron hand of Craig's Dragoons soon crunched a croppy dove.

Big McAteer and Currie, Gerry Fitt and others too,
Were fool enough to lead the van, expecting to get through.
But our hero commandos, let loose at last to play,
Did annihilate the rights of man in noontime of a day.

They downed women with children, for Teagues all over-breed,
They used the baton on men's heads, for Craig would pay no heed,

6. The information on Heaney's uncollected works is derived in part from Michael J. Durkan's, "Seamus Heaney: A Checklist for a Bibliography," *Irish University Review* 16 (1986): 48–76. Because an extensive bibliography on Heaney's poetry has yet to be compiled, these numbers should be considered as tentative. However, Michael Durkan is currently compiling a bibliography of Heaney's work, which should be published soon. Also, Durkan and Rand Brandes are collaborating on a bibliography of critical responses to Heaney's work, which is also forthcoming.

And then the boys placed in plain clothes, they lent a loyal hand
To massacre those Derry ligs behind a Crossley van.

O William Craig, you are our love, our lily and our sash,
You have the boys who fear no noise, who'll batter and who'll
    bash.

They'll cordon and they'll baton-charge, they'll silence protest
    tunes,
They are the hounds of Ulster, boys, sweet William Craig's Dra-
    goons.[7]

The epithet *Craig's Dragoons* links the home minister, William
Craig, and the Royal Ulster Constabulary with the king's soldiers,
or dragoons, who massacred thousands of the poorly armed and
trained United Irish Army during the rebellion of 1798. The poem
is more a political slogan than a poetic expression of Irish
troubles.

"Intimidation," another overtly political poem that Heaney excluded from *Wintering Out*, focuses on the anger of an unidentified though obviously Catholic speaker who resents the annual
Loyalist bonfires that the Protestants light on July 12 to celebrate
William III's 1690 victory at the Battle of the Boyne:

Their bonfire scorched his gable.
He comes home to kick through
A tumulus of ash,
A hot stour in the moonlight.

Each year this reek
Of their midsummer madness
Troubles him, a nest of pismires
At his drystone walls.

Ghetto rats! Are they the ones
To do the smoking out?
They'll come streaming past
To taste their ashes yet.

7. Karl Miller, "Opinion," *The Review* 27–28 (1971/72): 41–52. According to Miller,
"Craig's Dragoons" was circulated anonymously. Quoting the poem approvingly, Miller
calls it a "true and effective public poem which deserves to be printed" (47).

He sits long after bedtime
With the light out.
Moondust drifts down the street
And soot, off his blackened gable.[8]

The use of abstracted figures, the unidentified "him" and the collective "they" and "their," promotes a sense of alienation and division unlike the differences Heaney explored in *Death of a Naturalist* and *Door into the Dark*. "Craig's Dragoons" and "Intimidation" fall prey to the political/poetic dilemma Heaney needed to overcome: they both rearticulate the old antagonisms of Ulster politics from a single and exclusionary perspective.

In "Intimidation," however, Heaney experiments with a method that he would later use to escape this dilemma when he chooses the Latin *tumulus* over the Irish *cairn* in the first stanza to describe the piles of ash that remain after the bonfires. The choice of *tumulus* orthographically recalls *tumult*, which corresponds with *stour* and reinforces the sense of vertiginous violence. Also, the use of *stour* emphasizes not only the sense of violence and unease in the poem, but reasserts the factional divisions along religious and nationalist lines that characterize Ulster society.

The word *stour*—meaning armed combat or conflict, a death struggle—is a form of British and Scots dialect. The word was often used by Edmund Spenser to mean a time of turmoil or stress.[9] Spenser, who also appears as a lingering vestige of Ireland's cultural ties to the English monarchy in "Bog Oak," was an undertaker in Ireland for the settlement of Munster, and his home, Kilcolman Castle, was a planter's estate in County Cork. "Intimidation" bespeaks Heaney's growing awareness of what he would later call the "cultural depth-charges latent in certain words" (P 150). A word such as *stour* carries an array, even an arsenal, of meanings and associations that strongly resonate throughout the poem. Eventually, Heaney will use Irish (as well as English and

8. Seamus Heaney, "Intimidation," *Malahat Review* 17 (1971): 34.

9. See, e.g., Spenser's *The Faerie Queene*: 1, ii, 7; 3, ii, 6; 4, ix, 39 and *The Shepheardes Calender*: January, 51; May, 156, in *Spenser: Poetical Works* ed. J. C. Smith and E. De Selincourt (Oxford: Oxford UP, 1970).

Scots) words and local dialects as cultural depth-charges that explode in a traditional English line of verse to create a form of poetry that circumvents political monologism by celebrating linguistic pluralism.

Heaney's previous poetry had conspicuously lacked the inveterate acrimony and factional antagonism so evident in "Intimidation." Heaney reveals one reason for his change of heart and change of poetic stance in his article "Old Derry's Walls": "Two years ago, in an article on Belfast, I tried to present both sides as more or less blameworthy. But it seems now that the Catholic minority in Northern Ireland at large, if it is to retain any self-respect, will have to risk that charge of wrecking the new moderation and seek justice more vociferously."[10] Heaney makes the same point in his essay "Feeling into Words" when discussing the violence of the summer of 1969:

> From that moment the problems of poetry moved from being simply a matter of achieving the satisfactory verbal icon to being a search for images and symbols adequate to our predicament. . . . I mean that I felt it imperative to discover a field of force in which, without abandoning fidelity to the processes and experience of poetry as I have outlined them, it would be possible to encompass the perspectives of a humane reason and at the same time to grant the religious intensity of the violence its deplorable authenticity and complexity. . . . Now I realize that this idiom is remote from the agnostic world of economic interest whose iron hand operates in the velvet glove of 'talks between elected representatives', and remote from the political manoeuvers of power-sharing; but it is not remote from the psychology of the Irishmen and Ulstermen who do the killing, and not remote from the bankrupt psychology and mythologies implicit in the terms Irish Catholic and Ulster Protestant. (P 56/57)

Heaney clearly realizes that the times demand a poetry commensurate with their social and political upheaval, but the overtly political or propagandistic poem is not the answer. The "idiom" that Heaney is searching for is remote from that of political activism, which is exactly the type of idiom he uses in "Craig's Dragoons."

10. Heaney, "Old Derry's Walls," *The Listener* 24 (Oct. 1968): 552. Heaney is referring to his article "Out of London: Ulster's Troubles," *New Statesman* 1 (July 1966): 23–24.

The references to "the velvet glove" and the "iron hand," alluding to Prime Minister Captain O'Neill's political and economic policies, occur in both "Craig's Dragoons" and in the above passage from "Feeling into Words."

Although less propagandistic but no less inflammatory, "Last Camp" is another poem with a singular political agenda excluded from *Wintering Out*:

I
Our Lars always at stud—
Battering out a spore
Of fouled whitewash and tar—

Now haunts the charred gables,
Poison curd on the walls,
Abandoned urinals.

II
Here in the tundra we
Trot among our icons,
Old dung scattered like brains

Hardening underfoot.
We gather and burn it,
Reeking our lives.

III
Purses shrivelled like figs,
Cast-offs, spent cartridges—
God, we will defend these

Scraps with nails and canines,
Our bonded detritus,
Pieties, rare droppings.[11]

In "Last Camp," the past lingers in a pitiful and violent present, the speaker's vision that of a nearly decimated tradition enduring in its own ruins. The whitewash is used to write political graffiti and slogans on buildings, a practice Heaney discusses in his essay "Christmas, 1971" (P 31). The tar perhaps alludes to the practice of punishing Irish women who collaborate with British troops by

11. Seamus Heaney, "Last Camp," *New Statesman* 12 (June 1970): 840.

tarring them, a topic Heaney will return to in "Punishment." The stench of dung that fuels the fire, "Reeking our lives," pervades the poem, recalling the "reek / Of their midsummer madness" in "Intimidation."

The perspective in "Intimidation" and "Last Camp" is unusual for Heaney. Previously, he had used the first person plural primarily in narrative contexts where several people participate in an activity together, as in "Blackberry Picking" or "Dawn Shoot." In "Intimidation" and "Last Camp," though, Heaney uses the collective pronouns *we* and *our* to articulate a distinct and defiant collective consciousness, as if all Catholics were united in their resolve to pursue political unrest: "we will defend these / Scraps with nails and canines." Only once before had Heaney used the first person plural in a similar way, in the opening lines of "Bogland," the last poem in *Door into the Dark*: "We have no prairies / To slice a big sun at evening" (55). Here, however, the political agenda is not the militant one of "Intimidation" and "Last Camp"; instead, Heaney contrasts the "national consciousness" he voices from the American consciousness (P 55). This consciousness is, moreover, peculiarly Irish rather than particularly Catholic or Protestant, or otherwise assignable to a factor or myth that might be used to distinguish one Irish citizen from another.

Exemplifying the poems Heaney excludes from *Wintering Out*, "Craig's Dragoons," "Intimidation," and "Last Camp" are all characterized by their preoccupation with factional strife and violence. These three poems are, in other words, emblematic of the unproductive and polarizing discourse from which Heaney was trying to escape. Seamus Deane explains the trap of recapitulating the established political discourses in Northern Ireland:

The acceptance of a particular style of Catholic or Protestant attitudes or behaviour, married to a dream of a final restoration of vitality to a decayed cause or community, is a contribution to the possibility of civil war. It is impossible to do without ideas of a tradition. But it is necessary to disengage from the traditions of the ideas which the literary revival and the accompanying political revolution sponsored so successfully.[12]

12. Seamus Deane et al., eds. *Ireland's Field Day* (Notre Dame, Ind.: U of Notre Dame P, 1986) 56

Among the poems first published in magazines or journals between 1969 and 1972, approximately fourteen were significantly
revised before being included in *Wintering Out*.[13] One of these,
"Tinder," which became the final poem in "A Northern Hoard,"
saw significant revisions before its appearance in *Wintering Out*
and offers a useful indication of Heaney's changing poetic directions. "Tinder's" first nine stanzas, as they appeared in the *New
Statesman*, remained substantially the same as the version that appeared in *Wintering Out*, but its final stanzas were revised as
Heaney began to discover a direction for his poetry. A comparison
of the final stanzas is revealing:

> [*New Statesman* version]
> But the man came with a tinder-box
> And left ash like brown phlox
>
> Settling after the flames' soft thunder
> On blackened wall and live cinder
>
> He came with face blank as anvil
> His kettle-drum, the kick and rattle
>
> Of flint on iron
> From the box tossing at his groin.[14]

> [*Wintering Out* version]
> Now we squat on cold cinder,
> Red-eyed, after the flames' soft thunder
>
> And our thoughts settle like ash.
> We face the tundra's whistling brush
>
> With new history, flint and iron,
> Cast-offs, scraps, nail, canine.

(WO 44)

---

13. See Arthur McGuinness, "The Craft of Diction: Revision in Seamus Heaney's
Poems," *Irish University Review* 9 (1979): 62–91. McGuinness observes that Heaney nor-
mally makes his revisions between the worksheet and journal versions and that "the journal and book versions of a poem are identical or very similar" (68). While Heaney may
have adopted this practice with *North*, which is the focus of McGuinness's essay, he revised *Wintering Out* at other stages as well.

14. Seamus Heaney, "Tinder," *New Statesman* 15 May 1970: 704.

The *Wintering Out* version eliminates the intrusion of the Loyalist and his kettle drum, a reference, like that in "Intimidation," to the annual Protestant celebration on July 12 of the victory at the Battle of the Boyne, often referred to as the Orangemen's "walking day."

The revised ending of "Tinder" is less political and less polemical. Factional elements—images that promote a polarizing "us" versus "them" mentality—are modified to form a perspective that explores the connections between Ulster's violent past and its violent present. Heaney is clearly revising his poems to break with entrenched and apparently unproductive debates among exclusive groups and discourses. He revises moreover in order to suggest an emancipating discourse that retains the capacity to address current issues but without taking *a* side. Since the "new history," which might be the product of such an emancipating discourse, remains conjecture or even wishful thinking at the end of "Tinder," Heaney's revisions merely point to a goal and a means of pursuing it which he will explore in his other poems.

While "Tinder" was revised to suggest a "new history," the other poems in the sequence "A Northern Hoard" illustrate the burden of history that the "new history" must discard. The speaker in "A Northern Hoard" reflects upon the violence in Northern Ireland and the stance he must take toward that violence. The title of the sequence, "A Northern Hoard," is both a reference to the ancient Celtic clans (or hordes) of Ireland's past, those who sit about the primitive fire in the early stanzas of "Tinder," as well as to the diverse voices, myths, and languages that exist in the North—a hoard of traditions that do now and always have waged war with one another. The sequence of poems is set, however, in contemporary Ulster, a sign of the continuing Irish struggle for survival and homeland.

The speaker in the first poem, "Roots," makes no reference to the past, only to a present moment when two lovers, bathed in moonlight, are startled from their solitary world by the intrusion of the violent world outside their room:

> . . . the din
> Of gunshot, siren and clucking gas

Out there beyond each curtained terrace
Where the fault is opening. The touch of love,
Your warmth heaving to the first move,
Grows helpless in our old Gomorrah,
We petrify or uproot now.

(WO 39)

Their love, a temporary respite from the Troubles, "Grows helpless" in the face of gunshots and siren. The line "We petrify or
uproot now" warns that the constant and recalcitrant repetition
of Nationalist and Unionist discourses over time "petrify" into
unproductive political positions unless they are "uprooted now."
The clichés and catchphrases in "Whatever You Say, Say Nothing" also fall into this category of petrified discourse. Uprooting
the petrified discourses of hatred, sectarianism, and exclusion
portends the only source of hope for these two lovers.

The reference to Gomorrah in the lines quoted above encourages an alternative interpretation of the poem that does not require a connection with the Celtic clans. In the story of Sodom
and Gomorrah, Lot, his wife, and his family—the only righteous
people left in the city and thus the only ones spared the wrath of
God—were forced to leave their home or be destroyed with the
city. As the story goes, Lot's wife could not resist a final look back
at the city, despite God's warning against it, and was turned into
a pillar of salt. In light of this biblical reference, the line "We petrify or uproot now" becomes as an urgent plea for change, proclaiming, If we look back on the old ways, the way Lot's wife did,
we will be petrified, turned into a pillar of salt. But, the plea continues, if we uproot ourselves, as Lot did, we might be able to escape the inevitable destruction. Such an interpretation provides
no solution to the violence except escape—for the lovers to leave
the North, as Heaney and his family did in 1972.

The act of uprooting recurs in the final stanzas when the
speaker tells his lover that he will dream of a way to escape the
violence:

I've soaked by moonlight in tidal blood

A mandrake, lodged human fork,
Earth sac, limb of the dark;

And I wound its damp smelly loam
And stop my ears against the scream.

(WO 39)

The title of the first poem in the sequence, "Roots," refers to tradition and to an actual root, as the speaker mentions the mandrake root in the final stanzas. The mandrake root is a common symbol for man because its forked shape resembles a human trunk and legs. When a mandrake root is pulled, or uprooted, the shriek it supposedly emits is the cry of the dead murderers buried where the root now grows. Also, the mandrake root supposedly holds healing powers. Uprooting the mandrake in this sense both underscores the many people killed during Ulster's long history of violence and expresses the speaker's desire to halt the violence. The only solution the speaker finds, ineffective as it may be, is to wind the mandrake and stop his ears and thereby silence the screams.

In the subsequent poems in "A Northern Hoard," the speaker contemplates the consequences of his solutions. In "No Man's Land," the speaker finds respite only by leaving and thereby shutting out all signs of violence. Having temporarily escaped the sounds of their wounds, the speaker returns to "confront my smeared doorstep." The violence has continued in his absence. The reference to the smeared door recalls the Passover, another violent biblical reference regarding the impending wrath of God. The speaker's lament—"Why do I unceasingly / arrive late to condone / infected sutures / and ill-knit bone?"—suggests that his presence there condones the violence in some way (WO 40). "A Northern Hoard" is a sequence of poems that challenges and questions the speaker's personal versus public obligation toward the violence that plagues his country. Similar to the image of Long Kesh Prison in the prefatory poem, "A Northern Hoard" creates the political context in which all the poems of *Wintering Out* exist.

"Linen Town" is another poem that saw significant revision before its appearance in *Wintering Out*.[15] The most substantial

---

15. The poem was published under the title "High Street, 1786," *The Honest Ulsterman* 19 (Nov. 1969): 4–6, and then as "High Street, Belfast, 1786," *Critical Quarterly* (Winter 1969): 293–95.

change occurs in the fourth stanza, where the speaker describes the corpse of Henry Joy McCracken, hanged for his part in the 1798 uprising, as "the swinging tongue of his body" (WO 38). From this point on, voice, language, the spoken word, and the tongue become central concerns for Heaney in *Wintering Out*. The image of the hanged McCracken as a swinging—that is, still articulate—tongue links Ireland's history of repression and violent uprisings with language and the spoken word. Heaney explores the way the history of the Irish tongue corresponds with its history of colonialism. In "Midnight," the speaker contemplates the simultaneous loss of his country's native spirit and its language, described as a wolf hunted by dogs:

> Since the professional wars—
> Corpse and carrion
> Paling in rain—
> The wolf has died out
>
> In Ireland.
>
> (WO 45)

The reference to "paling," beyond the image of exsanguination and loss, recalls the Pale, the area around Dublin under English dominance.[16] The poem ends opprobriously as the speaker struggles to speak but finds that the "tongue's / Leashed in my throat" (WO 46). "Midnight" and "Linen Town" reveal the new direction Heaney's verse takes in *Wintering Out*. Many of the subsequent poems focus upon the topic of language and the spoken word. References to the tongue abound. Heaney chooses, after approximately eighteen months of experimentation, to address Ulster's violent Troubles, not with political rhetoric or propaganda, but with poetry that exposes the diversity of language and speaks with many dialects and in many voices.

16. John Wilson Foster examines John Montague's *The Rough Field*, written about the same time as Heaney's *Wintering Out*, and finds that the word "'pale' or a variant is used twenty-one times in the poem and suggests a dispirited counterbalance to the land's indigenous darkness." John Wilson Foster, "The Landscape of the Planter and the Gael in the Poetry of John Hewitt and John Montague," *Canadian Journal of Irish Studies* 1.2 (1975): 18.

In contrast to the period directly after the publication of *Door into the Dark*, when Heaney seemed dissatisfied with much of his work, the beginning of 1972 was a time of renewed productivity. Heaney discovered a way to unleash the cultural tongue that had been silenced by the clamor of factional violence and hatred as well as by the intrusion of the English tradition and language on the Irish consciousness. Anthony Bailey recounts that in May 1969 Heaney "wrote twenty-two poems in one week; a number of these survived and appeared in his third book, *Wintering Out*."[17] Of the eighteen poems published in journals or magazines after January 1972, fourteen appeared in *Wintering Out*, and one, "Orange Drums, Tyrone 1966," appeared in *North*.[18] Heaney had clearly found the polyphonic voice he wanted for *Wintering Out*. Such poems as "Fodder," "Anahorish," "Gifts of Rain," "Toome," "Broagh," "The Backward Look," and "Traditions" were first published during this period in 1972. In his essay "Feeling into Words," Heaney refers to poems that "explode in silence," but many of poems written during this creative burst convey the vernacular problematic of the Irish speaker/writer and explode in dialect and word-play (P 46). Heaney received some inspiration, interestingly enough, from several British writers.

In his essay "Englands of the Mind," Heaney discusses Geoffrey Hill's and Ted Hughes's use of dialect, etymology, and variations on literary traditions in order to create a poetry that is linked to the past but distinct unto itself. Heaney begins the essay, though, with an analysis of T. S. Eliot's "auditory imagination":

One of the most precise and suggestive of T. S. Eliot's critical formulations was his notion of what he called 'the auditory imagination', 'the feeling for syllable and rhythm, penetrating far below the conscious levels of thought and feeling, invigorating every word; sinking to the most primitive and forgotten, returning to the origin and bringing something back', fusing 'the most ancient and the most civilized mentality'. I pre-

---

17. Anthony Bailey, *Acts of Union* (New York: Random House, 1977) 135.

18. The poems include "Gifts of Rain," "Fodder," "Oracle," "Traditions," "Bog Oak," "Cairn-maker," "Nerthus," "The Backward Look," "The Other Side," "Anahorish," "Toome," "Broagh," "Bone Dreams," and "Land."

sume Eliot was thinking here about the cultural depth-charges latent in certain words and rhythms, that binding secret between words in poetry that delights not just the ear but the whole backward and abysm of mind and body; thinking of the energies beating in and between words that the poet brings into half-deliberate play; thinking of the relationship between the word as pure vocable, as articulated noise, and the word as etymological occurrence, as symptom of human history, memory and attachments. (P 150)

Heaney's provocative analysis explains as much about his own poetry as it does about Eliot's. In *Wintering Out* (as well as in subsequent volumes), the reader is often sent to the *OED* or the *English Dialect Dictionary* in order to verify or expand his or her understanding of certain words, their roots, and their usage. Like the word *stour* in "Intimidation," such words resonate with literary and historical associations. In poetic contexts, these words do act as "cultural depth-charges"; they do discharge "energies" as they beat against one another. As a result, friction, even turmoil, develops between the synchronic placement of the words in the line — perhaps a verse form from the English tradition — and the words' diachronic associations. Derek Attridge asserts that "the use of etymology fissures the synchronic surface of the text, introducing diachronic shadows and echoes, opening the language to shifts of meaning that can never be closed off."[19]

It is important to note that Heaney does not presume to use words as a means of reaching back to a Golden Age, a stable origin that, in the form of an all-inclusive "tradition," can invigorate the individual talent in enervated times. Rather, Heaney's diachronic "shadows and echoes," to use Attridge's terms, portends a "new history," a polyvocal history that celebrates its own differences

19. Derek Attridge, "Language as History/History as Language," in *Post-structuralism and the Question of History*, ed. Derek Attridge, Geoff Bennington, and Robert Young (Cambridge, Mass.: Cambridge UP, 1987) 203. Challenging Saussure's attempt to separate the diachronic from the synchronic, Attridge first recognizes "the feedback of history" within the linguistic present and then asks the following question: "Doesn't my knowledge of past forms of language (whether accurate or not) necessarily affect my present use and understanding of it? And aren't the coincidences of sound upon which word-play is based continually subverting the dictionary's attempt to keep words (and meanings) in separate compartments?" (200).

and its many voices. If tradition cannot be defeated from without, as political activists and terrorists attempt to do, then it might gradually be reinscribed from within. Consequently, "their" language, imbued with seemingly "binding secret[s]," becomes both theirs in part and ours in part through a calculated process of linguistic disruption, assimilation, and change. What Stephen Dedalus in response to his conversation with the dean sees as a breach in communication exposing a lengthy history of cultural and political hegemony, Heaney purposefully uses to create an emancipating discourse. Thus, Heaney's poems serve as a textual space in which competing discourses, conflicting experiences, discontinuous thoughts, interrupted action, questions without answers, and contradictory cultural messages cohabit.

Although many of Heaney's individual words may send the reader to a dictionary or lexicon, those words do not remain there. The reader brings new insight back to a reading of the text, where the words enter the social context of an individual reading of the text. Stephen Dedalus after all seeks the authority of a dictionary after his encounter with the dean, only to discover that *tundish* is in actuality "good old blunt English."[20] Discussing the Bakhtinian "factors that make the understanding of speech and writing possible," Caryl Emerson states that "Words in discourse always recall earlier contexts of usage, otherwise they could not mean at all. It follows that *every* utterance, covertly or overtly, is an act of indirect discourse."[21] The reader must, however, avoid treating etymologies and meanings as icons that represent a preferred or stable perspective. They are, instead, social entities that cannot be divested of their historical pretexts, their social contexts, or their political subtexts, what Bakhtin calls "heteroglossia."[22]

A reading of "Broagh" evokes such interrelationships among words, their etymologies and pronunciations, and their social

20. Joyce, *Portrait of the Artist* 251.

21. Caryl Emerson, "The Outer Word and Inner Speech: Bakhtin, Vygotsky, and the Internalization of Language," *Critical Inquiry* 10 (1983): 247/48.

22. See M. M. Bahktin, *The Dialogic Imagination*, trans. Caryl Emerson and Michael Holquist (Austin: U of Texas P, 1981) 272–75.

and political contexts. Like "Fodder," "Anahorish," and "Toome,"
"Broagh" is a poem in the *dinnséanchas* tradition, which considers
the sounds of a word, its pronunciation and usage, and the people
who use the word. Not restrained by its graphic representation
on the written page, the poem begins with the spoken word
"Broagh" in the title. In turn, the first word of the body of the
poem functions as an appositive or translation of the title:

> *Broagh*
> Riverbank, the long rigs
> ending in broad docken
> and a canopied pad
> down to the ford.
>
> The garden mould
> bruised easily, the shower
> gathering in your heelmark
> was the black *O*
>
> in *Broagh*,
> its low tattoo
> among the windy boortrees
> and rhubarb-blades
>
> ended almost
> suddenly, like that last
> *gh* the strangers found
> difficult to manage.
>   (WO 27)

Since the word *broagh* means riverbank, a reading of the poem
involves not only the articulation of the dialect word, but its
translation and pronunciation as well for those "strangers" who
find the word "difficult to manage." Immediately after the appositive or translation, the speaker shifts from the word itself to a particular scene that locates the word and its usage within a context
or setting. This transition from word to place then draws the
reader into a linguistic and regional community.

Some of the words used in this linguistic and regional community may be unfamiliar to readers, especially American readers.
Rigs, for instance, is northern and Scots dialect, derived from

"ridge" in placenames, meaning furrows in a field. *Docken* is a Scots and Irish dialect term for dock. *Pad*, originally vagabond's cant but now dialect—introduced, like so many dialect terms, by the Scots in the sixteenth century—can be both noun, meaning a path, and a verb, meaning to travel on foot. *Boortrees* is a variant spelling of "bourtrees," a word with a complex history in English and other languages. It is Ulster dialect for the elder tree, probably derived from the Scots pronunciation of "bower tree." A reader who is unfamiliar with or intrigued by these words can find each of them in the *OED*, the *English Dialect Dictionary*, or the *Dictionary of Modern English Usage*. The word *broagh*, however, is conspicuous in its absence from these dictionaries.

The Irish poet and critic Tom Paulin contends that many Irish dialect terms exist in various local forms that are unknown to most people, even some Irish citizens, because there is no dictionary of Irish English:

[M]any words are literally homeless. They live in the careless richness of speech, but they rarely appear in print. When they do, many readers are unable to understand them and have no dictionary where they can discover their meaning. The language therefore lives freely and spontaneously as speech, but it lacks any institutional existence and so is impoverished as a literary medium. It is a language without a lexicon, a language without form. Like some strange creature of the open air, it exists simply as *Geist* or spirit.[23]

23. Tom Paulin, "A New Look at the Language Question," in *Ireland's Field Day* ed. Seamus Deane et al. (Notre Dame, Ind.: Notre Dame UP, 1986) 11. John Braidwood scratches the surface of this complex issue in his *Ulster Dialect Lexicon* (Belfast: Queens UP, 1969). Loreto Todd does not attempt to document all dialect terms and their pronunciation, but does classify and explain the diversity of dialects in Ireland, such as the following: Anglo-Irish, Hiberno-English, Northern Hiberno-English, Southern Hiberno-English, Northern Ireland English, and Ulster Scots. See Todd, *The Language of Irish Literature* (London: Macmillan, 1989). Michael Toolan interprets Paulin's argument as a passionate but misguided plea for a standardized Irish English. See Toolan, "Language and Affective Communication in Some Contemporary Irish Writers," in *Cultural Contexts and Literary Idioms in Contemporary Irish Literature*, ed. Michael Kenneally (Gerrards Cross: Colin Smythe, 1988) 138–53. In his review of Heaney's *North*, Simon Curtis felt the need to gloss sixteen terms that appear in the volume—not all of which were Irish English or dialect terms. See Curtis, "Seamus Heaney's *North*," rev. of *North*, by Seamus Heaney, *Critical Quarterly* 18.1 (1976): 81–83.

The word *broagh* is just such a spirit, but in the hands of Seamus Heaney it is not "impoverished as a literary medium." In fact, its intrusion upon a poem written in English at once celebrates the oral tradition of Irish literature, broadens the scope of Anglo-Irish literature, and underscores the dynamics of Ireland's history and literature.

The word's lack of what Paulin terms an "institutional existence" calls attention to cultural differences and diversity that cannot be secured under the rubric of the "English" (i.e., British) language. For instance, the analogy of the "heelmark" in the "garden mould," which reminds the speaker of "the black O / in Broagh," emphasizes the fact that for hundreds of years some of the people who use this term have been the objects of colonial domination. The speaker is, after all, walking with an eye to the ground —certainly a gesture of submission. A word such as *broagh* exists outside the institutions of dictionaries and, like the heelmark in the rain, appears for a short time and then disappears back into its native environment, thereby resisting conformity to outside influences.

The word *broagh*, as well as the other dialect terms in the poem, accentuates the cultural diversity of Northern Ireland. *Broagh* is not a term used by Catholics to the exclusion of Protestants, nor is it used by those of Irish origin to the exclusion of Ulster-Scots. Rather, the term is native to the inhabitants of a particular district of Ulster, Protestant and Catholic alike. Although strangers may find the term "difficult to manage," *broagh* is not presented as a term that invaders could not conquer, that the English could not subsume within their dictionary, that Protestants could not master. The term is difficult but not impossible to manage, and the reader, in some measure, enters its community of users.

In his book on Heaney, Neil Corcoran astutely observes that this "community of pronunciation is an implicit emblem for some new political community"; that is, the poem "acts as a linguistic paradigm of a reconciliation beyond [or in spite of] sectarian division."[24] The "new political community" that Corcoran

24. Neil Corcoran, *Seamus Heaney* (London: Faber, 1986) 90.

perceives in "Broagh" stands as a microcosm in the "new history" anticipated in "Tinder" — a new history built on the emancipating discourse of linguistic pluralism rather than political antagonism and monologism. References to a "new history" or a "new political community" also recall Stephen Dedalus's desire to forge the uncreated conscience of his race. Whatever the terminology, such goals are easier to conceive than realize, but Heaney's poetry suggests that the first steps occur through a conscious use of the "cultural depth-charges latent in words" and a willingness to accept the vast and varying diachronic associations such words carry with them. This approach is inclusive rather than exclusive, and its inclusiveness at times points to the possibility of "a reconciliation beyond sectarian division." At other times, though, it engenders a problematic text in which the differences of language — as well as the traditions giving rise to them — abound and coexist in all their diversity, calling attention to themselves and refusing to be marginalized, subsumed, negated, or lost to a silent memory.

As in "Broagh," the title of Heaney's "Anahorish" becomes the first word of the poem, a word linked with the local environment in which it is used. The speaker describes "Anahorish" as "soft gradient / of consonant, vowel-meadow" (WO 16). In "Toome," the speaker's "dislodged / slab of the tongue" utters the sound of the poem's title over and over: "My mouth holds round / the soft blastings, / *Toome, Toome*" (WO 26). The speaker finds that speaking the word is a form of "prospecting." Just as the speaker in one of Heaney's first poems, "Digging," is able to unearth and excavate the past with a pen, the speaker in "Toome" speaks the past with every word, and the uttered word refers to both a political and historical terrain.[25] Toome Bridge was the site of the Irish rebellion of 1798 as well as the site of archaeological finds. The sound of the word *Toome,* then, evokes the "blasting" of British cannon fire as well as the pun on *Tomb.*

In "A New Song," the speaker describes meeting "a girl from

---

25. Heaney admits that Irish or regional words did not always invoke the kind of egalitarian response that "Broagh" indicates. Often words were linked so closely to painful historical events that they aggravated old wounds, as in "Toome." See "Forked Tongues, Ceilís and Incubators," *Fortnight* 197 (1983): 20.

Derrygarve," and the name of that place, like *Toome* and *Anahorish*, resonates with a living history that the speaker had thought "was just, / Vanished music" (WO 33). As in so many of Heaney's poems, the speaker shifts abruptly to the present moment:

> But now our river tongues must rise
> From licking deep in native haunts
> To flood, with vowelling embrace,
> Demesnes staked out in consonants.
>
> And Castledawson we'll enlist
> And Upperlands, each planted bawn—
> Like bleaching-greens resumed by grass—
> A vocable, as rath and bullaun.
>
> (WO 33)

This passage recalls both "Toome" and "Anahorish" in that the "river tongues" swell their banks and "flood" the fields and meadows of the country. In his prose, Heaney associates the Irish language with the "feminine" vowel and the English language with the "masculine" consonant (P 34). In "A New Song," as in "Anahorish," the flooding of vowels and consonants is the means of creating a new song.

In the linguistically dense final stanzas quoted above, *demesnes* associates the consonant with the British but also reveals how the land can be reclaimed from exclusive British control. The etymology of *demesne* is Latin and Anglo-French, meaning land belonging to a lord or land attached to a manor: *domain* is a closely linked variant. In Germanic and English law, *demesne* denotes possession rather than land tenure by ownership. The Irish countryside, then, may be under the temporary possession of the British, "staked out in consonants," but the flooding of the land, evocatively described in terms of lovemaking rather than aggression, will result in a "vocable," a new song that accommodates rather than marginalizes Irish English words such as "rath and bullaun."

Blake Morrison claims that the verb *must* in the above passage is ambiguous.[26] Does it mean "ought to" or "will inevitably"?

26. Blake Morrison, *Seamus Heaney* (London: Methuen, 1982) 42.

Stated differently, is "must" a call to action or a recognition of the inexorable? Perhaps the answer is both. As long as people speak and writers reinscribe Irish English, thereby continuing the "vowelling embrace," the flooding will necessarily follow. The result of this "vowelling embrace" is not the dominance of the consonants by the vowels, which would render the speaker mute. Instead, the water will soak into and irrigate the land. A flooded land is valueless. But when the water soaks into the land, the land is enriched and fertilized, and both the land and the water are changed.

The places mentioned in the final stanzas, Castledawson and Upperlands, are "planted bawn[s]." The word *planted* recalls the Plantation of Ireland by Scots immigrants in the seventeenth century. *Bawn* is a variant of the Irish *Babhun*, meaning a bulwark, rampart, or a fold for cattle. The references to Castledawson and bawn are personally charged for Heaney because his childhood home, Mossbawn, was located between Castledawson and Toome. Heaney has written at length about the origins of his home's name: *moss* is a Scots word meaning bog, and *bawn* is English meaning a fortified farmhouse. However, *bawn* came to be pronounced like the Irish *bán,* meaning white, thus the confluence of pronunciation and meanings yields "the white moss, the moss of bog-cotton" (P 35). Is *mossbawn* Scots, Irish, or English? It is a vocable—a word, term, statement, or designation—that speaks with many tongues, and the Irish vocable "must" be the polyvocal mixture of vowels and consonants. As a consequence of this polyvocal mixture, the speaker in "A New Song" claims that the "bleaching greens"—a reference to the Protestant linen trade that long controlled the economy of Ireland—will be "resumed by grass," returned to the "soft gradient / of consonant, vowel-meadow" of "Anahorish."

It would be excessive to claim that Heaney proposes a utopian society in which differences jubilantly yet benignly abound, where racial and religious distrust and antipathy succumb to a humane pluralism. For example, in "Traditions," anger over the intrusion of the English language is evident when the speaker caustically remarks: "Our guttural muse / was bulled long ago / by the alliterative tradition" (WO 31). The word *bulled* suggests anything but a peaceful and consenting relationship between the Irish muse and the English tradition. Later, the speaker sarcastically concedes that "We are to be proud / of our Elizabethan English."

The speaker in "The Wool Trade" similarly alludes to the dismantling of the Irish social, political, and economic systems — following Hugh O'Neill's surrender in 1603 — and does so in terms of a lost language and a lost tradition: "Unwound from the spools / of his vowel" (WO 37). The Flight of the Earls at the beginning of the seventeenth century coincides with the influx of Scots settlers and the beginning of the Plantation period:

> O all the hamlets where
> Hills and flocks and streams conspired
>
> To a language of waterwheels,
> A lost syntax of looms and spindles,
>
> How they hang
> Fading, in the gallery of the tongue!
>
> And I must talk of tweed,
> A stiff cloth with flecks like blood.
>
> (WO 37)

"The Wool Trade" is prefaced by the quotation from *Portrait of the Artist* discussed earlier in chapter 1 where Stephen contemplates the breach in communication between himself and the dean of studies: "*How different are the words 'home', 'Christ', 'ale', 'master', on his lips and on mine*" (WO 37). Yet the *must* of the final stanza in "The Wool Trade" is less elusive in its meaning than the *must* in "A New Song." The speaker in "The Wool Trade" seems to choke when he "must talk of tweed." The prosaic alliteration, "talk of tweed," signifies the speaker's acerbic acceptance of Ireland's economical and political facts of life. Like the speaker in "Midnight" whose tongue is "leashed," the speaker in "The Wool Trade" knows that linguistic change and diversity in Ireland are trace elements of British colonialism. The fact that Heaney commends diversity in other poems does not evade the historical and political determinants of that diversity.

In "The Backward Look," the speaker describes the deterioration of the Irish language as the flight of a snipe fleeing a hunter. The snipe flees "its nesting ground / into dialect, / into variants" (WO 29). The speaker then hears the echoes of the snipe's flight, its "tail-feathers / drumming elegies / in the slipstream," in "the vaults / that we live off." The snipe eventually disappears among the "gleanings and leavings / in the combs / of a fieldworker's archive." In one sense, these lines invoke a pastoral vision, a coveted connection with or continuation of the true Irish tongue through those rural farmers who still speak Irish as their primary language. Such a vision, though, acquiesces to the red-eyed old man Stephen Dedalus rails against in his diary. For Stephen, the old man from the west of Ireland who speaks Irish represents another version of those nets he must fly by: "It is with him I must struggle all through this night till day come, till he or I lie dead, gripping him by the sinewy throat till. . . . Till what? Till he yield me? No. I mean him no harm."[27] In Heaney's case, it seems more likely that the fieldworker is an archaeologist, linguist, or poet whose archive is the "English" language, with all its dialects and variants, through which the snipe's flight might still be traced. Heaney, who lacks Stephen's talent for histrionics, cannot escape the question of language by simply adopting the language of his ancestors. However, he has no intention of grasping the old man's throat in a death struggle either. In contrast to Stephen's highly emotional response to a vestige of the past, the "backward look" for Heaney entails, not a longing for a banished language, but a calculated encounter with and intrusion of Irish words and dialect in the language which he cannot escape.

"The Other Side," an expression used both by Catholics and Protestants to refer to those people who are not part of their group, is a poem where a Catholic speaker comes face-to-face with the patriarchal discourse of a Protestant neighbor. The speaker's farm borders his neighbor's, "his lea sloped / to meet our fallow" (WO 34). The speaker does not describe the neighbour, only his language and his gestures. To the speaker's ears, the neighbor

27. Joyce, *Portrait of the Artist* 252.

speaks with a "fabulous, biblical dismissal, / that tongue of chosen people." The reference here is to the Protestant's assurance that his religion is true because his faith is steeped in the biblical word of God. The word *dismissal* conflates the Protestant's use of the Bible to dismiss the Catholic Church as an unauthentic faith with the Protestant's rejection of the Catholic missal, the readings and prayers of the Mass.

The neighbor stands and waves his blackthorn like Moses or an Old Testament prophet, casting a shadow and prophesying over the fields before turning back toward "his promised furrows." The neighbor speaks a "patriarchal dictum," and "His brain was a whitewashed kitchen / hung with texts, swept tidy / as the body o' the kirk." In short, the speaker's Protestant neighbor is a product of his "side." Even though the neighbor speaks as one of the elect, he is not disrespectful of those from the other side. At one point, he remarks, "'Your side of the house, I believe, / hardly rule by the Book at all.'" While invoking the Protestant practice of basing doctrine on the direct teachings of the Scriptures, the neighbor's words remain friendly and accommodating, as if he were merely trying to learn more about the other side. Even his metaphor of the house implies that both sides live under the same roof, despite their differences. Moreover, on days when the speaker's family is saying the rosary, it has been this neighbor's practice to wait quietly outside until the final bead has been fondled before knocking on the door.

"The Other Side" ends in the present moment, like so many of Heaney's poems: "But now I stand behind him / in the dark yard, in the moan of prayers" (WO 36). The speaker attends a funeral, perhaps a member of the neighbor's family or some other Protestant who has been laid to rest. The speaker is out of place but still feels compelled to pay his respects. The speaker can only consider chatting with him about the weather or grass seed because their religion, a centuries-old wedge, separates them, despite their life-long proximity to one another: "Should I slip away, I wonder, / or go up and touch his shoulder / and talk about the weather or the price of grass-seed" (WO 36)? The discourse of "the other side" has, on both sides, excluded the other for so long that it seems impossible for the two neighbors to reach each other in any way except a touch on the shoulder or an inconsequential conversation about everyday matters.

Both men clearly recognize the alterity that defines their relationship—most, if not all, of their encounters over the years having been mediated by and bear the inscriptions of one side or the other. Even the talk of grass seed, if indeed it eventually occurs, will not escape the traces of biblical prophecy, religious differences, and social and political conflicts. However, the touch on the shoulder, minor as that gesture is, spans a cultural chasm—acknowledging and responding to a sense of empathy that, despite their differences, exists nonetheless between those who stand on either side of that chasm. The touch on the shoulder the speaker contemplates carries neither the taint of submissiveness nor the bile of revolt and reveals the struggle for even the most basic communication.

Earlier in this chapter, Heaney was described as being torn between two minds in the late 1960s and early 1970s. This duality shows most clearly in comparing such poems as "Broagh," "Anahorish," or "A New Song" with poems such as "Midnight," "The Wool Trade," or "Traditions." Pluralism and difference may be realities, but they do not necessarily lead to reconciliation. The tension among the various poems in *Wintering Out* indicates that diversity both recalls and creates friction. It is appropriate, then, that Heaney should choose to describe Eliot's auditory imagination as "energies beating in and between words . . . and the word as etymological occurrence, as symptom of human history, memory and attachments" (P 150), for the auditory imagination—the sound of words and the associations they conjure—plays an active role in *Wintering Out*. Often those associations evoke social contexts or political subtexts, and often those associations involve a history of colonial oppression and marginalization. Equally often, though, those associations explore new ways of addressing an old problem. A new song can provide an alternative to the discourses of exclusion so evident in poems such as "Craig's Dragoons" and "Intimidation" or in the political arena of Northern Ireland.

Heaney obviously has not directly solved any of the problems of Northern Ireland, but he has chosen poetically to address the Troubles by means of linguistic inclusiveness—despite, or because of, the friction it generates—rather than the discursive exclusiveness characteristic of political dogmatism. Even the Irish critic Edna Longley, who has often criticized Heaney's work, claims that "The Other Side" "does not minimise difference" or "its cultural vision" but "spans two languages to create a third." Longley also grants that "'The Other Side' stresses its own language to raise the language question at another level: not as a power-struggle but as a struggle towards expression."[28] However, "self-expression" and "power-struggle" are not mutually exclusive terms or practices, especially when self-expression is hampered or rejected by those whose political and ideological discourses—whether they be nationalist, unionist, or colonial—assume a position of authority by which self-expression is defined, classified, or marginalized. The struggle between self-expression and the counterexpression of power becomes an increasingly important factor in Heaney's poetry after *Wintering Out*.

My focus in this chapter has been the manner Heaney chose to address the suffocating political discourses of Northern Ireland and their attendant violence. I tend to be in agreement with Vicki Mahaffey when she insists that a knowledge of the personal, cultural, or political conflicts that gave rise to a writer's art—whether we agree with the conflict or the author's responses or not—energizes the text and avoids an exclusive or laundered reading of the text, which is more likely to occur as the text assumes a position of "status":

Art, like life, is most joyous when not calcified by homage, but when seen as a participatory process in which painful or even culpable representations coexist with productively revisionary ones, training us not only to admire, but to revise, with a flexible independence of mind that can continue to change in response to changing circumstances. Distrust of status and a view of writing as a continuing, complex *process* of interpretation

28. Edna Longley, "Poetry and Politics in Northern Ireland," *The Crane Bag* 9 (1985): 34.

and response can prompt us not only to revise and expand the canon . . .
but also to demystify the legacy of works that have attained a certain pon-
derous status. . . .[29]

In *Wintering Out*, Heaney attempts to reinscribe or revise what
Seamus Deane calls the "outmoded" terms that malinger in the
Irish consciousness: "the continuation of the Northern 'problem', where 'unionism' and 'nationalism' still compete for su-
premacy in relation to ideas of identity racially defined as either
'Irish' or 'British' in communities which are deformed by be-
lieving themselves to be the historic inheritors of those identities
and the traditions presumed to go with them."[30] For Deane,
Joyce—as opposed to Yeats, who strove to create an all-inclusive,
univocal, mythic, heroic tradition—atomized the sense of community in his novels through his use of a "multitude of equivalent, competing styles"; that is, the Joycean text is a "polyglot
mixture of styles (in *Ulysses*) and of languages (in *Finnegans
Wake*)."[31] The same point holds true for *Wintering Out*, though
the outcome is less playful and less extensive, as Heaney unleashes the linguistic diversity of the Irish English language in his
poems. It is not surprising, then, that "Traditions" ends with a
pair of allusions, one to the consummate English playwright and
the other to the most highly noted Irish novelist. On the one
hand Shakespeare's MacMorris "gallivanting" across the Globe
stage—a caricature of the Irish character, an invention known as
the stage Irish—asks, "'What ish my nation?'" That question is
then in turn answered several centuries later by an unlikely
source, "The wandering Bloom / [who] replied, 'Ireland,' said
Bloom, / 'I was born here. Ireland'" (WO 32). Diversity alone does
not solve the dilemmas of exclusivity. However, diversity exposed
and unleashed subverts attempts to create and sustain traditions
rooted in myths of exclusive origins. In *Ulysses*, Stephen, bor-
rowing the image from Oscar Wilde, maintains that the symbol

29. Vicki Mahaffey, "The Case against Art: Wunderlich on Joyce," *Critical Inquiry* 17
(Summer 1991) 671.
30. Seamus Deane, "Heroic Styles: The Tradition of an Idea," in *Ireland's Field Day*, ed.
Seamus Deane et al., (Notre Dame, Ind.: Notre Dame UP, 1986) 53.
31. Deane, "Heroic Styles" 52/53.

of Irish art is a "cracked lookingglass of a servant."[32] A cracked lookingglass necessarily reflects a multitude of images rather than a single, unified image. And Heaney shows himself aware of such multiple refractions of light.

In his essay "Forked Tongues, Ceilís and Incubators," Heaney addresses both his multiple literary traditions and his role as an Irish writer who uses local dialect. While acknowledging the influence of Yeats and Patrick Kavanagh on the one side and Keats and Shakespeare on the other, Heaney defends his espousal of dual traditions—a position he will strengthen and explore more fully with time: "To belong to Ireland and to speak its dialect is not necessarily to be cut off from the world's banquet because that banquet is eaten at the table of one's own life, savoured by the tongue one speaks. . . . I do not yield to the notion that my identity is disabled and falsified and somehow slightly traitorous if I conduct my casual and imaginative transactions in the speech I was born to."[33] Beyond acknowledging diversity, Seamus Deane insists that "Everything, including our politics and our literature, has to be rewritten—i.e. re-read. That will enable new writing, new politics, unblemished by Irishness, but securely Irish."[34] To that end, in *Wintering Out* Heaney explores one method of reinscribing Ireland's politics, literature, and languages.

32. James Joyce, *Ulysses* (New York: Vintage, 1986) 6.
33. Seamus Heaney, "Forked Tongues, Ceilís and Incubators," *Fortnight* 197 (1983): 20.
34. Deane, "Heroic Styles" 58.

4 ❧ From Artifact to Artifice:
A Disjunctive Transformation in *North*

The power of a poetic voice to ascribe mythic immortality upon those who at one time seemed so ordinary is evident in the final lines of Yeats's "Easter 1916":

> I write it out in a verse—
> MacDonagh and MacBride
> and Connolly and Pearse
> Now and in time to be,
> Wherever green is worn,
> Are changed, changed utterly:
> A terrible beauty is born.[1]

Literature can seem to act as a means of transcendence and, consequently, forge a cultural conscience steeped in a mythic heroism that is elevated above the divisiveness of political unrest. According to Richard Kearney, Thomas MacDonagh, whom Yeats memorialized in "Easter 1916," "described the recurring aspiration for national renewal as the 'supreme song of victory on the dying lips of martyrs,'" and that MacDonagh's words articulated the "overall *mythos* of the 1916 Rising which gained common currency in the popular imagination—particularly after the signatories were executed."[2] Yet, such mythic visions of sectarian and political violence, especially when articulated through the power of verse, can so dominate a culture that they assure the perpetuation of the violence that gave rise to the mythic visions in the first place. In other words, the joint forces of politics and aesthetics

---

1. W. B. Yeats, *Collected Poems of W. B. Yeats* (New York: Macmillan, 1956) 179–80.
2. Richard Kearney, "Myth and Motherhood," in *Ireland's Field Day*, ed. Seamus Deane et al., (Notre Dame, Ind.: U of Notre Dame P, 1986) 75.

may result in politics with the power of the poetic and a poetic whose aesthetic practices cannot escape a predetermined political premise.

Edward Said maintains that Yeats was trapped in such a revolving or self-perpetuating and self-informing scenario. In his Field Day essay, Said contends that Yeats realized that Irish nationalism, on the one hand, and Ireland's cultural heritage, bound as it is to England, on the other, overlapped, resulting in an "urgently political and secular tension." As a result, Yeats tried to resolve this tension "on a 'higher,' that is, nonpolitical level. Thus the deeply eccentric and aesthetic histories he produced in *A Vision* and the later quasi-religious poems are elevations of the tension to an extraworldly level."[3] Many critics have taken similar approaches to the poetry of Seamus Heaney. For these critics, Heaney, rather than elevating the tension he cannot resolve to an extraworldly level as Yeats did, burrows into a realm of "atavisms" and "archetypes" in an attempt—at times successful and at others not so—to understand and address—and perhaps even to escape—the problems of Northern Ireland.

I would like to propose a reading of Heaney's *North* that differs somewhat from previous readings. I need to begin, however, with a simple question: Is it Heaney's objective to "address" the issues of politics and aesthetics as the topic or focus of his poetry—in the sense that the result is a poem that either extricates the poet from the dilemma Said sees in Yeats or maps the way others might avoid the same trap? As I have discussed in previous chapters, the issues of Irish nationalism, identity, conflicting traditions, and politics are constant concerns in Heaney's poetry. However, that fact does not mean that Heaney necessarily writes verse with a narrow political agenda, nor does it mean that Heaney always writes in his own voice.

In both *Wintering Out* and *North*, Heaney incorporates the voices of mythic characters and the victims of the Iron Age sacri-

---

3. Edward Said, "Yeats and Decolonization," in *Nationalism, Colonialism, and Literature*, ed. Terry Eagleton et al., intro. by Seamus Deane (Minneapolis: U of Minnesota P, 1990) 80.

fices in poems that juxtapose—or cohabit—the recent violence in Northern Ireland and its history of violence and hegemony. Heaney is not, however, striving for a mythic discourse through which the victims of recent violence will be "Transformed utterly," as the slain revolutionaries of the Easter Uprising are in Yeats's poem. Nor is Heaney, as Ciarán Carson accuses him, "the laureate of violence—a mythmaker, an anthropologist of ritual killing, an apologist for the situation, in the last resort, a mystifier."[4] The opposite, indeed, is usually the case as the various speaking voices question and interpret the myths of the past. These various speaking voices—quotation marks appear frequently in *North*—share the duties of narration and description with the primary speaking voice in a manner that neither valorizes the victims, past or present, nor avows an unbroken—and therefore, perhaps, acceptable—tradition of sacrificial victims and martyrs.[5]

Many of the poems in these two volumes challenge the writer's ability to profess a mythic transforming power through language. In the place of a mythic discourse, the speakers in Heaney's poems at times adopt an ethical discourse and at other times a self-reflexive discourse of demythification—both of which comprehend and question rather than transform. Such ethical and de-mythifying discourses, which are often polyphonic, explore the limits of the conceptual structures of language without at-

4. Ciarán Carson, "Escaped from the Massacre?" rev. of *North*, by Seamus Heaney, *The Honest Ulsterman* 50 (1975): 183.

5. Edna Longley argues effectively that the "transforming power of Yeats's poetry contemplates an equivalent transformation in the outer world ('changed utterly')." Longley argues further that Yeats also has contrary or competing voices in "Easter 1916," though she believes that they are variations of the poet's voice, a shift between poet and politician: "In 'Easter 1916' Yeats's bardic voice as spokesman ('Now and in time to be, / Wherever green is worn'), alternates with the poet as man speaking, 'troubled' by 'Hearts with one purpose alone'. The pronouns of the poem, 'they and I' and 'We', approximate to Yeats's shifts between solitariness and solidarity" (27). An argument that stems from the belief that Yeats has two sides is more than credible; however, my argument is that the voices in Heaney poems often question the power of the bardic voice itself. It is not a shift between solitary and solidarity voices, but between voices that create myth and voices that deconstruct myths. See Longley, "Poetry and Politics in Northern Ireland," *Crane Bag* 9.1 (1985): 26–40.

tempting to make the leap to a realm outside those structures. In contrast, a mythic discourse, which is often monologic, relies upon such a leap as a means of empowering itself or its subject and as a means of achieving an eternal state that is supposedly uninhabited by the structures of language. Just because the ethical and demythifying discourses frequently result in indeterminacy (several of the speakers seem inhibited, intimidated, or uncertain), it does not mean that Heaney is choosing to "escape the massacre" in any evasive sense, fleeing to a realm of detached abstraction or political isolationism. The opposite, in fact, is true in that the speakers in these poems perceive—even to the point of being haunted by—both the victims of violence as well as the mythic discourse that perpetuates their victimization.

To examine this issue, I must back up in the Heaney canon for a moment to "The Tollund Man," from *Wintering Out*, a poem that acts as a prelude to the bog poems and other historical poems of *North*. Divided into three sections, the poem can be read as a tentative or optative syllogism: "Some day I will go to Aarhus / To see his pet-brown head"; then "I could risk blasphemy, / Consecrate the cauldron bog"; and as a result "Something of his [the Tollund Man's] sad freedom / As he rode the tumbril / Should come to me / / [and] I will feel lost, / Unhappy and at home" (WO 47/48). If the poem is read in such a manner, the speaker is seeking a source of mythic power in the Tollund Man through which he can germinate, mythologize, or immortalize the victims of a ruthless attack by the B Specials during the 1920s.[6]

With such a reading, Heaney's poem resembles Yeats's "Easter 1916" in several ways. Written in the first person by a poet or writer, both poems affirm the power of the poetic voice to ascribe mythic immortality upon its subject matter. In both poems the

6. Heaney is perhaps alluding to the Owen McMahon family that lived on Antrim Road. The B Specials took McMahon, his five sons, and a barman who lived with the family into the sitting room, lined them all against the wall, and then shot them. Two of the victims survived. This may not be the particular case, however, because there were so many instances of violence against entire families during the wars in the twenties. Michael Farrell documents many of the specific cases of violence perpetrated against both Protestants and Catholics during this period. See Farrell, *Northern Ireland: The Orange State* (London: Pluto, 1976).

speakers imaginatively stand over the bodies of the slain victims and invoke—or imagine invoking in Heaney's case—the powers attendant to their verse—similar to Antony's myth-creating speech over the body of Caesar in Shakespeare's *Julius Caesar*. And then a transformation occurs: in Yeats's poem, the four revolutionaries are inseparably joined to their political cause so that "Wherever green is worn," there they will be also; in Heaney's poem, the victims of the recent violence might germinate and find everlasting life in the annals of Ulster martyrdom. The speaker in Heaney's poem is also transformed in that he will, perhaps, find the "sad freedom" that the Tollund Man experienced— to span the centuries and discover a mythic freedom, a connection between sacrifice and survival, that has since been lost.[7]

In his reading of the poem, Neil Corcoran emphasizes the mythic power of the Tollund Man, who becomes "like the miraculously incorrupt bodies of Catholic hagiology, and may be prayed to as a saint is prayed to in Catholic worship: he may make these recent dead 'germinate' again, as his original killers hoped he would make their next season's crops germinate."[8] In contrast, Elmer Andrews, de-emphasizing the mythic qualities of the Tollund Man, reads the poem as the means by which the speaker of the poem can reconcile himself to the current violence in Ulster: "By presenting contemporary events in Ulster as elements of a timeless continuum they [the recent victims] are rendered smaller, more manageable, bearable. It is a technique of assuagement, an effort to find the grounds for endurance and continuance."[9] These two readings resemble one another in that each focuses upon one aspect of the poem while de-emphasizing the other. Also, both readings ignore the pivotal role of the speaker. In the case of Corcoran's reading, the speaker must have the

7. Heaney's source for the bog poems is now well-known as P. V. Glob's *The Bog People*. The Tollund Man is described in Glob's book, like other victims found in the bogs of Jutland, as a sacrifice to Nerthus, an earth goddess, for fertility purposes. Heaney also has a poem entitled "Nerthus" that follows the "Tollund Man" in *Wintering Out*.

8. Neil Corcoran, *Seamus Heaney* (London: Faber, 1986) 79.

9. Elmer Andrews, *The Poetry of Seamus Heaney: All the Realms of a Whisper* (Basingstoke: Macmillan, 1988) 64.

power to manifest the Tollund Man in a way that transforms him into a member of the Catholic tradition of saints. In the case of Andrews's reading, the speaker seems more concerned with his own responses to and feelings about the violence than he is about the victims themselves, a pan-historical perspective that is more a trivialization of than an assuagement of violence. A reading of "The Tollund Man" must entail both of these perspectives, without ignoring the speaker's uncertainty.

The speaker perceives the Tollund Man as a potential objective correlative, perhaps even a mythic figure who could be the impetus for poetic creation. In section 1, the speaker describes the bog in which the Tollund Man was found as "She," and her actions are that of an Earth Goddess, who is seductress, slayer, and deifier. The Earth Goddess "tightened her torc" (a collar, necklace, or bracelet, often in gold), which is both an act of aggression and an act of adornment. The sexuality of the Goddess opening her fen and engulfing the Tollund Man is also aggressive in that it is the mode of death for the Tollund Man. Once in her grasp, the Tollund Man is saturated and kept by the Goddess's "dark juices," resulting in his transcendence or eternal life. The apotheosis of the Tollund Man, however, stands in contrast to the two preceding descriptive stanzas, in which the speaker describes in stark fashion both the Tollund Man and the environment in which he was found. The pivotal line between the description of the Tollund Man—in which all that is preserved is a poor, starving victim of an Iron Age sacrifice—and the Tollund Man's mythic deification by the Goddess's "dark juices" is the speaker himself saying, "I will stand for a long time."[10] The speaker is a poet and the apparent medium of the Tollund Man's deification, and it is the

10. David Lloyd makes the point that a slippage occurs in this passage between speaker and the speaker's subject: "The distance of the historical observer rapidly contracts in this first section into an imaginary immediate relation to the corpse, and ultimately to the putative goddess . . . " (332). This is an astute point; however, I would argue that such a contraction may indeed be contemplated by the speaker, but the speaker ultimately does not in the poem actually choose such an abandonment into a mythic unity. See Lloyd, "'Pap for the Dispossessed': Seamus Heaney and the Poetics of Identity," *Boundary 2* 13 (1985): 319–42.

speaker's thoughts and words that will or could bring about the apotheosis of this sacrificial victim.

The speaker is aware of his potential roles, as either deifier or archaeologist. In the second section of the poem, he contemplates his role as deifier if he were to consecrate the bog and speak the Tollund Man ("pray / Him") into a transcendent power that will "germinate / The scattered, ambushed / Flesh of labourers, / [and] Stockinged corpses" which have littered the countryside of Ulster. In the initial line of section 2, though, the speaker is not at all certain that germinating the recent victims is what he wants to do when he says, "I could risk blasphemy." Blasphemy against what? None of the speakers in Heaney's poems have been particularly religious, so blasphemy against the Holy Catholic Church seems unlikely. Perhaps the blasphemy is against those "scattered, ambushed" "labourers, [and] / Stockinged corpses." The speaker senses that he could deify the Tollund Man's death in such a way that the Tollund Man could then be used as the impetus to "germinate" those modern-day victims, to transform those corpses into sacrificial victims as well. The speaker is, then, contemplating doing to the unnamed victims what the speaker in Yeats's poem did for the political martyrs of the Easter Uprising.

But does the speaker choose to do this? Could it be that blasphemy for the speaker is just such an apotheosis? Although the speaker comprehends the transforming and eternalizing power of myth, as seen in the fourth stanza of section 1 regarding the goddess's powers, he also recognizes that power as a blasphemy because it averts his, and the reader's, eyes away from the specific victims and from the horror of the individual violent act. Thus, the victims of recent violence in section 2 are described in stark terms similar to those used to describe the Tollund Man in section 1—not as the "Bridegroom to the goddess," but as a poor and hungry victim of violence. In fact, many of the bog victims have frailty and poverty in common.

To deify a victim is, to a certain extent, to perpetuate the need for that victim; to look directly at the victim is to perceive the need for a solution to the violence. The former is mythical, the latter ethical. From this perspective, the speaker wants to direct the reader's eyes upon those "corpses / Laid out in the farmyards," and to do otherwise is blasphemy against the individual lives of each victim. By focusing upon the individual victims, the speaker gives voice *in absentia* to those victims who can no longer speak, and they speak of senseless violence. Conversely, to mythify the victims' death, the speaker must silence their individual voices in favor of a single, monologic voice that ascribes some greater good, some greater power, some greater purpose, some universal theme that unites all these victims with the living. And this the speaker does not or will not do.

The last section of "The Tollund Man" from this perspective is the speaker's identification with the Tollund Man — not as the sacrificial victim embraced by the Earth Goddess — but as a victim of violence whose "sad freedom" is the uncertainty of finding himself pulled by forces outside of his control. In such a naturalistic, nonmythic context the speaker "will feel lost, / Unhappy and at home" (WO 48). The speaker in these lines imagines himself traveling in Jutland, and the similarity between the violent context of the Tollund Man and the violent context of the speaker's home is that sense of "sad freedom." In other words, "sad freedom" for the speaker involves seeing life without all-encompassing and transcendent myths, seeing violence for what it is without glorifying it. The speaker "will feel lost, / [and] Unhappy," but he will also feel *at home*, not part of a mythic abstraction. "Sad freedom" severs bonds to the past, as familiar or assuaging as they may be, and imagines a present and a future without the benefit of a prefabricated, mythic past. Violence will not, then, be valorized or deflected. While the speaker may see the bog victims as an objective correlative of his own culture, he will choose to explore that objective correlative with a critical, questioning voice rather than a mythic, transforming voice.

In similar fashion, the speaker in "Punishment" imaginatively places himself in the past, during the ritualized murder of a young woman accused of adultery. Critical of his own dispassionate ability to observe, discern, and tacitly condone the violence of clan life, the speaker concedes that he too "would have cast / . . . the stones of silence" and not stood up to defend the young girl from her accusers (N 38). Pulled by conflicting allegiances, the speaker has a sense of "civilized outrage," but he also understands "the exact / and tribal, intimate revenge." Thus, despite his great empathy for the young girl — "I almost love you" — the speaker detects something endemic and ineffable about the violence.

"Bog Queen" conveys a similar impression of violence. In this poem, the victim speaks and describes her own murder, her burial in the bog, and her eventual excavation from the bog: "My diadem grew carious / gemstones dropped / in the peat floe / like the bearings of history" (N 33). The words *bearings of history* express both progression, the ball bearings upon which history rolls, as well as orientation or location, that is, to establish one's bearings. In either case, the ritualized murder of victims like the Bog Queen is the means by which the history of humankind progresses — what is called the "floe of history" in "Kinship" — and the means by which humans know their place in the scheme of things. Separating history from its victims is impossible, for the victims are first used as catalysts for and then act as signposts of history.

The speakers in "Punishment" and "Bog Queen" make some painful and unpopular observations, but that does not make them mythmakers. A mythmaker would not perceive the young girl in "Punishment" with the kind of paralyzed compassion to which the speaker admits: a mythmaker would announce her place as martyr or as saint, as *pharmakos* or as sacrifice. One has to read Heaney's poems, not in isolation, but as a series of dialogues on related subjects. The speakers in Heaney's poems do not make monologic proclamations; rather, they observe and question events, both past and present, as well as their own response to those events, and each poem explores those events from various perspectives. This practice of questioning and self-questioning myth continues in *North*, a collection that contains not only the famous "bog poems," but other poems that juxtapose mythic, historical, and personal experiences. These poems contain many voices, along with the primary speaking voice, and fluctuate between a distant, archaeological past and a more personal present.

The speaker in "The Grauballe Man," for example, takes a position similar to that of the speakers in "Punishment" and "Bog Queen" when he describes the body of the ancient victim:

> but now he lies
> perfected in my memory,
> down to the red horn
> of his nails,
>
> hung in the scales
> with beauty and atrocity.
>   (N 36)

While the Grauballe Man, like the Tollund Man, may be perfected in the speaker's mind, he is "hung in the scales / with beauty and atrocity," between myth and violence. Rather than perceiving Yeats's "terrible beauty," which fuses myth and violence, the speaker in "The Grauballe Man" acknowledges the beauty of the artifact and its mythic resonances, but he also recognizes the "atrocity" of the violent act. The first he may apprehend, but the latter he will never condone. The reference to "the scales" furthers this sense of tension between the two, a tension explored throughout the poems of *North*.

Part 1 of *North* begins and ends with poems about Antaeus, focusing upon the myth of the nurturing earth and upon territorial—and sexual—conquest. Antaeus, who finds his strength through contact with the maternal earth (his mother was Gæa), speaks for himself in the opening poem of part 1: "I am cradled in the dark that wombed me / And nurtured in every artery / Like a small hillock" (N 12). In the final poem of part 1, Antaeus wrestles with Hercules, whose "mind [is] big with golden apples, / his future hung with trophies" (N 52). During their wrestling match, Hercules raises Antaeus from the earth, separating Antaeus from his source of strength, and thereby defeating him. When Antaeus is separated from the earth, he is lifted "out of his element / [and] into a dream of loss / and origins," and the result is "a sleeping giant, / pap for the dispossessed."

On one level, the wrestling match between Hercules and Antaeus is an allegory of the Irish and British struggle in which the

British finally defeat the Irish.[11] In this reading, the Irish have created a tradition of "loss and origins" — that is, "pap for the dispossessed" — in order to compensate for their defeat at the hands of the British. The connections between Antaeus and Ireland on the one hand and Hercules and England on the other are striking. First, Antaeus is the defender, Hercules the aggressor. Second, Antaeus is described in terms that link him with his native soil (reminiscent of Heaney's earlier poems about rural life), while Hercules seems rational and dispassionate, a positivist. Third, Antaeus is associated with the defeated (Balor, Byrthnoth, and Sitting Bull), while Hercules, as Brian Hughes points out, raises his hands in triumph, a "*remorseless* [Churchillian] *V.*"[12]

The struggle between Hercules and Antaeus, however, also represents competing forces or discourses particularly Irish — a struggle not with the British, but within the Irish themselves. Antaeus, rooted as he is in the earth, is representative of the Irish tradition and the myth of origin; he is a voice of monumentality who imagines to speak as a unity. Hercules, on the other hand, is the force or discourse of demythification, the constant struggle of an Irish writer to circumvent monumentality; he is a voice aware that tradition is a teeming conflict of ideologies, perspectives, and systems. The struggle between the two, then, is a form of self-inflicted violence by the Irish writer, for Hercules severs what Antaeus attempts to unify. From this perspective, once the assumed unity of Antaeus is severed, it persists in the form of a "dream of loss / and origins," the "pap for the dispossessed." This conflict between the discourse of myth and the discourse of demythification is a topic Seamus Deane and Richard Kearney address in their

11. Brian Hughes in his article "Myth and History in the Poetry of Seamus Heaney" and Brian Arkins and Patrick F. Sheeran in their article "Coloniser and Colonised: The Myth of Hercules and Antaeus in Seamus Heaney's *North*" analyze and explore various interpretations of the myth and the battle between Antaeus and Hercules. None of these critics, however, suggests the alternative that the battle may be between competing discourses. See Hughes, "Myth and History in the Poetry of Seamus Heaney," *Revista Canaria de Estudios Ingleses* 13/14 (1987): 109–23; and Arkins and Sheeran, "Coloniser and Colonised: The Myth of Hercules and Antaeus in Seamus Heaney's *North*," *Classical and Modern Literature* 10.2 (Winter 1990): 127–34.

12. Hughes, "Myth and History in the Poetry of Seamus Heaney" 120.

respective Field Days essays. For these two writers, Yeats is an Antaeus-like mythmaker and Joyce a Hercules-like demythifier.[13] Yeats himself makes the connection with Antaeus in "The Municipal Gallery Revisited," a poem in which he and the other modern Irish writers establish the means and test of art:

> John Synge, I and Augusta Gregory, thought
> All that we did, all that we said or sang
> Must come from contact with the soil, from that
> Contact everything Antaeus-like grew strong.
> We three alone in modern times had brought
> Everything down to that sole test again,
> Dream of the noble and the beggar-man.[14]

In Heaney's poem "Hercules and Antaeus" the last line from Yeats's poem becomes a "dream of loss and origins," which is "pap for the dispossessed."

Brian Arkins and Patrick F. Sheeran point out that "Pap is mother's milk, sustaining yes — but for infants. Pap is also cheap fiction, the diet of fantasies on which the semi-literate gorge. Finally, it carries an echo of Joyce's dismissal of 'the old pap of racial hatred,' which Joyce felt pervaded Irish nationalism."[15] The censorious tone of "pap for the dispossessed" aggressively challenges Antaeus's claims of territorial primacy. Likewise, the Joycean echo encourages a reading in which Hercules is not necessarily the British colonial impact on Ireland, but one in which a competing Irish discourse, a discourse of demythification, confronts the claims of solidarity and primacy of those who "dream of loss / and origins."

Both of these readings of "Antaeus" and "Hercules and Antaeus" — that of the Irish/British political and cultural conflict on the one hand and the specifically Irish myth of origin/demythification conflict on the other — complement and compete with one

13. See, e.g., essays by Richard Kearney, Seamus Deane, and Declan Kiberd in *Ireland's Field Day*, ed., Deane et al. Heaney has made similar points in several essays as well. See, for instance, "The Interesting Case of John Alphonsus Mulrennan," *Planet* (Jan. 1978): 34–40, and "Forked Tongues, Ceilís and Incubators," *Fortnight* 197 (1983): 18–21.

14. Yeats, *Collected Poems* 318.

15. Arkins and Sheeran, "Coloniser and Colonised" 130.

another and influence a reading of all the intervening poems in *North*. In fact, just as the tension between mythification and de-mythification were key to a reading of "The Tollund Man," so too is it important to *North* as a whole; otherwise, as a poet Heaney is just what Carson proclaims him to be—a mythmaker, an Antaeus who has either evaded Hercules or acts as a purveyor of "pap for the dispossessed."

In "The Tollund Man," the speaker takes a questioning or un-certain stance toward the power of mythic signification. In the Antaeus poems demythification wrestles with the myth of a lost origin and its constituent sense of dispossession. In "Belderg," the speaker questions that origin or lost tradition only to discover a complex interplay of traditions that cannot be isolated, unified, or traced to an absolute origin. The speaker in "Belderg" recounts a conversation with an unnamed person whose voice occasion-ally enters the poem. This alternative voice speaks of Ireland's past as "A congruence of lives," a collection of traditions that can-not be isolated and made exclusive from others, what in "Viking Dublin: Trial Pieces" is described as "interlacings elaborate / as the netted routes / of ancestry and trade" (N 22). The discussion in "Belderg" begins when the two voices comment upon the quern-stones that rise out of the earth. In the initial lines of the poem, the alternative voice states that "'They just kept turning up / And were thought of as foreign'" (N 13). It becomes clear as the poem continues that, despite what some might think, these quern-stones are not at all "foreign," that they are part of Ireland's com-plex past, its "congruence of lives."

The primary speaking voice recounts the etymology of *Moss-bawn*, Heaney's childhood home, and states that he had con-templated finding "sanctuary" in thinking the word exclusively "Irish." This speaker admits, though, that he cannot avoid the word's "forked root," and that he must accept the etymological intrusion of *bawn*, meaning "an English fort, / A planter's walled-in mound." The reference to the forked root signifies not only a dual etymology, but a dual tradition that cannot be separated, de-spite the fact that branches have broken off from the original stem. The alternative voice is quick to compound the forked tradition by pointing to the "older strains of Norse" in *moss*, "the Norse ring on your tree."

After this discussion on the "forked root" of "Mossbawn," the speaker's imagination takes over:

> I passed through the eye of the quern,
>
> Grist to an ancient mill,
> And in my mind's eye saw
> A world-tree of balanced stones,
> Querns piled like vertebrae,
> The marrow crushed to grounds.

(N 14)

The imagery in this final stanza is dense—a tree of stones that looks like vertebrae. The reference to a "world-tree" recalls the tremendous Yggdrasil tree of Norse mythology that supported the cosmos—its roots extending to Niflheim, the netherworld; to Midgard, the home of man; to Jotunheim, the place of the giants; to Asgard, the home of the gods. Read in the context of the multiple etymologies and multiple traditions that precede it, however, the stanza is more accessible. The word *quern* recurs in some form or another in many branches of the Indo-European family of languages: Scotch, Old English, Old Frisian, Old Saxon, Dutch, Middle High German, Old Norse, Icelandic, Gothic (from a pre-Teutonic stem), Swedish, Lithuanian, Old Slavonic, Russian, Polish, Old Irish, and Welsh. Variants of *quern* probably exist in so many cultures because a millstone to grind grain would be one of the fundamental tools of any agricultural society. Furthermore, the recurrence of the word *quern* in so many languages suggests a genetic relationship among languages and cultures, a coexistence of similarities and differences.

The "marrow crushed to grounds" depicts the function of a quernstone to grind grain into flour, and references to a "marrow" hints at but does not confirm an essence crushed to grounds over time. Thus, the wide and varied occurrence of the word *quern* in the Indo-European branches of languages belies the foreignness of both the word and the quernstone that "just kept turning up" at the beginning of the poem. The speaker's vision is not of a utopia, but of an etymology and tradition forked in so many directions that it is difficult to determine what is actually "foreign." If Antaeus's separation from the earth resulted in a "dream of loss / and origins" that compelled a dispossessed people to long for a time of unity or a rediscovered origin, then the constant appearance of quernstones from that earth and the "forked root" of such words as *Mossbawn* act as reminders that such an origin is itself a myth.

The ideas and conflicts that occur in "The Tollund Man," the two Antaeus poems, and "Belderg" recur throughout the other poems of *North*: multiple etymologies and traditions, violence, the potential to create myths and the value of demythification, the longing for a lost origin, and a sense of dispossession and loss. In reading *North*, though, it is important not to isolate these elements as themes or motifs that act independently of one another. They are collectively, to use Bakhtin's term, the heteroglossia of *North*—tension, juxtaposition, and interrelationships that defy reconciliation. Such heteroglossia challenges the speaker as well as the reader because both are as susceptible as anyone to the "dream of loss / and origins," and "sad freedom" carries an overwhelming responsibility, as the speaker in "Funeral Rites" makes clear.

The speaker in "Funeral Rites" contemplates a mythic baptism on a cultural level after burying yet another relative who died, a victim of "neighborly murder." In the opening lines of the poem, the speaker describes the funeral and the corpse of his relation: "I shouldered a kind of manhood / stepping in to lift the coffins / of dead relations" (N 15). These lines anticipate the speaker's thoughts of a mythic baptism that might result in a cultural rebirth and end the violence. The first line refers to the speaker helping lift the coffins, but the reference to "shoulders" suggests responsibility, as does a "kind of manhood." "Stepping in" suggests both the speaker adding his strength to lift the coffins as well as the speaker stepping in to take a stance. The shifting meaning in these opening lines identifies not only the living's obligation to bury the dead, their funeral rites, but the living's obligation to see that the dead do not die in vain.

The speaker begins section 2 by adding that "Now as news comes in / of each neighborly murder / we pine for ceremony" (N 16). The speaker's idea of ceremony is a massive ritual baptism in which he "would restore / the great chambers of Boyne." The speaker imagines each family driving its car through the sepulchre and emerging renewed, the sins of the past and the divisiveness of the present left inside the tomb:

> When they have put the stone
> back in its mouth
> we will drive north again
> past Strang and Carling fjords
>
> the cud of memory
> allayed for once, . . .
>
> (N 17)

The resealed tomb inverts the resurrection when Christ's tomb was unsealed. The Christian baptism resulting from Christ's resurrection has not brought peace, so a pagan baptism might. Once the tomb is sealed, the "cud of memory" — the slow, constant contemplation of the past and its injustices that must be avenged — will be "allayed for once." As a result, each family will drive home "past Strang and Carling fjords," emblems of Ireland's varied and violent past, and leave "those dead by violence . . . unavenged." The speaker cannot possibly shoulder the mythic baptism contemplated in "Funeral Rites." Such a baptism longs to create a community and a communion through a symbolic act. Moreover, the speaker recognizes that the "cud of memory," what is referred to as "memory incubating the spilled blood" in "North," exerts a powerful influence that will not be allayed so easily.

The opening lines of "North" could be the same speaker just after the funeral in "Funeral Rites." The speaker listens to the "ocean-deafened voices," and a Viking's "longship's swimming tongue" specifies how he should write of the past:

> It said, 'Lie down
> in the word-hoard, burrow
> the coil and gleam
> of your furrowed brain.

Compose in darkness.
Expect aurora borealis
in the long foray
but no cascade of light.'

(N 20)

The creative process is described in these lines as a foray, both a journey and a battle. Insight and composition occur in the refracting, bending, changing light of the aurora borealis rather than a single, directed, divine shaft of light. But writing poetry whose source of inspiration is ever-changing, refracting light is more challenging and less certain that writing from an inspiring single shaft of light. And Heaney addresses this challenge in "Viking Dublin: Trial Pieces."

Heaney defines "trial-pieces" as "little stiff inept designs in imitation of the master's fluent interlacing patterns, heavy-handed clues to the whole craft" (P 45). "Viking Dublin: Trial Pieces" comprises a mosaic of compositional moments as a writer self-consciously contemplates his craft. The poem begins with the speaker describing, perhaps to himself, an artifact. The object itself is described in sections 1, 2, and 3 but not identified specifically as the speaker creates a narrative through which he can envision the artifact in its original form and function. The word *anyhow* is an informal intrusion in the opening stanza as the speaker abandons his associational attempt at identifying the object and begins describing it. Section 4 begins with the line "That enters my longhand, / turns cursive," which indicates the point at which thoughts about the artifact become a resource for writing. The pronoun *That* is ambiguous, as if the antecedent is still in the speaker's mind but has begun to find its way onto the page. The speaker then becomes immediately self-conscious as to his role and responsibility as a writer, envisioning himself as Hamlet, the "skull-handler," one who comes into consciousness "by jumping in graves, dithering, blathering" (N 23). The speaker's words are a commentary on his role as a writer, a self-conscious parablist, a teller of moral tales. The speaker senses the obligation of allegory, but the words he speaks and the lessons he teaches are described as "dithering, blathering." The speaker perceives himself as a literary and cultural descendant of the Danish prince, and while thinking and writing, the speaker sees this genealogical connection most clearly. He adopts the persona of Hamlet, or perceives himself as a new Hamlet who must, since something is rotten in the state of Ireland, go to extremes to adopt voices, and conjure up old ghosts in order to explore "the worm of thought."

Section 5 of "Viking Dublin" begins in the imperative and ends in the vocative mood. Someone, whether the speaker/poet or someone from the imaginary Viking longship, calls out to "Come fly with me" (N 23). That journey follows the savage invasions of the Vikings who attack and kill with "a butcher's aplomb" (N 24). In the final stanza of section 5, the speaker calls out to his violent ancestors: "Old fathers, be with us. / Old cunning assessors . . ." (N 24). The allusion to the final lines of Joyce's *Portrait of the Artist* is clear enough: "Old father, old artificer, stand me now and in good stead."[16] These lines from *Portrait of the Artist* occur immediately after Stephen's famous proclamation to forge the uncreated conscience of his race. The forefathers in Heaney's poem are "assessors" rather than artificers. An artificer is one who creates something new, while an assessor is one who sits beside and shares another's rank, position, or dignity. An assessor can also be an assistant or an advisor as well as one who assesses taxes. Therefore, the speaker's forefathers in "Viking Dublin" significantly differ from Stephen Dedalus's forefathers in that they do not contribute or create anything new. Although they have undoubtedly contributed to the forging of the Irish conscience, their continued influence acts more as a detriment than an asset. Further-

16. There is also a less obvious source to this reference, Yeats's "Meditations in Time of Civil War," section 4 entitled *"My Descendants"*:

> Having inherited a vigorous mind
> From my old fathers, I must nourish dreams
> And leave a woman and a man behind
> As vigorous of mind, and yet it seems
> Life scarce can cast a fragrance on the wind,
> Scarce spread a glory to the morning beams,
> But the torn petals strew the garden plot;
> And there's but common greenness after that.
>   (201)

more, they lack the subtlety or creativity of Stephen Dedalus's mythic forefather. Nonetheless, the words *be with us* have the sound of a mythic litany, as if the speaker were combining a Christian prayer with a pagan magical incantation, a practice that also occurs in "Funeral Rites."

Section 6 entails a shift to the words of Jimmy Farrell from act 3 of Synge's *Playboy of the Western World*. The speaker's words and Jimmy's words are interlaced throughout section 6, and the naive Jimmy stands in contrast to the "cunning assessors" of section 5. As the quotation marks indicate, Jimmy is telling a story that someone had told him. In light of Jimmy's tale, the speaker's reference to a "compounded history" signifies Ireland's secular and religious history—a history of many skeletons from many countries—as well as a history composed of many stories told by one person or generation to another.

The intrusion of Jimmy Farrell's words in the final section of "Viking Dublin" complicates the poem because Jimmy—while a character from literature, the Irish rather than British tradition—is no Prince Hamlet, no Stephen Dedalus. Jimmy's role in *Playboy of the Western World* is primarily to facilitate the plot: he is a naive gossip who both initiates and perpetuates many of the myths about Christy Mahon. Once the stories about Christy are exposed as false, Jimmy becomes the most vociferous of Christy's antagonists. Unlike Hamlet and Stephen Dedalus, Jimmy is a victim, even a dupe, to the stories that surround him. He is not forging the uncreated conscience of his race, nor is he a tragic hero driven by a desire for justice. After five sections that span a vast period of time and allude to various cultural and literary antecedents, the poem reaches the final section and the words of Jimmy Farrell telling a tale told to him by someone else, a thrice-told tale.

"Viking Dublin: Trial Pieces" ends with the speaker's words licking "around / cobbled quays" (N 24). Here, as in the previous sections, the speaker is conscious of himself as a writer. His words, now on the page, are no monumental revelation, no mythic transformation, no unified vision or experience. The speaker's words move around, digging in the cracks and crevices of everyday life; they seek the lost and the dispossessed that have been trampled under and ignored. The poem begins with thoughts and imaginative speculation and follows the writing process through the initial stages where thoughts turn to print and ends where the writer looks at his own writing in action. Likewise, the poem begins with references to the tongue, a recurring reference in *Wintering Out* as well, in the image of a "child's tongue / following the toils / of his calligraphy" and ends with reference to the speaker's words licking into the crevices of everyday life. There is an implied violence in words that "go hunting," but these words go not with the violence of the speaker's cultural ancestors, those "Old fathers," but lightly over the cobbled way.

"Viking Dublin: Trial Pieces" and "Bone Dreams" are parallel in several ways. Both poems begin with the speaker, who is a writer or a poet, contemplating an object. In both poems the object is an artifact or remnant from the past, but the object, while identified, is not described in great detail because the focus of the poems is not the object in the writer's hands but the writer's thoughts on and responses to that object. Both poems, then, delve into the process of writing poetry — from the initial stimulus through the thoughts and associations that spring from that initial stimulus. Both "Viking Dublin" and "Bone Dreams" are divided into sections, and the final sections include the words of another voice, someone other than the speaker's voice: Jimmy Farrell in "Viking Dublin" and an unnamed neighbor or friend in "Bone Dreams." Both poems include a section in which the poet-speaker imagines traveling through time: in "Viking Dublin" to a cultural/historical past when the invading Vikings raided Ireland, and in "Bone Dreams" to a literary past of kennings, etymologies, and poetic conceits. Consciously allusive, the poet-speaker refers to Shakespeare, Joyce, and Synge in "Viking Dublin" and to Anglo-Saxon poetry, Elizabethan diction, Provençal poetry, Petrarch, and seventeenth-century Renaissance poetry in "Bone Dreams."

Even though both of these poems about writing poetry self-consciously tap a vast resource of myth, tradition, and history, they do not lead to an epiphany, a spot of time when stimuli and thought coalesce into a poetic utterance that has some kind of transforming or restorative power. In fact, the section breaks in the two poems—rather than leading to a form of culmination, fusion, or unity—accentuate the disparate thoughts that cannot be unified through or into a single poetic vision. Moreover, the Roman numerals that separate the various sections act as a suture to bind them, but that suture only punctuates the dissonance among the parts rather than truly binding them together into a unified whole. Each section correspondingly entails shifts in voice, focus, and tone as well. The final sections of both poems undercut or call attention to the lack of any all-encompassing, unifying poetic utterance. Any appearance of continuity, development, or transformation is disrupted by the section breaks that result in a disjunctive progression and gaps that the speaker and reader must leap.

All the conflicting elements in *North* occur in "Kinship": the bog—"slime kingdom" and references to other poems by Heaney such as "Digging," "Personal Helicon," and "Bogland"; violence—"strangled victim," "incisions," "gallows," "casket," "fearful dead," "inhumed faces of casualty and victim," and "slaughter"; history—"Ruminant ground" and "floe of history"; language—"hieroglyphic" and "the vowel of the earth"; personal experience—"I stand at the edge of centuries" and "I grew out of all this"; literary references—to Yeats's "Easter 1916" and "The Second Coming" and to Tacitus; myth and religion—"Insatiable bride," "mother ground," "sacred heart," "the goddess swallows our love and terror" (N 40–45). However, all these juxtaposing and competing elements are not reconciled into a unified and transforming experience. In fact, the opposite is true. The speaker believes that "nothing will suffice," which answers the question posed in Yeats's "Easter 1916": "Too long a sacrifice / can make a stone of the heart / O when may it suffice?"[17] The rhyme on "sacrifice" and "suffice" in Yeats's poem in conjunction with the speak-

17. Robert Garratt sees Heaney's words here as a "negative allusion to Wallace Stevens' well-known poetic axiom 'The poem is the act of the mind / Finding something that will suffice'; Heaney echoes Stevens' lines to contrast his own poetic failure 'where nothing will suffice.'" See Garratt, *Modern Irish Poetry: Traditions and Continuity from Yeats to Heaney* (Berkeley: U of California P, 1986) 237.

er's response in "Kinship" leads to the conclusion that the thirst for sacrifice is unquenchable and the need for victims—like those in "The Tollund Man," "The Grauballe Man," and "Punishment"—recurrent and inevitable.

"Kinship" begins with references to the bog as a form of ur-text:

> Kinned by hieroglyphic
> peat on a spreadfield
> to the strangled victim,
> the love-nest in the bracken,
>
> I step through origins. . . .
>
> (N 40)

Hieroglyphics is a sign system that is difficult to interpret, often associated with the dead, and the peat bog tells many tales of violence. Although an "unstopped mouth," the bog is not easily "sounded." To sound the bog, to interpret the hieroglyphics, the speaker must "step through origins." The speaker describes himself as a dog circling a kitchen mat contemplating its past in the wilderness, lines that echo the "dream of loss / and origins" from "Hercules and Antaeus." The speaker in "Kinship" faces the challenge of avoiding the simple interpretation of the peat, the "pap for the dispossessed," and discovering an interpretation that is not simply a longing for times past. Also, stepping through origins reenacts the passage through the eye of the quernstone in "Belderg," as a result of which the speaker perceives a vast and complex "world-tree."

The *OED* defines *kin* as relatives or descendants, people of a common background, but it also cites the word as northern dialect meaning a crack, chink, or slit; a chasm or fissure in the earth or breaks in the skin—which recalls the doubled meaning of "cured wound" in "The Grauballe Man." The word *kinned* is defined as chipped or cracked. Thus, *kin* and *kinned* signify both a line of descent and fractures and fissures in an otherwise uniform surface, a double inscription indicating the disjunctive process of history, despite its apparent progress or "floe."

The imperative mood recurs with some frequency in *North*. Of-

ten it is unclear whether the speaker of the poem is commanding
the reader or if some unnamed voice is commanding the speaker
to do something. Several of the commands echo one another:
"Come back to this / 'island in the ocean'" in "Kinship"; "Come
back past / philology and kennings" in "Bone Dreams"; "Come
fly with me" in "Viking Dublin: Trial Pieces"; and "Compose in
darkness" in "North." Whoever or whatever the voice in "Kinship," the demand that the speaker/reader "Come back / / [and]
Read the inhumed faces of casualty and victim; / report us fairly"
is not a call for transformation or mythification. It is rather a call
to portray the recurring violence—the "inhumed faces"—accurately and with all fairness. It is a voice of reason rather than emo-
tion, *ethos* rather than *mythos*. The first person plural indicates
a group, perhaps a collective consciousness, speaking in relative
harmony, a group who has not been heard or listened to before,
demanding that the crimes against each of them and their individual tragedies be told. The fact that the speaker/reader is told to
"Read" involves a reenvisioning of Irish history and tradition that
looks unblinkingly at the process of violence and reports that process without mythologizing it for some greater good and without
reducing it to some predetermined, clichéd expression. The voice,
in the end, demands that something be said. Also important is the
fact that the speaker stands "at the edge of centuries / facing a goddess" that "swallows / our love and terror" (N 42/45). That goddess
cannot be simply reduced to an invader, whether Viking or British: she is a product of the speaker's kin. Like the quernstones, she
is neither an alien nor a foreign figure.

The questioning and self-questioning in these poems belies any
unified position or stance to the violence, then or now. Instead of
making cultural connections, the speakers in these poems often
discover cultural splinters that truncate any hope of a single perspective, unified tradition, or monologic voice. To read the
poems of *Wintering Out* and *North*, then, is to participate in a complex juxtaposition or cohabitation of voices, traditions, and
myths that defy any unified expression. Party to this debate is the
the poet, who can choose to speak with an all-encompassing,

monologic voice, or who can admit that he or she must compose in the aurora borealis that is Ireland's disparate, and at times contradictory, heritage.

The pull of these various forces or influences is great. Yeats, echoing the voice of Hamlet's father, commands future Irish poets from the grave to "Swear . . . Swear."[18] The speaker in Heaney's "Whatever You Say, Say Nothing" quotes the same scene from *Hamlet*. In this case, though, the speaker is the son sworn to act on the father's behalf because "The time is out of joint." The Shakespearean allusion begins in Yeats's "Under Ben Bulben" and resonates through Heaney's poem. Robert Garratt argues that "the self-doubt and dramatization of the poetic voice questioning itself appear as a version of the Yeatsian dialogue in which the mind turns in upon itself and, in the process of a quarrel, produces art."[19] This is a fine point that might be taken a step further so that the quarrel also includes the old artificer himself, the legacy of Yeats and his poetry. If it is the poet's duty to the father to write a verse in which "a terrible beauty is born," then perhaps "whatever you say, say nothing."

18. Yeats, *Collected Poems* 341.
19. Garratt, *Modern Irish Poetry* 244.

5 ✤ Tradition(s) and the Individual Talents: Heaney, *The Crane Bag*, and the Field Day Theatre Company

In 1983 Seamus Heaney published his "Open Letter" through the Field Day Theatre Company, of which he was a director. The letter is addressed specifically to Blake Morrison and Andrew Motion, who included some of Heaney's poetry in the *Penguin Book of Contemporary British Poetry*. The purpose of the letter is to voice Heaney's objection to being subsumed by the British literary tradition. Heaney wanted to call attention to the fact that traditions tend to include or exclude on caprice or prejudice and that what is often included under a particular banner is not always homogeneous.

It is not just that Heaney wants the adjective *Irish* as part of his literary appellation; it is that words such as *British* and *Irish* are not exclusive: they deserve careful scrutiny; they need to be liberated from recalcitrant myths of origin and descent; and, because they are products of language, they must be constantly reinscribed by writers. Such had been Heaney's objective in his poetry up to and following his 1983 letter to Morrison and Motion, and such has been the overall objective of the Field Day Theatre Company.

Heaney's first four volumes of poetry entail a detailed and at times painful examination of the dissonance of tradition, the complexities of language (its role in British hegemony, the resilience of local dialect, unresolvable etymological questions) as well as the dangers of mythic discourse. However, these poems always sprang from and existed within a cultural context. Throughout this study I have presented readings of Heaney's poetry within a cultural context that is neither stable nor unified. In this chapter, I discuss Heaney's "Open Letter" and his other Field Day endeavor, the play *The Cure at Troy*, within this complex cultural context in order to show that the word *Irish* is more than just a term designating a particular writer's residence. As a result, it will be clear that much of Heaney's poetry is an investigation and definition of that word *Irish*.

In order to appreciate the critical objectives of the Field Day Theatre Company—and its objectives certainly have not received unanimous approval—it is important first to examine *The Crane Bag*, in whose critical wake Field Day emerged. That is, *The Crane Bag*—an interdisciplinary journal of cultural criticism first published in 1977, organized and edited by Richard Kearney and Mark Patrick Hederman—acted in many ways as the critical harbinger of Field Day. The title of the journal was derived from an Irish myth, according to which the crane bag was owned by Manannan, god of the sea, and held all that was precious to Manannan. When the sea was full, all the treasures in the crane bag were visible; when the sea ebbed, they disappeared. Also part of the legend is the story of the first Irish alphabet, letters formed in the sky by cranes, the meaning of which was known only to those who knew the code. In the editorial that precedes the first issue of the journal, the editors claim that "*The Crane Bag* is not a tangible object. It exists only as a metaphor or symbol which cannot be expressed in other words. There can be no definitive exegesis. It is a container rather than a content itself."[1] The editors go on to discuss the mythic fifth province of Ireland. Although Ireland has had only four provinces for centuries (Ulster, Leinster, Munster, and Connacht), the Irish word for province is *cóiced*, which means fifth, giving rise to speculation of a lost province that may have been the middle or center of Ireland.[2] While *The Crane Bag* editors are unable to determine precisely where the fifth province might

1. Mark Patrick Hederman and Richard Kearney, eds., *The Crane Bag Book of Irish Studies (1977–1981)* (Dublin: Blackwater, 1982) 10.

2. See also Mark Patrick Hederman, "Poetry and the Fifth Province," *The Crane Bag* 9.1 (1985): 110–19. For a more thorough discussion of the fifth province, see chapters 5, 6, and 7 of Alwyn and Brinley Rees's book *Celtic Heritage: Ancient Tradition in Ireland and Wales* (New York: Grove, 1961).

have existed geographically, they assert the possibility of an imaginative or discursive province:

Uisneach, the secret centre, was the place where all oppositions were resolved. The discovery of points where unrelated things coincided was the art of seers, poets, and magicians. The constitution of such a place would require that each person discover it for himself within himself. Each person would have to become a seer, a poet, an artist. The purpose of *The Crane Bag* is to promote the excavation of such unactualized spaces within the reader, which is the work of constituting a fifth province.[3]

With such rarefied notions as the crane bag, existing somewhere beyond the realm of exposition, and an imaginatively attained fifth province, *The Crane Bag* endeavor might seem more metaphysical speculation than critical cultural analysis. But such is only the case because critical cultural analysis is no small feat in Ireland a decade or so after the beginning of the Troubles.

Heaney wrote the introduction to the collected edition of the first five years of *The Crane Bag*. He places *The Crane Bag* within a cultural context so choked with divisiveness that dialogue and debate no longer seem possible, a topic Heaney had already addressed in his poem "Whatever You Say, Say Nothing":

To contemplate for too long the stalled politics of Northern Ireland, the rickety economy of the republic, the general lack of trust in a fulfilling future, is to confront a gorgon more withered than withering, one which does not even have the power anymore to petrify us but can indeed induce inertia and self-rebuke. The extreme reaction to all this is a sterile violence, the petulant reaction is a hollow post-colonial resentment and a masquerade of codified feelings as a unique ethnic resource. In formulating the idea of a fifth province of the imagination, a second centre for the country independent of the centre of power, *The Crane Bag*, then, does not seek to evade the contingent realities. It is, rather, a response to them.[4]

The objective of *The Crane Bag* was to allow a polyvocal expression of ideas on subjects relevant to contemporary Ireland, such as art

3. Hederman and Kearney, *The Crane Bag* 11.
4. Hederman and Kearney, *The Crane Bag* 8.

and politics, a sense of nation, mythology, tradition, and the northern issue.

Many of those who now write for Field Day first wrote for *The Crane Bag*, and while the focus may have narrowed (some critics saw *The Crane Bag* as eclecticism run amok), the basic objective of addressing issues that apparently cannot be solved through the political discourses that dominate both Northern Ireland and the Republic. In fact, the motto of *The Crane Bag* and Field Day, assuming either were inclined toward epigrammatic pronouncements, might be the opposite of Sinn Féin's position on art and politics. For Sinn Féin, "Art evolves from the nation, not the nation from art," a position that renders art—and by extension literary and cultural criticism—the minion of politics—good if it promotes the cause, bad if it does not. Art becomes then an extension of and medium for polemics. In contrast to Sinn Féin's position, art and the nation coexist as art and criticism act as the textual space—or container, to use *The Crane Bag* terminology—in which the nation's competing discourses resound. Valuable and stimulating art and criticism, therefore, do not perpetuate a predetermined agenda or proceed along a teleological track, which the word *evolves* in Sinn Féin's motto suggests. Rather, art and criticism unleash a complex interplay of overlapping, interpenetrating, and often contradictory discourses that constitute the nation.

In the preface to the American edition of the first six Field Day pamphlets, published in 1986, the directors state that the objective of the Field Day pamphlets, the plays written and staged by the group's members, as well as its (then only anticipated) anthology is a "reappraisal of Ireland's political and cultural situation [made] explicit and urgent . . . [and the directors] believed that Field Day could and should contribute to the solution of the present crisis by producing analyses of the established opinions, myths and stereotypes which had become both a symptom and a cause of the current situation."[5]

5. Seamus Deane et al., eds., *Ireland's Field Day* (Notre Dame, Ind.: U of Notre Dame P, 1986) vii. The following publications represent an incomplete but useful list of Field Day's efforts to this date: **Plays,** Brian Friel, *Translations* (1980), *Three Sisters* (1981), *The Communication Cord* (1982), *Making History* (1988); Tom Paulin, *The Riot Act* (1985);

Over the years, Field Day writers have focused on the various political and literary traditions in Ireland; how those traditions calcify into exclusivity, ideology, sectarianism, repression, and violence; and, in turn, how those influences might be combated in order to forge "a new speech, a new history or life story that would give it rational and coherent form."[6] Seamus Deane identifies the ultimate goal of Field Day as a rewriting of Irish literature and politics. Deane and other Field Day writers argue that literature, history, and politics are interwoven in Ireland: "It is possible to write about literature without adverting in any substantial way to history. Equally, it is possible to write history without any serious reference to literature. Yet both literature and history are discourses which are widely recognised to be closely related to one another because they are both subject to various linguistic protocols which, in gross or in subtle ways, determine the structure and meaning of what is written."[7] Field Day strives to analyze those "protocols" in its pamphlets and dramatize them in its plays in order to focus attention upon the discursive factors that control, mar, or truncate attempts by the Irish to address their own troubling situation.

Derek Mahon, *High Time* (1985); Thomas Kilroy, *Double Cross* (1986); Stewart Parker, *Pentecost* (1989); Terry Eagleton, *Saint Oscar* (1989); Seamus Heaney, *The Cure at Troy* (1990); **Books**, Seamus Heaney, *Sweeney Astray: A Version from the Irish* (1983); **Pamphlets** (published separately, in groups of three): (1) Tom Paulin, "A New Look at the Language Question" (1983), (2) Seamus Heaney, "An Open Letter" (1983), (3) Seamus Deane, "Civilians and Barbarians" (1983), (4) Seamus Deane, "Heroic Styles: The Tradition of an Idea" (1984), (5) Richard Kearney, "Myth and Motherland" (1984), (6) Declan Kiberd, "Anglo-Irish Attitudes" (1984) (see also Deane et al., 1986), (7) Terence Brown, "The Whole Protestant Community: The Making of a Historical Myth" (1985), (8) Marianne Elliot, "Watchmen in Sion: The Protestant Idea of Liberty" (1985), (9) Robert L. McCartney, "Liberty and Authority in Ireland" (1985), (10) Eanna Mulloy, "Emergency Legislation: Dynasties of Coercion" (1986), (11) Michael Farrell, "Emergency Legislation: The Apparatus of Repression" (1986), (12) Patrick J. McGrory, "Emergency Legislation: Law and the Constitution: Present Discontents" (1986), (13) Terry Eagleton, "Nationalism, Irony, Commitment" (1988), (14) Fredric Jameson, "Modernism and Imperialism" (1988), (15) Edward Said, "Yeats and Colonialism" (1988) (see also Eagleton et al., 1990); **Anthology**, Seamus Deane et al., eds., *Field Day Anthology of Irish Writing*, (New York: Faber, 1991).
    6. Terry Eagleton et al., eds., *Nationalism, Colonialism, and Literature*, intro. by Seamus Deane (Minneapolis: U of Minnesota P, 1990) 14.
    7. Deane et al., *Ireland's Field Day* 45

Arguing that critical dialogue takes place within a cultural context, Deane has steered Field Day in a course away from the austere epistemic doubt of Derridean deconstruction, with its emphasis on undermining determinant meaning in favor of the freeplay of signification and its disassemblance of texts with little or no concern for the political, social, or economic powers that operate through, within, or by virtue of those texts. Instead, Deane urges a genealogical or social text approach that discourages critical debate from escaping its distinct and conflicting cultural features — the scabrous and infected body politic — in favor of a realm where such factors are blurred or blended away in an unrelenting flow of signification:

The bulk of the Irish people are ignorant of and alien to the Irish language and its ancient literature; northern Protestants are alien to both that and to their own complex earlier history in Ireland. To remove ourselves from that condition into one in which all these lesions and occlusions are forgotten, in which the postmodernist simulacrum of pluralism supplants the search for a legitimating mode of nomination and origin, is surely to pass from one kind of colonizing experience into another. For such pluralism refuses the idea of naming; it plays with diversity and makes a mystique of it; it is the concealed imperialism of the multinational, the infinite compatibility of all cultures with one another. . . .[8]

In such a critical approach, competing discourses exist within a cultural framework. These discourses are not universal or even global, but tied to the histories, traditions, literatures, and religions of the culture. The goal of Field Day, then, is to call into question notions of an uncontested consensus or singular community in Ireland as well as supposedly neutral and innocent definitions of the word *Irish*. The answer to the question "What does it mean to be Irish?" entails a politically and culturally constructed, ideologically charged, and ever-shifting dialogue that attempts to include a diverse and heterogeneous population.

Field Day is not without its critics, though. Edna Longley, a critic of Field Day long before the recent objections to the exclu-

---

8. Eagleton et al., *Nationalism, Colonialism, and Literature* 18–19.

sion of many female voices in the *Field Day Anthology*, has identified an inclination among Field Day writers that she terms the
"de-Yeatsisation" of Irish literature.[9] Certainly, Seamus Deane,
Richard Kearney, and to some extent Declan Kiberd acknowledge
a dualism in Irish literature, usually presented as Yeatsian mythification contrasted with Joycean demythification. However, it is
unlikely that critics could, even if they wanted to, entirely elimi-
nate W. B. Yeats from the Irish poetic landscape, any more than
critics could de-Whitmanize American poetry. Nonetheless, Yeats
and his poetry have been interrogated by several Field Day authors.[10] Longley has also criticized Heaney's poetry—particularly
North—and the Field Day project for rearticulating old antagonisms in new terms:

Deane's polarized vista of endlessly 'competing discourses'—rival propa-
gandas?—frighteningly rules out any objective language of fact or value.
. . . [Field Day's] ability to use the English language contradicts their inclination to abuse it. Friel's clever device in *Translations* of making the audience believe that English is Irish may imply more irrevocable loss than
intended. . . . Paulin creates division where unities already exist. And his
own writing proves that excessive awareness of linguistic difference, of
'competing discourses', the loss of creative innocence once language is
comprehended as political, can damage your style. Propaganda breeds
antithesis: black-and-white readings, black-and-white writings. . . . All
this antithesis yearns for Edenic oneness (as opposed to pluralistic 'fusion'), a monolithic nation.[11]

These are intriguing words. Longley asserts that competing discourses invariably denotes only two discourses and that those two

9. Edna Longley, "Poetic Form and Social Malformations," in *Tradition and Influence
in Anglo-Irish Poetry*, ed. Terence Brown and Nicholas Grene (London: Macmillan, 1989)
159. I have intentionally avoided the controversy over the anthology in my discussion
here because my focus is the critical background and context of Heaney's "Open Letter."
10. See also Heaney's "The Interesting Case of John Alphonsus Mulrennan," *Planet*
(Jan. 1978): 34–40; "A Tale of Two Islands: Reflections on the Irish Literary Revival," *Irish
Studies 1*, ed. P. J. Drudy (London: Cambridge UP, 1980) 1–20; and his introduction to
Yeats in the Field Day anthology, Seamus Deane et al., eds., *Field Day Anthology of Irish
Writing* (New York: Faber, 1991).
11. Longley, "Poetry and Politics in Northern Ireland," *The Crane Bag* 9.1 (1985):
30/31.

discourses represent unified traditions—specifically "Protestant" vs. "Catholic." (Other binary distinctions might include Unionist vs. Nationalist, Orange vs. Green, North vs. South.)[12] Neither *The Crane Bag* nor Field Day restricted itself to just Catholic positions, and many opposing voices—even among those of the same religious affiliation or background—found residence in these two mediums.[13]

More importantly, Longley does not identify where "unity already exists." Conflating competing discourses, the political aspect of language (which Longley ties to a loss of innocence), and propaganda inverts Field Day's critical goals. Propaganda is by definition a form of writing that attempts to silence opposing voices; it is a noncompeting discourse that conceives of itself as the only valid discourse. Moreover, recognizing and charting competing discourses does not negate the power and authority attendant to interpretation.

Identifying competing discourses does not result in a loss of innocence, but in the realization that there never was a state of innocence in the first place—that language was always political, whether we believed it to be or not. Longley's essentialist beliefs are articulated clearly when she approvingly quotes Edward Thomas: "'Only when a word has become necessary to him can a man use it safely; if he try to impress words by force on a sudden occasion, they will either perish of his violence or betray him.'"[14]

12. In his interview with Monie Begley, Heaney discusses two different types of Catholics: "There's a Papish house, definitely nationalistic in their approach. They thought of themselves as Irish. They were against the Unionist majority and against the British connection, but had no active political Sinn Fein ideology. The other kind of house belonged to the Republican, or Sinn Fein, tradition. There are, and were, families who maintain that tradition from the 1920's." See Begley, *Rambles in Ireland* (New York: Methuen, 1977) 161–62. See also the opening chapter of Deane's *Celtic Revivals* for a fascinating discussion of the events that led to a unification of race and religion in the English/Irish question.

13. For example, pamphlets 7–9, written by Terence Brown, Marianne Elliot, and Robert McCartney respectively, present Protestant perspectives, and Brown, W. J. McCormack, and John Wilson Foster—none of whom, as George Watson points out in his review of the anthology, are "plaid-clad croners of aisling"—all make contributions to the *Field Day Anthology*.

14. Longley, "Poetry and Politics in Northern Ireland" 31.

From this perspective, meaning exists independently of human-kind, preformed and awaiting, sometimes even resisting, articulation, and if a writer misperceives the essence of a word and uses it before he or she is capable, or it is ready to be used, then a violence results. This "violence" is not the violence of reinscription or competing discourse—that is, textual violence—but a crime against nature, a violation or perversion of an essentially pure word through inappropriate usage. Such a view places words in an extratextual dimension, abstracted from the cultural context in which meaning is located.

In another essay, however, Longley articulates quite well the complexities of competing discourses that adopt terms for their own exclusive purposes while ignoring or suppressing alternative perspectives:

Take three often unexamined buzz-words: 'crisis', 'colonialism', 'identity'. Republicans and Marxists insist on their undifferentiated application to the whole of Ireland, but the poetry discussed in this essay supports plural usages. Contrasting vocabularies define 'crisis' as chiefly territorial in the North; chiefly one of faith and identity in the South: 'Holy Ireland' battling it out with forces of pluralism, secularisation and liberalisation.[15]

My intent here is not to isolate a single critic. Instead, I hope to show the challenge facing the Field Day agenda: uprooting myths, exposing contingencies and contradictions, circumventing old and established antagonisms and suspicions, all the while reflecting back upon itself in an attempt to avoid becoming what it strives to undo. To the extent that Longley questions the Field Day "agenda on the grounds that . . . a distinctively Northern Nationalist formation was claiming wider validity that it had earned" and that Field Day was politicizing "a literary movement whose relation to Northern Irish culture and politics was more complex than their categories allowed" she forcefully challenges the interpretive authority of Field Day.[16]

15. Longley, "Poetic Form and Social Malformations" 176.
16. Edna Longley, "Hospitable Meta-Narrative or Hegemonic Bid?" rev. of *The Field Day Anthology of Irish Writing*, ed. Seamus Deane, *The Canadian Journal of Irish Studies* 18.2

It is within this debate that Heaney's "Open Letter" exists—within the competing discourses of Irish nationalism and against the consuming influence of the British literary tradition. The letter is written in verse form, thirty-three stanzas that fluctuate in style. Beyond challenging the classification of "British," Heaney reveals that he has expanded his scope to include a wide range of influences, what he calls "a new commonwealth of art" (OL 9). The word *commonwealth* on the one hand signifies countries that have some kind of dependent political connection to another—stronger, patriarchal—country. The term also suggests *common / wealth*, as in wealth or value that is available to, interactive with, and influential upon all. The first meaning is colonial, the second communitarian. While both senses of the terms convey the influence of eastern bloc writers on Heaney, the second sense poses the problematic of a pluralism that must resist homogenizing impulses that equate one culture essentially with another—that is, faith in a benign, or highly abstract and textualized, pluralism.

Self-consciously allusive and self-critical, Heaney refers to authors such as Philip Larkin, Donald Davie, Miroslav Holub, Michel Foucault, W. B. Yeats, T. S. Eliot; to traditions such as Latin literature, Gaelic literature, the classical tradition underpinning the English literary tradition; and to the English lyric, modern Irish literature, and international modernism. The self-consciously educated style accentuates colonial influences and assimilation through education. The point of the letter, though, is that, beyond resenting the classification of "British," the modern writer, Irish or otherwise, is eclectic, willing or even compelled to excavate the various traditions at his or her disposal. Heaney is not unaware, however, that his success, not to mention his income, has been a direct result of his British publishers, Faber, and British periodicals, LRB, TLS, and *The Listener*, and Heaney admits he "hate[s] to bite / Hands that led me to the limelight" (OL 13).

John Wilson Foster questions the authenticity of Heaney's

(Dec. 1992): 119. Longley lists eight specific objections to the Field Day agenda and its anthology in her review. See also Longley's pamphlet *From Cathleen to Anorexia: The Breakdown of Irelands* (Dublin: Attic, 1990) 9–13.

stance when he points out that Heaney would have had to give permission for Blake Morrison and Andrew Motion to include his poetry in their collection.[17] But there is more to this issue than just contracts and royalties. Originally Morrison and Motion's collection was to be titled *Opened Ground*, a term derived from one of Heaney's "Glanmore Sonnets." Consequently, there was no classification system along cultural or national lines in the preliminary title of the collection. While the exact sequence of events regarding permission and contracts remain unclear from the letter, the letter's intent seems more critical and personal than antagonistic. Like the other works in the Field Day series, Heaney speaks to the narrowing, restricting, or exclusionary traits that terms such as "British Verse" can have.

References to marginalization and colonization recur throughout the letter. In the opening stanza, Heaney identifies his anxiety as an Irish poet being labeled as "British": "My anxious muse, / Roused on her bed among the furze, / Has to refuse / The adjective" (OL 7). The word *furze* refers to an evergreen shrub abundant on the waste lands of Europe, which recalls the whin described in Heaney's poem "Whinlands." The etymology of *furze* is ambiguous. The *OED* is suspect about the Latin root and finds no connection in the Old English. Thus, beyond being a term signifying something considered on the fringe, the word's background is complex and not completely known. Also, the reference to waste lands adds a double inscription to the word *refuse*, the distinctively British homonym for waste products.

In stanza 3, Heaney speaks of "Caesar's Britain" and uses the Latin terms for Britain and Ireland—*Britannia* and *Hibernia*—which accentuates both the distinction between Ireland and the *partes tres* of Britain (United England, Scotland, and Wales) and the fact that the colonizer was once the colonized. Heaney uses the word *colon* in stanza 4, emphasizing the word through italics. Beyond its biological and punctuation meanings, the word *colon*

17. John Wilson Foster, "Post-war Ulster Poetry: A Chapter in Anglo-Irish Relations," in *Cultural Contexts and Literary Idioms in Contemporary Irish Literature*, ed. Michael Kenneally (Gerrards Cross: Colin Smythe, 1988) 170–71.

refers to a husbandman or farmer, echoes of the Plantation period in Irish history, and its orthographic resemblance to *colony*, *colonial*, and *colonize* is unmistakable: "The 'British' word / sticks deep in native and colon / Like Arthur's sword" (OL 7). The half rhyme on *word* and *sword* recalls the topic of linguistic and geographical dispossession in John Montague's *The Rough Field*, Brian Friel's *Translations*, and Heaney's poems in *Wintering Out*. Moreover, the half rhymes and vocalic rhymes that end many of the stanzas carry an acerbic twist: "worse"/"verse" in stanza 9, "equally"/"poesie" in stanza 11, "green"/"*The Queen*" in stanza 14, "home"/"name" in stanza 16, "Wilde"/"self-exiled" in stanza 18, and "awkwardness"/"Seamus" in the final stanza of the letter. These twists indicate an overall complexity in the letter, revealing that Heaney is far from certain about his conviction to write the letter.

References to Hamlet and Prufrock, two indecisive characters from British literature, occur as well in the early stanzas. Heaney is nonetheless aware, as I have discussed in earlier chapters, that he is as much a product of the British literary tradition and its language as he is the Irish tradition and language. Thus, it is more than biting the hand that signs the royalty checks; it is a double influence, an interconnection of diverse traditions, that Heaney cannot distinguish and compartmentalize—though he knows that he does not want to lose the Irish portion in favor of the exclusive "British" classification. He knows too that he must "Steer between Scylla and Charyb / A middle way that's neither glib / Nor apocalyptic" (OL 12). As a result, Heaney decides to face the "awkward facts" and, in contrast to the speaker's indecision and worry in "Exposure," admits that it is "time to break / Old inclinations" and take a stance.

The most intriguing portion of the letter is the latter half, in which Heaney discusses his *patria*—his influences, origins, and traditions. The British influence is at once a violation but a violation that seems to have been the product of inexorable history. For instance, the historic paradigm of Yeats's "Leda and the Swan" is used to describe the British influence on Ireland:

> Who long felt my identity
>   So rudely forc'd.

Tereu. Tereu. And tooraloo.
A shudder in the loins. And so
The twins for Leda. And twins too
    For the hurt North,
One island-green, one royal blue.
    An induced birth.

One a Provo, one a Para,
One Law and Order, one Terror—
It's time to break the cracked mirror
    Of this conceit.
It leads nowhere so why bother
    To work it out?

The hidden Ulster lies beneath.
A sudden blow, she collapsed with
The other island; and the South
    's been made a cuckold.

                    (OL 11)

In Yeats's poem, the aggression and violence of rape is described in stark detail, but the emphasis—perhaps even the sympathy—of the poem lies more with the power of the swan and its historical imperative than with the victimization of Leda. Rape is less a personal horror in Yeats's poem and more a vehicle for history. (The opposite, to some extent, is true in two of Heaney's poems in *North*—"Act of Union" and "Ocean's Love to Ireland.") In the "Open Letter," history *is* the horror of rape, the nightmare that Stephen Dedalus wants to escape. On the cultural level, the "shudder of the loins" in Heaney's letter engenders a schizophrenic offspring brought about by an "induced birth." On the personal level, Heaney, like Montague in *The Rough Field*, perceives his own identity "so rudely forc'd" as a product of that cultural schism.

The four stanzas on Donald Davie preceding the reference to Yeats's poem are more pointed than they appear. Replying to an essay written by Davie in an issue of *Critical Inquiry* dedicated to "The Politics of Interpretation," Heaney objects to Davie's expression "the pang of ravishment." This term appears in the article at the point when Davie downplays the debilitating influence of colonialism. Responding to Edward Said's story about the British officer who confiscated and destroyed his mother's passport when she registered her marriage with the authorities, Davie dismisses what he sees as a feminist objection to this sexist act of taking away the woman's passport but not the man's. Davie's next point is particularly revealing, which I shall quote at length:

> Even further beside the point is the ready-made vocabulary about "colonialism." For the British officer's explanation was not that of the colonizer addressing the colonized but, on the contrary, was offered according to the utilitarian logic of "the greatest good of the greatest number." He spoke not the language of the master race but the language of international philanthropy, the language of "concerned" and enlightened liberalism, of social engineering. And that language, which is still by and large the language that we all use when speaking of these matters, has no words for *the pang of ravishment* that a person feels when his or her national identity is symbolically cancelled before his or her eyes. What was taken from the woman was her patria; and her sense of having been violated, though it may have been "irrational," was thoroughly reasonable. Anyone who cannot sympathize with her has become a slave to the terms of accepted discourse and has no access to the different vocabulary of literature, where reality and rightness of such responses are continually asserted or taken for granted [emphasis mine].[18]

Of course there are "words for the pang of ravishment," and Davie uses them himself at the beginning of this passage when he dismisses the issue of colonialism as "beside the point." Being *beside the point* is to be marginalized. In turn, Davie's dismissal is the point of Heaney's response. Whether called the "master race" or the "language of international philanthropy . . . [and] 'concerned' and enlightened liberalism," the point is the same: one group establishes a system whereby others are categorized, named, assimilated, or expelled—to repress and regiment another's identity by means of an authoritarian bureaucracy. The British officer's actions were more than a symbolic cancellation of the women's national identity, for the passport was an official text within an overall colonial discourse in which an individual

18. Donald Davie, "Poet: Patriot: Interpreter," *Critical Inquiry* 9 (Sept. 1982): 34.

can be defined and redefined as deemed appropriate by the colonizer who creates, justifies, and enforces that discourse.[19]

Essentially the same point can be derived from the epigraph that precedes Heaney's poem "Freedman" in *North*. The passage comes from R. H. Barrow's *The Romans*: "*Indeed, slavery comes nearest to its justification in the early Roman Empire: for a man from a 'backward' race might be brought within the pale of civilization, educated and trained in a craft or a profession, and turned into a useful member of society*" (N 61). This passage at once veils and unveils the effects of colonialism: the marginalized ("*backward*") figure is *re*-educated and *re*-trained in the ways of the colonizer, ways that no longer make him or her "*backward.*" Once reeducated, the metamorphized figure becomes ("*turned into*") a member of the colonizer's society who can do something of value for that society. Barrow's revealing reference to being "*brought within the pale of civilization*" links the Roman practice of conquest and occupation with the same behavior on the part of the British in Ireland. Such a colonial metamorphosis is what Heaney refers to as "my identity / So rudely forc'd" (OL 11).[20]

There is more to be concerned about, though, than just the British influence. Heaney refers to Daniel Corkery's *The Hidden Ireland*, a book with a nationalist and essentialist vision of an Ireland

19. Heaney dedicated a recent poem to Davie. "The Flight Path," published in 1993, exposes powerful, competing forces that have in the past and continue as well today to rudely force Heaney's poetic identity — the first a humorless passport official at Heathrow airport who rejects and officially terrorizes Heaney for his facetious comment on his Embarcation Card: "Under Purpose of Visit, this bard wrote / "TO EDUCATE (IF POSS.) SOME ENGLISH PEOPLE"; the second an unnamed but recognized figure solicits Heaney's assistance in a car bombing and angrily derides Heaney for refusing, "'When, / For fuck's sake, are you going to write / Something for us?'" "The Flight Path," *The Threepenny Review* (Winter 1993): 5.

20. For a valuable discussion of colonial influences, see the following essays in an issue of the *Oxford Literary Review* 13.1–2 (1991) focusing on neocolonialsm: Clair Wills, "Language Politics, Narrative, Political Violence," 20–60; David Lloyd, "Race under Representation," 62–94; and Luke Gibbons "Race against Time: Racial Discourse and Irish History," 95–117. For a Northern Protestant perspective on such matters, see John Wilson Foster, "Culture and Colonisation: View from the North," *The Irish Review* 5 (Aut. 1988): 17–26. Richard Kearney advocates "a new form of *Federalism* [that] may be balanced with a democratic form of *regionalism*" (581). See Kearney, "Postmodernity and Nationalism: A European Perspective," *Modern Fiction Studies* 38 (1992): 581–93.

that has been stripped of its past by the violent, colonial intrusion of the British—what Heaney has elsewhere called Corkery's "potent monocular vision."[21] In stanza 17 of the letter, Heaney states that "The whole imagined country mourns / Its lost, erotic / *Aisling life*" (OL 10). This unrestrained nationalism—a side effect of the induced birth of colonialism—is the "dream of loss / and origins," the "pap for the dispossessed" described in "Hercules and Antaeus." In short, the "whole imagined country" is undoubtedly a product of the rape, but is nonetheless a response as unhealthy as the terror of the Provos.

Heaney wrote his "Open Letter" in verse, while all the other Field Day publications have been essays. Thus, Heaney's points are made in a form that dynamically portrays the complex interrelationship between the two traditions. The verse format also allows Heaney a certain amount of playfulness, when for instance he abandons hope of reconciling Stephen's (and Wilde's) "cracked looking-glass of a servant." Heaney knows that the refractions of a "cracked mirror" can never be reconciled, and the whole thing is a just conceit anyway.

Heaney's contribution to the Field Day Theatre Company has continued beyond his "Open Letter," but the intent of his letter is to insist that the Irish part of his voice not be ignored, that the historical and political fact of colonization does not silence alternative voices or shepherd all into the fold of the colonizer. Diversity rather than homogeneity has been the focus of Heaney's poetry since *Death of a Naturalist*, and that focus does not change in his "Open Letter." While he refuses to exclude his Irish voice, Heaney opens new vistas for himself and other writers when he speaks of a "new commonwealth of art" and when he alludes to writers such as Miroslav Holub.

Holub's prose poem "On Necessity of Truth" is a fable of sorts that recounts an episode in a movie theater when a man sitting in front of the speaker becomes increasingly agitated at a narrator in a short film who insistently refers to muskrats as beavers. Even though no one in the theater could change the inaccurate words,

---

21. Seamus Heaney, "Forked Tongues" 19.

the man rages against their falsity: "'Damn, I said it was a musk-rat! . . . No . . . that's a muskrat.'"[22] The speaker of the poem con-cludes from the event that "Nobody can live without the truth he knows. In one way or another. Nobody can tolerate croolneck squash being called turnips, or Sirius Aldebaran. The right name is the first step toward the truth which makes things things and us us."[23] The lesson of Heaney's "Open Letter," to continue in the fable-telling mode, is that the right name does make "things things and us us," but some people can and do call a croolneck squash a turnip if it serves their purpose. However, that does not prevent the lone agitated individual from talking back to the "au-tomated voice" and demanding truth.

Beyond the "Open Letter," Heaney's contribution to Field Day is the play *The Cure at Troy*, a version of Sophocles's *Philoctetes*, which was Field Day's production for 1990. Regarding Field Day's theatrical enterprises, Seamus Deane states that "the central pre-occupation has been with a particular experience of what we may call translation."[24] Translation includes the adaptation of texts written by other writers to particularly Irish contexts. Tom Paulin, for instance, whose play *The Riot Act* is a version of Sophocles's *Antigone*, incorporates Ulster vernacular into his version that adds a historical immediacy—as well as occasional humor—to the age-old question of personal responsibility versus legal mandate.

Since Heaney's play is a version of Sophocles's play, the cul-tural context of the play is more important than any particular lines in the play. And that context is established in part by the two stanzas from Auden's poem "As I Walked Out One Evening," which Heaney includes as an epigraph to the play:

"O look, look in the mirror,
   O look in your distress;
Life remains a blessing
   Although you cannot bless.

22. Miroslav Holub, *Saggital Section: Poems New and Selected*, trans. Stuart Friebert and Dana Habova (Oberlin, Ohio: Oberlin College, 1980) 89.
23. Holub, *Saggital Section* 90.
24. Eagleton et al., *Nationalism, Colonialism, and Literature* 14.

"O stand, stand at the window
As the tears scald and start;
You shall love your crooked neighbor
With your crooked heart."[25]

As is often the case with Auden's poetry, the poem resonates with conflicting voices and implications. The nursery rhyme quality of these lines evokes the Christian virtue of loving one's neighbor as oneself. But the type of love remains ambiguous in the poem. In the poem's second stanza, for example, the speaker hears a lover calling out:

And down by the brimming river
I heard a lover sing
Under an arch of the railway:
"Love has no ending.

"I'll love you, dear, I'll love you
Till China and Africa meet
And the river jumps over the mountain
And the salmon sing in the street.[26]

This list of romantic hyperboles continues throughout the following stanza. The nursery rhyme elements is evident here as well, with a variation on the cow jumping over the moon. While the lover's words have the sound of a love poem, the lover stands "Under the arch of the railway," which opens the possibility that this lover could be calling out to a departed love or could be a prostitute calling out to prospective clients: I'll love you a good long time. The fusion of the sordid and the ethereal forces a constant readjustment on the part of the reader, who is at one moment drawn into the conventions of a love poem, while pushed away the next. The result is a poem in which time is not a winged chariot, but "watches from the shadow / And coughs when you would kiss." The reader is not encouraged to expect anything but a "crooked neighbor," whom he or she must love with a "crooked

25. W. H. Auden, *Selected Poems*, ed. Edward Mendelson, (New York: Vintage, 1979) 62.
26. Auden, *Selected Poems* 61.

heart." The hope of transcendence is merely a trope, but that fact does not free the reader from responsibility. Rather, it places the responsibility of accepting both one's neighbor, wound and bow, upon each person, just as Odysseus and the Greeks had to accept both in Philoctetes. Therein lies not only the cure at Troy, but the cure at Ulster.

Such a reading might seem excessively didactic, like that nursery rhyme morality that Auden undermines in his poem. This might also indicate why members of Ireland's intellectual and political left have dubbed Field Day "toffs against terrorism." Sophocles' *Philoctetes*, though, is a tragedy that ends not with death, but with, if not complete reconciliation, at least mutual acceptance and adaptation. Philoctetes, who has embraced his destiny with bitterness and hatred for ten years alone on an island, must relinquish his grip upon the past: "The past is bearable, / The past's only a scar, but the future— / Never" (CT 73). Odysseus, on the other hand, must accept Philoctetes, wound and bow, not just the politically expedient portion needed at the time. Heaney's version of the play ends, like Auden's poem, with a command. Speaking through the Chorus, Hercules requires not peace, not acquiescence, not escapism, but "fair combat":

> Go, with your bow. Conclude the sore
> And cruel stalemate of our war.
> Win by fair combat. But know to shun
> Reprisal killings when that's done.
>
> (CT 79)

Heaney speaks through and co-opts a Sophoclean voice, resulting simultaneously in a familiarized and de-familiarized voice, a sense of the immediacy of and the distance from the experience of the play. This is similar to the case of Sweeney, in whom Heaney finds a companion voice, a voice he can use in place of his own in *Sweeney Astray* and a voice whom he can modify and return to in "Sweeney Redivivus."

Consequently, in *The Cure at Troy*, the character of Neoptolemus, who has been torn throughout the play between his personal sense of ethics and the political needs of his country, can make a searing comment to his countryman, Philoctetes, that carries with it a naked political indictment that Heaney is loath to make in his poetry: "Stop just licking your wounds. Start seeing things" (CT 74). The word *just* qualifies the statement because Philoctetes does have a severe wound that he cannot ignore, but he can choose to do something other than *just* lick his wounds. He can start seeing things. What Philoctetes might start seeing is beyond the scope of the play, but what Heaney wants his fellow Irish citizens to see is revealed in *The Haw Lantern* and his most recent volume, *Seeing Things*.

6 ❦ "Alive and Violated": Acknowledging both Song and Suffering in *Field Work* and *Station Island*

Field Work represents a shift in focus for Heaney that actually begins with part 2 of *North* and continues through *Station Island*, and even into his more recent volumes. This shift, or perhaps more accurately this inversion, of focus entails an examination and interrogation of the poet-figure. In contrast to the poems in part 1 of *North* in which the speakers examine the topics and practice of poetry, the speakers thereafter contemplate and question the poet's role in society. While the poet's role in society is, undoubtedly, a matter of personal, artistic, and civic responsibility, it also inescapably involves questions of identity, influence, and perspective. And these questions are probed in part 2 of *North*.

"The Unacknowledged Legislator's Dream," whose title mimics Shelley's famous treatise on the role of poets, begins part 2 of *North*. The first several lines of the poem establish a somewhat whimsical dialectic:

> Archimedes thought he could move the world if he could find the
>   right place to position his lever. Billy Hunter said Tarzan
>   shook the world when he jumped down out of a tree.
> I sink my crowbar in a chink I know under the masonry of state
>   and statute, I swing on a creeper of secrets into the Bastille.
>
> (N 56)

On the one hand, Archimedes, the mathematician and physicist, is a force of intellect and science: a plan, a principle, a repeatable and reliable method for making sense of the world. On the other hand, Tarzan, Lord of the Jungle, is a childhood influence of story and myth: power and strength, a controlling will, a sheer weight of presence. The speaker, apparently more inclined toward Tarzan than Archimedes, envisions himself swinging "on a creeper." The reference in this line to the Bastille separates the speaker, both in time and space, from the actual problems he imagines himself attacking. The speaker, then, is engaging in a game of imaginative cowboys and Indians. As might be expected, the speaker, in his imagined incursion, does not shake the world: his gesture only succeeds in getting him captured and imprisoned. Subsequently, the speaker can jump only from a corner of his cell onto the cell's flagstone floor, a gesture that merely elicits a quick peep through a hatch in the door.

Neil Corcoran links the title of Heaney's poem with Auden's pessimistic observation that "in our time the unacknowledged legislators are the secret police."[1] To what extent is this dream a sign that the poet-figure is impotent, merely "a silhouette," as the speaker in "Sandstone Keepsake" concludes, "not worth bothering about" (SI 20)? This question must be answered within the context of modern Ireland and the context of the British influence upon the Irish writer. Within such a context, the writer's choice is more complex than taking sides or making gestures. That is, the difference between potency and impotency is not a matter of political gestures and slogans, as assuaging and immediately appealing as they may be, but a matter of writing in which contradictory or negative experiences and influences are not ignored in favor of—or even transformed into—an abstract, aesthetically exclusive art. The poet cannot luxuriate in the perfect, abstract symmetry and postulations of a mathematician, nor can the poet abandon reason altogether for the Tarzan-like gestures of the political activist that have an immediate and visceral appeal but do little to address the root problem of violence and tyranny.

The poet's responsibility lies in capturing the moment when song and suffering coexist. Chekhov came to this realization at Sakhalin when the sound of the cognac glass he smashed against the rocks resounded in "the convict's chains / That haunted him"

1. Neil Corcoran, *Seamus Heaney* (London: Faber, 1986) 123.

throughout his stay and throughout his life. In Heaney's poem "Chekhov on Sakhalin," the artist is neither Archimedes nor Tarzan, nor, however, is the artist paralyzed by or indifferent to the suffering that surrounds him:

> In the months to come
> It rang on like the burden of his freedom
> To try for the right tone—not tract, not thesis—
> And walk away from floggings. He who thought to squeeze
> His slave's blood out and waken the free man
> Shadowed a convict guide through Sakhalin.
>
> (SI 18–19)

In the poetry of *Field Work* and *Station Island*, song and suffering shadow one another like the convict shadowing the free man. At times, the song is the substance with suffering its shadow; at other times, the reverse is true. But in part 2 of *North* that coexistence is still a troubling union.

In "Freedman," for instance, the speaker explores the paradox of being educated by and subjugated by the dominant culture in the same stroke—depicted in the play of such Latin terms as *Manumitted* (to release from slavery; to graduate) and *optimi* (one who has been placed in second or third division in the Mathematical Tripos at Cambridge), and in the contrast of the Latin of dominance and education with the Latin of the Mass, "*Memento homo quai pulvis es*," the ashes on the forehead being a sign of the Catholic "caste" (N 61). In classical antiquity, the act of *manumittere* (meaning to send forth from one's hand) bestowed a certain level of humanity upon a slave. No longer was the slave or bondsman considered property or chattel, but neither was the slave raised to the level of his former master: "The freedman—*libertinus*—bore the mark of his former state, a mark impossible to wash out, sometimes up to the third generation. His was a wholly negative status; he was *not* a slave. . . . Freedmen had to be *made* free."[2] The status of the freedman creates an unusual nexus between two otherwise separate and incompatible worlds. That is, the freedman

2. Zygmunt Bauman, *Freedom* (Minneapolis: U of Minnesota, 1988) 30.

straddles the line distinguishing the privileges of freedom and the deprivation of nonfreedom. Moreover, this unusual status is one conferred upon the freedman by those with the power to define the status of others—the power to dispense or deny freedom.

The paradox of "Freedman" is that the speaker gains a clearer vision of himself as a product of an imperialist system from the very education derived from and rooted in that system. The religious mark of ashes on the speaker's forehead, hence, is not the only mark he bears: the education he receives is the education of the empire, determined and levied by the oppressor. Despite its mark, education brings a form of freedom as the speaker learns to use his education through poetry: "Then poetry arrived in that city— / I would abjure all cant and self-pity— / And poetry wiped my brow and sped me" (N 61). Once the freedman begins to speak, he is accused, in turn, of biting the hand that fed him, the typical backlash of colonial paternalism against those who do not acquiesce. This paradox, involving a conflation and juxtaposition of influences (literary, political, and cultural), is the topic of the six autobiographical poems collectively entitled "Singing School," which conclude *North*.

The poems of "Singing School" are a collocation of moments, memories, historical events, pieces of advice about writing, and questions about the writer's role. Threads of race, religion, literary antecedents, and the inescapable politics of everyday life are woven together in a series of poems in which Heaney recounts some of the factors that have molded his poetic identity. These factors play no small part in his decision in the final poem, "Exposure," to escape the massacre and to weigh his "responsible *tristia*" in the solitary woods of Wicklow.

Although the speaker, wandering alone in Wicklow's woods, has physically escaped the violent upheaval in the North, he cannot escape his poetic responsibility. Ironically, the speaker's longings in "Exposure" are essentially the same as those of the speaker in "The Unacknowledged Legislator's Dream." The one imagines that swinging on a creeper will somehow rescue his caged people, the other thinks, "If I could come on meteorite" (N 72)! Both speakers unrealistically contemplate all-encompassing moments of insight and inspiration that will somehow immediately make things right. Consequently, the speaker can do nothing but chastise himself for merely "blowing up these sparks / For their meagre heat, [and having] missed / The once-in-a-lifetime portent, / The comet's pulsing rose" (N 73). After the extensive exploration and questioning of part 1 in which the dangers of mythification and aesthetic transcendence are exposed, part 2 of *North* comes to a close with words disparaging artistic detachment. But the speaker's alienation may actually be a consequence of exposure — exposure to random, senseless violence, like the two berserks who "club each other to death" in "Summer 1969," as well as exposure to public scrutiny and the subsequent expectation of many that the speaker should act the Tarzan and "swing on a creeper" in order to rescue his caged people.

Artistic detachment is a luxury not easily sustained, and such detachment, the speaker in "Oysters" learns, if it even exists, is an impediment to artistic expression. "Oysters," the first poem in *Field Work*, provides some insight into the predicament of the speaker in "Exposure." While out with friends and dining on oysters, "Laying down a perfect memory / In the cool of thatch and crockery," the speaker is shaken by a sudden thought:

> Over the Alps, packed deep in hay and snow,
> The Romans hauled their oysters south to Rome:
> I saw damp panniers disgorge
> The frond-lipped, brine-stung
> Glut of privilege
>
> And was angry that my trust could not repose
> In the clear light, like poetry or freedom
> Leaning in from the sea.
>
> (FW 11)

The speaker's disquieting thought comprises the realization that being "alive and violated" is an inescapable quality of life — whether it be the violation of a mollusk "ripped and shucked and scattered" or the plunder of a colossal empire motivated by the "glut of privilege." This disturbing thought angers the speaker because his "trust could not repose" in such circumstances: such realizations carry the burden of response. This is the point at which being "alive" and being "violated" coexist, what Heaney has called the nexus of "Art and Life" or of "Song and Suffering" (GT xii).

Heaney explains this intersection in his introduction to *The Government of the Tongue*. One evening while he and David Hammond were traveling to a studio to record some songs and poems for the BBC, a number of explosions occurred, and the previously peaceful evening was suddenly filled with the cry of sirens. At that moment, the impotence of the speaker in "Exposure," whose guilt over "blowing up sparks / For their meagre heat" becomes manifest:

There was no sense of what to anticipate. And still that implacable disconsolate wailing of the ambulances continued. It was music against which the music of the guitar that David unpacked made little impression. So little, indeed, that the very notion of beginning to sing at that moment when others were beginning to suffer seemed like an offense against their suffering. He could not raise his voice at that cast-down moment. He packed the guitar again and we both drove off into the destroyed evening (GT xi).

The artist's voice, meager heat as it may be, is most needed at moments of desolation and suffering. Although certainly not the Tarzan gesture or one of coming as a meteorite, it is the gesture of the freedman who has gained the power to articulate his voice. The poet may be trapped within a system run by the secret police, as the aforementioned quotation from Auden maintains, but that does not mean that the secret police should have the only voice. The artist's voice, the Song, can coexist with the artist's political surroundings, the Suffering, whatever they may be.

Music and song recur in differring forms throughout *Field Work*: "armoured cars . . . / warbling on powerful tyres" (15), "bucket's clatter / And slow diminuedo / / the treble / Creak of her voice" (16), "'the raw bar! / Sing it by brute force'" (20), "music [that] hits off the place . . . / / glittering sound" (27), "*sprezzatura*" (29), "ringing with an armourer's music" (32), "an iron tune / Of flange and piston" (36), "John Field's *Nocturnes* — / / . . . pure drop notes" and "Hammond, Gunn and McAloon / in full cry till the

dawn chorus" (43). But that music is often accompanied by its opposite, at times the silence of absence at others the silence of suffering: "Silence / Has shoaled into the trawlers' echo-sounders"
(13), a stone that "Answered my silence with silence" (14), the
"Raw silence" of a cold day (22), the "quiet walkers" of a funeral
(23), "a deep no sound" (33), "the laden silent river" (45), "a silence of water / lipping the bank" (49), "the mellowed silence in
you" (58), or the "silence cored from a Boyne passage-grave" (60).
The coexistence of song and suffering is the lesson Heaney
learned from eastern bloc writers such as Osip Mandelstam and
Zbigniew Herbert, the urgency and the ethic that informs many
of the poems in *Field Work* and *Station Island*. It is here the poet-
figure finds his place: "The witness is any figure in whom the
truth-telling urge and the compulsion to identify with the op-
pressed becomes necessarily integral with the act of writing itself"
(GT xvi).

The speaker in "Oysters" cannot escape the call of his craft or
the responsibility that call demands. All the speaker can do at the
particular moment when the thought strikes him is to eat "the
day / Deliberately," a variation on *carpe diem*, which will quicken
him "into verb, pure verb." The grammatical and textual reference here is important in that the speaker does not say to
"quicken me into action," for the poet's action is the action of the
text, of verb and writing. The poet has it within his power to see
that his "poetry [is] added to the volume of good in the world"
(GT xix). In this vein, the speaker in "The Singer's House," a poem
that Heaney wrote to David Hammond after the incident in the
recording studio, encourages the singer to raise his voice in song.
Even though such questions as "What do we say any more /
to conjure that salt of our earth?" seem unanswerable, and even
though the beliefs that once bonded the community have faded,
the speaker senses something of value in the singer's raised voice:

> When I came here first you were always singing,
> a hint of the clip of the pick
> in your winnowing climb and attack.
> Raise it again, man. We still believe what we hear.
>
>   (FW 27)

The words *clip* and *attack* have military and violent associations that coexist with their musical ones. Thus, song and suffering do not completely eclipse one another, but nonetheless shadow each other.

The good that might be added as a result of the poet's or the singer's voice can be found in the ordinary pleasures and quiet joys of everyday life. In this way, "After a Killing" recapitulates "Oysters," though the sequence of events is reversed. The poem begins with an impression of "two young men with rifles on a hill," armed IRA men trekking across the countryside. The image is a manifestation of a collective memory, of the "unquiet founders" who, dead but not silent, still stalk the countryside in the form of these two young rebels. After seeing these armed young men, the speaker asks, "Who's sorry for our trouble? / Who dreamt that we might dwell among ourselves / In rain and scoured light and wind-dried stones" (FW 12)? The answer to the first question is, We should be. Of course, being sorry for oneself is in itself not enough unless it is infused with a spirit of forgiveness, which is Sibyl's point in the following poem. The answer to the second question has already been answered: the "unquiet founders" are those who "dreamt that we might dwell among ourselves." The answer is a startling indictment of the speaker's own people, rather than those who would control them, because the words *dwell among ourselves* echoes or varies upon *Sinn Féin*, "we ourselves" or "ourselves alone." The continued dream, manifest in the two armed young men, therefore, assures that after any killing there will be another killing, one moment of suffering following another.

"After a Killing" ends with the simple pleasures of everyday life like those that began "Oysters": a "stone house by a pier. / Elbow room. Broad window light." and "a basket full of new potatoes, / Three tight green cabbages, and carrots / With the tops and mould still fresh on them" (FW 12). In both "Oysters" and "After a Killing" the force of politics and history does not preclude the pleasures of life, so too the pleasures of everyday life do not trivialize or ignore the recurrent suffering that constitutes Ireland's politics and history. This is less a dichotomy or contrast than a coexistence and interweaving of antithetical elements. The speaker in "After a Killing" sees the armed young men, echoes of the "unquiet founders," walking upon the same ground as his "stone house by the pier," the same ground that brought forth a basketful of potatoes, cabbages, and carrots.

The poems of *Field Work* entail such a juxtaposition of and, often, a simultaneous existence of the volume of good and the volume of evil in Ireland. In some of the most heartbreaking poems, those who would seem to bring a volume of good into the world are snuffed out by those bent upon evil. Sean Armstrong, for instance, commemorated in "A Postcard from North Antrim," whose only sin was being "the clown / Social worker of the town," stops "A pointblank teatime bullet" (FW 19). Armstrong is another ghost, an image on a fading, sepia-toned postcard, who can be called back but will not return. The speaker attempts a resurrection that recalls Christ's command to the dead child to rise from her bed and walk: "Get up from your blood on the floor." Unlike the "unquiet founders," though, who return in the form of the armed young men, Armstrong, like Heaney's cousin Colum McCartney in "The Strand at Lough Beg," will not rise. He will never again recite poems or sing his songs:

> Your voice was a harassed pulpit
> Leading the melody
> It kept at bay,
> It was independent, rattling, non-transcendent
> Ulster—old decency
>
> And Old Bushmills,
> ....
> Wind through the concrete vents
> Of a border check-point.
>
> (FW 20)

Once again song and suffering intertwine in "independent, rattling, non-transcendent / Ulster." Armstrong's voice, it seems, could not reconcile the coexistence of song and the suffering, for his voice led "the melody / It kept at bay." The speaker of the poem, in contrast, embraces the melody by weaving the song and the suffering together. The poem ends as "Oysters" began, with a "perfect memory," but that perfect memory is not a means of transcendence or a means of escape, but an intertwining of "old decency / And Old Bushmills" along with "the concrete vents / Of a border check-point." This, in other words, is not two memories, but one.

The importance of the poet's song is clearly seen in "Casualty," in which a local man, whom the speaker knows, is killed in a retaliation bombing three days after Bloody Sunday. The speaker knew the old man, a common fisherman whose only crime was succumbing to the lure of a drink after curfew. The old man had asked the speaker one time about poetry, but the speaker, "always politic," silently declined an answer and switched the subject to other, more common topics. If there is a "once-in-a-lifetime portent" (N 73) to which the poet is obliged, the speaker in "Casualty" has certainly missed his chance; here the unacknowledged legislator has failed his duty. The speaker realizes too late that he could have had an influence upon this old man, that "my tentative art / His turned back watches too" (FW 22). The speaker's condescending silence circumvents his song and opens the door for suffering alone. The words of the old man indict the speaker's inaction: "'Puzzle me / The right answer to that one'" (FW 23). The speaker—aware that it is too late, as it is too late for Colum McCartney and Sean Armstrong—vainly calls the old man back: "Dawn-sniffing revenant, / Plodder through midnight rain, / Question me again" (FW 24). (Such attempts to call back the dead and the penance for reticence will be replayed in the "Station Island" sequence.) The speaker's reticence in "Casualty" is a liability, not because the secret police will come after the speaker if he talks, but because he allows suffering to exist unchecked by choosing to mute his song.

The elegies to Sean O'Riada and to Robert Lowell mourn for but also celebrate two artists whose uninhibited conviction to their song allowed them to make a difference in the lives of others. Both men are portrayed as boats sailing in rough waters—O'Riada "trusting the gift, / risking gift's undertow" while Lowell was "our night ferry / thudding in a big sea, / the whole craft ringing / . . . across / the ungovernable and dangerous" (FW 29/32). Although the speaker lacks the certainty and self-confidence of these two artists, he sees the need for such courage and conviction: "The way we are living, / timorous or bold, / will have been our life" (FW 31). Key to these two artists is their self-fulfilling, self-generating quality. O'Riada is described as a "quill flourishing itself," while the elegist, speaking to Lowell says, "you swayed the talk / and rode the swaying tiller / of yourself" (FW 29/31). These two passages contain a common trope that Christopher Ricks identifies as a "self-inwoven simile," a trope in which an action or object in a line of verse turns back upon itself, witnesses its own creation, or seems to blur the distinction between itself and something else. Ricks contends that the use of the trope, recurring with some frequency in Heaney's poetry as well as the verse of other contemporary Ulster poets, reveals two important traits:

[F]irst, an intense self-reflexive concern with the art of poetry itself in poems; and second, a thrilled perturbation at philosophical problems of perceptions and imagination . . . [and that a] . . . reflexive image simultaneously acknowledges the opposing forces and yearns to reconcile them. It is, like all paradoxes, 'a composition of contraries', and composition is not only a literary term but a civic one, of peace after differences.[3]

I would add, however, that the opposing forces that Ricks identifies are the impetus of both the song and the suffering, thus reconciliation seems less likely than the continued "composition of contraries." Specifically, O'Riada's artistic endeavors incorporated the very different traditions of classical and Irish music. O'Riada was then able to create a new music that expressed his own experience, a music less a reconciliation of different traditions than the coexistence of the two. So too the speaker in "Elegy" says to Lowell, your "eyes saw what your hand did / as you Englished Russian, / as you bullied out / heart-hammering blank sonnets" (FW 31). Thus, contraries need not be debilitating as

3. Christopher Ricks, *The Force of Poetry* (Oxford: Clarendon, 1984) 54–55.

they appear to be in "Freedman"; contraries can be quickening and productive for artists such as Sean O'Riada and Robert Lowell attuned to their times and their influences.[4]

A "composition of contraries" perfectly describes the figure of Francis Ledwidge, whose elegy is the penultimate poem in *Field Work*. Ledwidge was a loyal Irishman whose political sympathies ran toward Irish nationalism but whose personal sensibilities led him to fight for England during World War I. During his service, preparing for an assault on Ypres, Ledwidge was killed by shell-fire and buried in Artillery Wood cemetery in Belgium. To the speaker, Ledwidge is "our dead enigma" in whom "all the strains / Criss-cross in useless equilibrium," a rather harsh assessment in contrast to the one given of O'Riada and Lowell.

In contrast to the generative, productive O'Riada and Lowell, Ledwidge is frozen perpetually in the midst of contradictory, indeed self-annihilating, and unproductive action:

> The bronze soldier hitches a bronze cape
> That crumples stiffly in imagined wind
> No matter how the real winds buff and sweep
> His sudden hunkering run, forever craned
>
> Over Flanders.
>
> (FW 59)

Ledwidge's actions as a soldier for the enemy, frozen in time, create nothing except a criss-cross of strains and a "useless equilibrium." Of course, the elegies to O'Riada and Lowell are written to men the speaker knew personally, while the elegy to Ledwidge is written about an image frozen years before in bronze. The speaker admits that he cannot hear "the twilit note your flute should sound." The speaker, in other words, cannot hear the music of

---

4. Heaney has also expressed his respect for Robert Lowell in prose: "Lowell deliberately occupied — sometimes by public apostrophe and rebuke, sometimes by introspective or confessional example — the role of the poet as conscience, one who wakens us to a possible etymology of that word as meaning our capacity to know the same thing together. Such knowing also makes us vulnerable to poetry as a reminder of what, together, we also may have chosen to forget, and this admonitory function is one which Robert Lowell exercised, more or less deliberately, all his life" (GT 130).

Ledwidge, only the wind's whistling tune through "vigilant bronze" and the "confusing drum / You followed from Boyne water to the Balkans" (FW 60). (Both places, interesting enough, were sites of battles not without imperialist agendas.) The tragedy of Francis Ledwidge is that, despite his intentions, he "consort[s] now underground" with those "true-blue" Unionist and British subjects with whom Ledwidge was never "Keyed or pitched." Ledwidge died fighting upon the same ground as those who would subdue his native ground, those who were antagonistic toward his political convictions. Ledwidge "consorts underground" with those whom he has no chance of finding harmony, then or now.

The "Glanmore Sonnets," the centerpiece of *Field Work*, are a return in part to the poetry of *Wintering Out*, or even *Death of a Naturalist* and *Door into the Dark*. The references in the fifth sonnet to the speaker's role as "etymologist of roots and graftings" recall the language poems of *Wintering Out*. The sonnets unashamedly bespeak rural life and the pleasures — and difficulties — of everyday existence in the country. The poems are in this sense a celebration of Patrick Kavanagh's parish, what Kavanagh has called the needed return to the local: "Why do we always need to go back? What is it we want to return to? So it is . . . that I return to the local newspapers. Who has died? Who has sold his farm?"[5]

The "Glanmore Sonnets" can also be read as the poet's surrender to the elements that inform his verse: "art a paradigm of earth." This surrender — or, perhaps better stated as the poet's guilt-free acknowledgement of inspiration and influence — is not an escape from the massacre of political life, just as there is no escape from memory or the mark of caste and education. For the ghosts of the massacre haunt the countryside just as the massacre fills the city streets of Belfast with its own inescapable actuality. The speaker chooses, though, to pursue his own poetic practice rather than the practice — what Blake Morrison has called the "burden of spokesmanship" — prescribed by others:

> I used to lie with an ear to the line
> For that way, they said, there should come a sound

5. Patrick Kavanagh, *Collected Pruse* (London: MacGibbon, 1967) 283

Escaping ahead, an iron tune
Of flange and piston pitched along the ground,
But I never heard that.

(FW 36)

If the sonnet cycle suggests a rejection of poetic practices the speaker cannot use, then it also entails an acknowledgment of those he can.

The first sonnet is as rich as the soil that acts as both the poem's central image and its stimulus:

Vowels ploughed into other: opened ground.
The mildest February for twenty years
Is mist bands over furrows, a deep no sound
Vulnerable to distant gargling tractors.
Our road is steaming, the turned-up acres breathe.
Now the good life could be to cross a field
And art a paradigm of earth new from the lathe
Of ploughs. My lea is deeply tilled.
Old ploughsocks gorge the subsoil of each sense
And I am quickened with redolence
Of the fundamental dark unblown rose.
Wait then . . . Breasting the mist, in sowers' aprons,
My ghosts come striding into their spring stations.
The dream grain whirls like freakish Easter snows.

(FW 33)

Language ("Vowels"), violence ("gorge" and "Vulnerable"), new life ("breathe," "quickened with redolence," and "Breasting") co-exist with the "ghosts [that] come striding into their spring stations," a line that adumbrates the encounters of "Station Island." The speaker, experiencing the "mildest February for twenty years," is no longer wintering out, nor is he lost in Francis Ledwidge's poetic world of Georgian nature and tranquility. It is interesting to note the line "And art a paradigm of earth new from the lathe / Of ploughs." The earth is not the paradigm of art, hiding its secrets to be discovered by the writer who finds the right configuration of words to render their release. Rather, art—like digging—cuts, severs, overturns, violates as it "gorge[s] the subsoil of each sense."

Essentially the same experience is explored in "The Loaning," a poem from *Station Island* in which the speaker's words seem to arise from the "limbo of lost words" and exist in free-form flow running through and about all things:

> Then I knew why from the beginning
> the loaning breathed on me, breathed even now
> in a shiver beaded gossamers
> and the spit blood of a last few haws and rose-hips.
>
> (SI 51)

Though the speaker knows that "When you are tired or terrified / your voice slips back into its old first place / and makes the sound your shades make there," he also knows that those words must also account for "the click of a cell lock," "a blood-red cigarette," and "the shades, screeching and beseeching" (SI 52). The speaker's words are given to him on loan, and though they seem to emanate from local, peaceful "first place[s]," they are at times called upon to carry the image of "spit blood," the sound of "screeching and beseeching."

The second "Glanmore Sonnet" continues where the first leaves off. The last lines of the second sonnet directly echo the opening lines of the first:

> Sensings, mountings from the hiding places,
> Words entering almost the sense of touch
> Ferreting themselves out of their dark hutch—
> ....
> And from the backs of ditches hoped to raise
> A voice caught back off slug-horn and slow chanter
> That might continue, hold, dispel, appease:
> Vowels ploughed into other, opened ground,
> Each verse returning like the plough turned round.
>
> (FW 34)

Here again, this sonnet and "The Loaning" resemble one another in that the words spring up from "hiding places," but those words demand something of the speaker. He must raise a voice. The voice that "might continue, hold, dispel, appease" recounts the various practices Heaney has adopted throughout his career. The voice is not called merely to "continue" or merely to "dispel"; the voice is called to contradictory articulations. Moreover, the reference to "vowels ploughed into other" calls attention to the essential metaphor of writing, for the vowels are not ploughed into one another, but into something else, into "other." The resulting "opened ground" both breathes new life and releases old ghosts.

The ninth sonnet asks a question that recurs in Heaney's poetry: "What is my apology for poetry" (FW 41)? The answer lies in the need to begin singing even though others are suffering — to infuse, conflate, and juxtapose singing and suffering. The question is one, apparently, of process, like ploughing, rather than one of a singular response because the speakers in *Station Island* continue the same process. "Away from It All," for instance, one of the first poems in *Station Island* is almost a carbon copy of "Oysters." The speaker, enjoying an evening of conversation and lobster with friends, cannot escape memory and the call of responsibility, to which "quotations start to rise / like rehearsed alibis" (SI 16). The poem ends, as "Oysters" does, with the speaker haunted by the violations of life:

> And I still cannot clear my head
> of lives in their element
>
> on the cobbled floor of that tank
> and the hampered one, out of water,
>
> fortified and bewildered.
>
> (SI 17)

"Away from It All" differs from "Oysters" in one respect as Heaney's sympathies have shifted from mollusks to crustaceans. Beyond that variation, though, the poem's central concern is poetic responsibility, a topic addressed in the passage quoted from Czeslaw Milosz's *Native Realm*.

The quotation in "Away from It Away" comes from an essay entitled "Marxism." In this essay Milosz recounts an article written about him by a Communist critic that in many ways echoes the criticism of Heaney's poetry by Irish critics with predetermined political expectations. The critic accused Milosz of "want-

ing to keep [his] hands clean," which meant that Milosz had chosen not to embrace the political imperative of materialism, of
Marxism, and ultimately of the Soviet Union. The passage in
which Milosz responds to this critique, containing the passage
quoted by Heaney, reveals Milosz's approach to poetry and an imperative that is not an escape from politics, but a recognition of
the ineluctable politics of language and thought:

[T]hought and word should not submit to the pressure of matter since,
incapable of competing with it, they would have to transform themselves
into deed, which would mean overreaching their lawful limits. On the
other hand, I quite justifiably feared dematerialization, the delusiveness
of words and thoughts. This could be prevented only by keeping a firm
hold on tangible things undergoing constant change; that is, control over
the motor that moves them in a society—namely, politics. Marxists dis-
missed their opponents by treating them en masse as "idealists." Although such an indictment embraced too many elements to be philo-
sophically correct, it did contain a particle of truth. *I was stretched, therefore, between two poles: the contemplation of a motionless point and the
command to participate actively in history*; in other words, between transcendence and becoming. I did not manage to bring these extremes into
a unity, but I did not want to give either of them up [emphasis mine].[6]

The dual mind of Milosz, so evident in Heaney's poetry as well,
lent itself to a sense of guilt and inadequacy when the actions of
some politically zealous friends temporarily grasped the attention
of "the blockheaded authority of the state."[7] Milosz, admitting he
was "unable to accept [these individual's Tarzan-like] style of life
with a clear conscience," is cast into a state of self-doubt, as if the
actions of others whose behavior and intent he knows are wrong
nonetheless set the standard that others, like himself, must be
judged: "The greatest ally of any ideology is, of course, the feeling
of guilt, which is so highly developed in modern man that it saps
his belief in the value of his own perceptions and judgments."[8]
    Milosz ends his essay by advancing the actions of the poet. The

6. Czeslaw Milosz, *Native Realm* (New York: Doubleday, 1968), 124–25.
7. Milosz, *Native Realm* 125.
8. Milosz, *Native Realm* 125.

critical year for Milosz was 1939. If this passage were read and the year 1969 substituted for 1939, the passage could easily have been written by Heaney:

My fate was to grapple exclusively with the secret doctrine as I sought to discover where, in which of its segments, the falsehood lay, and what is the duty of a man who encounters an obstacle that is the creation of human beings, yet seems almost wholly to elude their reason and will. For many people, the answer may be easy, as hunting a whale is easy for those who have never run up against one. For us, however, beginning with the year 1939, the problem was no longer abstract; it had become a concrete situation which required daily decisions. Like the primeval hunter face-to-face with mysterious nature, we learned painfully that if one could hope to subdue the equally mysterious element that has replaced nature in the twentieth century, it was not by force but by wiles.[9]

Milosz's words echo Heaney's often quoted account of his own shift in poetic expectations that occurred in 1969 when longtime antagonisms violently erupted in Northern Ireland: "From that moment the problems of poetry moved from being simply a matter of achieving the satisfactory verbal icon to being a search for images and symbols adequate to our predicament" (P 56).[10]

The influence of guilt upon the psyche of the poet, so clearly stated in Milosz's words, acts as the motivating factor in several of the poems in *Field Work*, but especially so in the poems of *Station Island*. The entire "Station Island" sequence, on one level, involves the poet's attempt to purge the guilt of surviving when violence and death befalls others around him. It seems as though the poet ought to be able to do or say something, but the only things that arise, as the speaker in "Away from It All" laments, are "rehearsed alibis." The conversation in which the quotation from Milosz's essay takes place occurs at "twilight, twilight, twilight," when the "light at the rim of the sea / is rendered down to a fine /

9. Milosz, *Native Realm* 127.

10. Despite his formalist vocabulary in this quotation, Heaney's poetry neither before nor after 1969 had been a verbal icon, self-contained and separated from the world around it. Historical echoes, cultural resonances, personal recollections, political expectations, and practical necessities coexist and at times compete with one another in Heaney's poetry.

gradation, somewhere between balance and inanition" (SI 17). This crepuscular time, a time Yeats and the other Revivalists found most conducive for poetry, when features are blurred and all but general distinctions difficult, is the dominant atmosphere of "Station Island," as clouds and rain and night both impair the poet's sight and give rise to the poet's visions.

The paradox of being *"stretched between contemplation / of a motionless point / and the command to participate / actively in history"* is that neither alone can account for "lives in their element" nor can either strike at the heart of the problem. The impasse is worth exploring. The words *contemplation of a motionless point* require a level of abstraction and distance from life that poets such as Milosz and Heaney cannot afford. These words clearly recall T. S. Eliot's famous lines from "Burnt Norton" about the "still point of the turning world." While the still point promises a position of aesthetic stasis and permanence, Heaney warns that "it tends to eschew the local, the intimate, the word which reeks of particular cultural attachments."[11] That is, the aesthetic stasis of the still point can only be attained through an act of exclusion in which the quotidian is either transformed or ignored. Heaney's complaint about Yeats, the same complaint he renders against Synge, is that Yeats chose to ignore any portion of the actual that did not lend itself to imaginative transformation and symbolization:

Over against all [the] democratic buzz and huddle there stood the patrician figure of the artist, whose solitude and dignity linked him to all that was enduring and pure in the country . . . instead of living among the detritus of the filthy modern tide, this ideal artist/ Irishman would find himself by nature and by right haunting a territory between the ditchback where the beggar sang and the walled demesne where the patron conducted her salon . . . .[12]

In contrast to the stasis of the ideal, the "command to participate actively in history" invariably demands a submission to an

11. Note that Heaney is discussing the language of "Little Gidding" in this passage, but his comments are equally relevant to the discussion here. See Heaney, "Envies and Identifications: Dante and the Modern Poet," *Irish University Review* 15 (1985): 9.

12. Heaney, "A Tale of Two Islands: Reflections on the Irish Literary Revival," in *Irish Studies 1*, ed. P. J. Drudy (London: Cambridge UP, 1980) 3.

ideological imperative, Marxism in Milosz's case and nationalism in Heaney's case.[13] At its worst, the imperative results in hollow slogans, recalcitrant antagonism, or the "tribe's [silent] complicity" (FW 23). The two armed young men who appear in "After a Killing" manifest the problem of the "command to participate actively in history" in that their active participation succeeds only in perpetuating the inflexible commands of the "unquiet founders"—voices, now mythologized, that live on in perpetuity. Such ideological imperatives are invariably monologues and, therefore, result in a form of discursive stasis, which is essentially the same trap as the "motionless point." The paradox here resembles the conflicting impulses the speaker senses in "The Unacknowledged Legislator's Dream," the unsatisfactory choice between Archimedes and Tarzan.

Not surprisingly, the speaker in "Away from It All" sees his position as "somewhere between / balance and inanition"—between aesthetic stasis and discursive, and political, exhaustion. The title of Heaney's poem would seem to be a colloquial affirmation of escapism to the motionless point. However, the revelation of the poem is that no such escape is possible. Just as the speaker in "Oysters" could not escape memory and the obligation that comes with memory, the speaker in "Away from It All" finds that he cannot clear his head "of lives in their elements." Revenant lives and their element haunt this poem as well as many of the poems in *Station Island*.

"Chekhov on Sakhalin" is an important poem in *Station Island* because it asserts the artist's need to be involved in and aware of all aspects of his or her culture, not just the fashionable or artisti-

---

13. For an example of the various forms of nationalist thinking in Ireland—though the terms may vary from "Unionist," to "Republicanist," to "Loyalist"—see essays by George Boyce and Simon Murphy in *Contemporary Minority Nationalism*, ed. Michael Watson (London: Routledge, 1990); Liam de Paor, "The Rebel Mind: Republican and Loyalist," in *The Irish Mind*, ed. Richard Kearney (Dublin: Wolfhound, 1985); Terry Eagleton, "Nationalism: Irony and Commitment" in *Nationalism, Colonialism, and Literature*, ed. Eagleton et al., intro. by Seamus Deane (Minneapolis: U of Minnesota P, 1990); Conor Cruise O'Brien, "Nationalism and the Reconquest of Ireland," in *The Crane Bag Book of Irish Studies (1977–1981)* ed. Mark Patrick Hederman and Richard Kearney (Dublin: Blackwater, 1982): 95–100.

cally enlightened aspects. A close examination of Chekhov's account of his trip to the Russian penal camp on Sakhalin Island reveals some interesting parallels to Heaney's imagined pilgrimage to Station Island. My point here is not merely to assert a biographical or bibliographical influence that reveals what Heaney was thinking when he wrote "Station Island." Rather, I believe that a reading of "Station Island" is enriched if viewed as an intellectual and aesthetic journey in which the poet comes face to face with the violence and suffering of his country.

In 1890 Chekhov was thirty years old and at the height of his creative power and popularity. It was at this point that he chose to undertake the voyage across Russia to Sakhalin, an island off the Pacific coast of Russia, north of Japan. Chekhov's motive for the journey was private; the result of the journey public, in the form of a book, *The Island: A Journey to Sakhalin*. In his introduction to Chekhov's book, Robert Payne discusses the vague reasons behind Chekhov's fascination with Sakhalin:

To those who were especially close to him he would hint that there were more serious reasons for the journey. To one he hinted darkly that he did not expect to return, to another he spoke of the need for a Russian writer to venture into the forbidding landscape of imprisonment for his soul's sake, while to a third he spoke of a restlessness which had gripped him by the throat and would not give him any rest—only a long journey would quieten him.[14]

Heaney probably read and used the edition of Chekhov's book with Payne's introduction because the quotation attributed to Chekhov in Heaney's poem, "So, he would pay his 'debt to medicine'" (SI 18) comes from a letter written by Chekhov that Payne quotes at length in his introduction. So too, the story about the "troikas of Tyumin" is derived from a harrowing encounter Chekhov recounts in a letter to his sister, which Payne quotes. These sources are interesting as background information, but their value lies in the fact that Chekhov's voyage into suffering and human degradation parallels the poet's journey on Station Island.

14. Anton Chekhov, *The Island: A Journey to Sakhalin*, trans., Luba and Michael Trepak, intro. by Robert Payne (New York: Washington Square, 1967) xiv.

In a letter to his brother, Chekhov wrote that "Sakhalin is a place of intolerable suffering, and man alone, whether free or enslaved, is capable of making such a place." Later in that same letter, Chekhov says, "I am sorry that I am not sentimental: otherwise I would say we ought to go on pilgrimage to Sakhalin as the Turks go to Mecca."[15] The concept of a pilgrimage to a place of suffering created by human beings complements the Dantean pilgrimage to Purgatory, a place of suffering created by God; furthermore, it provides an insight into Chekhov's motives for going to Sakhalin in the first place. The artist has a responsibility, perhaps even a need or a calling, to encounter what Stephen Dedalus rather flamboyantly called "the reality of experience." The reality of experience can, of course, include the aesthetic but it must not deny the place of human-made suffering.

Chekhov was to see suffering as he never imagined. At one point, he describes a prisoner who was beaten so severely that he could only scream, "Oh, my God, my God!" repeatedly—cries of suffering that in another context could be cries of worship or praise. And it is here that one of the parallels with "Station Island" becomes apparent. Pilgrim's prayers and portions of the Holy Mass resonate throughout the poems of "Station Island" along with the voices of violence and suffering. Payne notes in his introduction that Chekhov's concern was "to catch the exact tone of voice, the expressions on the faces of these people who had become the playthings of an inefficient and ludicrously ineffective administration."[16]

Heaney makes the same point in his poem about Chekhov, that Chekhov was trying "for the right tone—not tract, not thesis" (SI 19). This explains the poet's encounter with William Carleton on the road to Station Island. Carleton's style of writing certainly captured the tone of the Irish peasantry, but his lust for fame compelled him to be used as tool by the anti-Catholic, evangelical Reverend Caesar Otway, editor of *The Christian Examiner*, who first published Carleton's stories. Carleton was a writer who, after

15. Chekhov, *The Island* xix.
16. Chekhov, *The Island* xxx–xxxi.

his conversion to Protestantism, did not distinguish between tone and tract and thesis. Carleton, like Francis Ledwidge, made himself a composition of contraries.[17]

Payne concludes that Chekhov was "lit by a flame of quiet indignation and furious sorrow," and such can also be said of Heaney.[18] In "The Strand at Lough Beg" Heaney discovers, cleans, and prepares his slain cousin Colum McCartney for burial. The poem certainly conveys powerful sorrow, but the only indignation occurs through the tacit contrast of the methodical Protestant murder and the ritualized Catholic funeral. McCartney reappears in section 8 of "Station Island" to condemn the poet for his allusive description of sectarian violence: "'you whitewashed ugliness and drew / the lovely blinds of the *Purgatorio* / and saccharined my death with morning dew'" (SI 83). Furious indignation and quiet sorrow seem to be the expected response for the Irish poet. In contrast to McCartney's condemnation, Seamus Deane praises Heaney's poetry—particularly *Field Work* and subsequent works—for "changing our conception of what writing can be because it is facing up to what writing, to remain authentic, must always face—the confrontation with the ineffable, the unspeakable thing for which 'violence' is our helplessly inadequate word."[19]

The lesson of Czeslaw Milosz and Anton Chekhov is that the artist cannot escape the massacre and remain an artist, that the artist must come face to face with the suffering and violence that plagues his or her culture, that the artist must deflect ideology's guilt and avoid the immediate and visceral political gesture in favor of a battle that strikes at the very heart of humanity's suffer-

17. It is only fair to note that Carleton was used by Otway as part of his zealous attempt to portray the superstitious mind of the Catholic peasantry. The short story, though, was to be Carleton's genre. And his stories were so rich in detail and texture that they went well beyond the two-dimensional portraits one might expect from a religious tract bent on stereotyping and ridiculing Catholics. Nonetheless, as James Cahalan points out, Carleton's "is a polemical rather than a complex fiction." See Cahalan, *The Irish Novel* (Boston: Twayne, 1988) 53.

18. Chekhov, *The Island* xxxvi.

19. Seamus Deane, *Celtic Revivals: Essays in Modern Irish Literature* (London: Faber, 1985) 186.

ıg. The influence of Milosz and Chekhov can be seen through-
⌐ut "Station Island" as the poet questions beliefs and practices
that have molded him and faces the suffering that threatens to
mute his song. For Heaney, though, it is always both a battle of
wiles and a battle against self-effacing reticence.

In "Sandstone Keepsake," for instance, the speaker out on an
evening stroll picks up a stone from the shore of Lough Foyle.
Looking across at the Magilligan detention and internment camp,
the speaker contemplates first the stone's color and texture and
then imagines the stone coming from hell's River Phlegethon.
From this point, the speaker's imagination takes over, but only
briefly:

> Evening frost and the salt water
>
> made my hand smoke, as if I'd plucked the heart
> that damned Guy de Montfort to the boiling flood—
> but not really, though I remembered
> his victim's heart in its casket, long venerated.
>
> (SI 20)

The Phlegethon, a river of fire, appears in the *Inferno* as a boiling
river of blood in which those who committed violence against
their fellow humans are punished. The reference to Guy de Montfort alludes both to Dante and English history. In 1272 during
Holy Mass at the church, Guy de Montfort, one of Charles d'An-
jou's emissaries, avenged his father's death at the hands of King
Edward I by stabbing to death Prince Henry, son of Richard the
Earl of Cromwell, and cousin of Edward. Henry's heart, supposedly placed in a golden cup above a column at the head of London
Bridge, dripped blood into the Thames, signifying that the murder had not yet been avenged. The speaker undercuts these references to political intrigue and violence by truncating the comparison between his own experience and that of Dante's when he
says, "but not really." When the speaker begins his next train of
thought with "Anyhow," his original thought deflates into ba-
thos. The speaker draws back from the allusions, then, to see just
"the wet stone / in my hand."

In his "free state of image and allusion," the speaker might imagine himself as Dante by the Phlegethon, but all such comparisons seems absurd. The centaurs, for example, who guard the river and keep its victims immersed to their designated position challenge Virgil and Dante upon their arrival at the river. In "Sandstone Keepsake," these centaurs become "trained binoculars" who "swooped on, then dropped" the speaker because he poses no threat, merely "a silhouette not worth bothering about." Moreover, the centaur Chiron can tell that Dante is an important presence, not a shade, not a silhouette, but a living human: "'Have you noticed, / how the one behind moves everything he touches? / This is not what a dead man's feet would do'" (12, 80–82). "Sandstone Keepsake" ends with a reference to *Hamlet* that Heaney used in "Whatever You Say, Say Nothing." The speaker, unlike Hamlet, is not about to take vengeance against Claudius, or Guy de Montfort, or anyone else for that matter. He, as "one of the venerators," has his keepsake and will leave it at that.

I would like to suggest a reading of the "Station Island" sequence that differs from previous readings. Several critics have focused upon the Dantean paradigm as a factor in Heaney's poetry.[20] While I do not dispute the influence of Dante on Heaney's poetry—Heaney himself has acknowledged it—I believe that the

20. See, e.g., Kieran Quinlan, "Forsaking the Norse Mythologies," *Studies in Medievalism* 2.3 (1983): 19–28; Alasdair Macrae, "Seamus Heaney's New Voice in *Station Island*," in *Irish Writers and Society at Large*, ed. Masura Sekine (Gerrards Cross: Colin Smythe, 1985): 122–38; Geert Lernout, "The Dantean Paradigm: Thomas Kinsella and Seamus Heaney," in *The Clash of Ireland: Literary Contrasts and Connections*, ed. C. C. Barfoot and Theo D'haen (Amsterdam: Rodopi, 1989): 248–64; Donald Davie, *Under Briggflatts: A History of Poetry in Great Britain 1960–1988* (Chicago: U Chicago P, 1989) 245–51; Henry Hart, *Seamus Heaney: Poet of Contrary Progressions* (Syracuse, N.Y.: Syracuse UP, 1992), chap. 6; and Seamus Heaney, "Envies and Identifications: Dante and the Modern Poet," *Irish University Review* 15 (1985): 5–19. Although the Dante connection is clear enough, it should be noted too that St. Patrick's Purgatory was the topic of pilgrimage tales prior to Dante, as Alwyn and Brinley Rees explain: "The adventures of a certain Knight Owen in this cave [to the Underworld located on Lough Derg] comprise one of the most widely known of medieval "Visions" prior to Dante's. He first encounters demons who show him the horrors of Purgatory and of Hell, and then, after he has crossed a narrow bridge over the River of Hell, two prelates conduct him through Paradise and show him the Gate of Heaven." See Rees, *Celtic Heritage: Ancient Tradition in Ireland and Wales* (New York: Grove, 1961) 304.

"Station Island" sequence can also be understood as the poet's aesthetic and intellectual journey into the his "native realm," to borrow the title of Milosz's book. Once in his native realm, the poet encounters various influences (what Heaney called "gravities" in *Death of a Naturalist*), various voices from the grave, and various memories of past experiences. Three poems that precede the "Station Island" sequence — "Away from It All," "Chekhov on Sakhalin," and "Sandstone Keepsake" — act as the critical compass points of "Station Island" and direct the poet's aesthetic and intellectual journey: "Away From It All" highlights the impasse of being abstracted from life or being active in an unproductive manner, "Chekhov on Sakhalin" asserts the necessary coexistence of song and suffering, and "Sandstone Keepsake" warns against turning aesthetic practices into historical necessities. Collectively, then, these poems map the journey of the poet through his native realm, a journey that does not have a specific end point as Dante's journey does. Nevertheless, the poet, like Chekhov, learns to "walk away from flogging" and thereby sets himself free, even from the master's influence, to pursue his own artistic vision, the responsibility of his own song.

Simon Sweeney is the first figure the poet encounters on the pilgrimage. Ireland's pagan past, its former resistance to the rigors and rituals of Christianity evident in *Buile Suibhne*, persists in modern Ireland in the semi-Druidic figure, the "old Sabbath-breaker," Simon Sweeney. Sweeney's advice to the poet is not that different from the advice that Joyce gives in the last section, though not quite as exhaustive a litany as Joyce's: "Stay clear of all processions" (SI 63)! The poet, nonetheless, had "fallen into step" with the other pilgrims along their "drugged path" after talking to Sweeney. The influence, the gravity, of religious faith still compels the poet to stay in line and obey the call of the bells. Carleton's condemnation of religious obedience in section 2 furthers Sweeney's sentiment: "'O holy Jesus Christ, does nothing change'" (SI 64)?

Carleton, while avoiding the drugged path of religion, acts as a fork in another drugged path, the "Obedient strains" of politics:

"I who learned to read in the reek of flax
and smelled hanged bodies rotting on their gibbets
and saw their looped slime gleaming from the sacks—

hard-mouthed Ribbonmen and Orange bigots
made me into the old fork-tongued turncoat
who mucked the byre of their politics.

If times were hard, I could be hard too.
I made the traitor in me sink the knife.
And maybe there's a lesson there for you."

(SI 65)

The poet responds to Carleton's harsh assessments by stating that he has had the same experiences, though now inanition has set in and the once politically potent Ribbonmen are now "a frail procession / staggering home drunk on Patrick's Day / in collarettes and sashes fringed with green" (SI 65). Both Carleton and the poet come from similar backgrounds, though a century divides them, but each has taken a different course politically. Carleton chose an aggressive tack in which "their politics" became a weapon he could use against his own people. The poet, on the other hand, has "'no mettle for the angry role'" (SI 65). This will not be the last time the poet defends himself for not heeding the "harp of unforgiving iron / the Fenians strung" (SI 65–66).

The drugged path of religion, "Habit's afterlife," recurs in section 3 as the poet kneels "among bead clicks and the murmurs / from inside confessionals" (SI 67). Section 3 represents a "Hiatus" in the procession of figures the poet meets, and the poet here recalls, not a person, but a trinket owned by a young girl, Agnes, the sister of Heaney's father, who died of tuberculosis.[21] The trinket over the years has reached the status of a sacred object to the poet, who has held it in "a shimmering ark, my house of gold / that housed the snowdrop weather of her death / long ago" (SI 67).

Instead of addressing the young girl directly, the poet explores the connection between the veneration of the dead and the power

21. I am indebted to Neil Corcoran for providing in his book the actual names of the figures who appear anonymously, or almost anonymously, in "Station Island."

of prayer. The veneration of the dead can reach a point of religious ardor whereby the individual is eclipsed by the symbols representing that person's absence or loss. The danger of the venerated dead has already been seen in the "unquiet founders" whose names and deeds influence the living, and that spirit will recur in section 9 in which an IRA prisoner martyrs himself for the cause, thus securing a place for himself among those founders. The symbolic image of the dead young girl, the trinket, is contrasted with the naturalistic image of the dog's carcass in the last stanza of the section. Another naturalistic image of death will appear in section 7 when a slain friend appears with the top of his head blown off.

The powerful influence of veneration for the dead is further compounded by the fact that suffering otherwise silent—Agnes's name is "hardly ever spoke"—finds its only voice in prayer and religious devotion: "*Health of the Sick* / fluttered its *pray for us* in the litany" (SI 67). Prayers, which appear primarily as incidental noise in "Station Island," become a means of replenishing what has come to nothing when the unnamed monk in section 11 tells the poet to "'Read poems as prayers'" (SI 89). Though the connection remains shadowy, the link between poetry and prayer suggests that poetry can give voice to silent suffering.

Section 4 portrays an encounter with Terry Keenan, a young clerical student when Heaney knew him, who went off to celebrate Mass with the inhabitants of the rain forest. The poet meets the priest, just as he is to begin his renunciation: "my back / to the stone pillar and the iron cross, / ready to say the dream words *I renounce.* . ." (SI 69). On first reading, it seems that the poet, having lost his religious faith, is about to renounce Christianity—to declare, as Stephen Dedalus did, *non serviam*. But the poet makes no such statement in the section. In fact, the poet could just as easily be beginning a renewal of his faith, as in the rite of baptism in which the participants proclaim, "I renounce Satan. . . ." The renunciation, like baptism, is a starting point or point of departure from which the Christian, turning his or her back on one path, begins a spiritual journey on another path. Renunciation can also be sacrificing something so that the individual may advance spiritually—foregoing, as an act of will, of certain pleasures

or certain objects of value. Lent, in other words, is a form of renunciation.

The priest's conclusion that the poet is there to take the last
look is conjecture on his part, perhaps even reflecting his own
questionable faith now that he believes "'what I thought was chosen was convention'" (SI 70). Whether real or habitual is no matter, for in either case, religion has made its imprint upon both
priest and poet. Just as the Ribbonmen from section 2 have influenced the poet politically and the various fosterers in section 5
have influenced the poet intellectually and aesthetically, the
Church has influenced the poet spiritually. William Carleton's
words ring true in this regard: "'all that / has gone through us is
what will be our trace'" (SI 66).

The sixth section of "Station Island" is another hiatus from the
sequence of figures who visit the poet. The poet's mind drifts back
instead to a first love, apparently in part a love from afar, and the
well-known Irish guilt over sexual attraction. The reference to
King Midas recalls the Ovidian story about the musical contest
that ensues when Pan has the temerity to compare his music with
that of Apollo. When Tmolus chooses Apollo's music and awards
Apollo the contest, Midas objects and questions the justice of the
award. Enraged, Apollo gives Midas a set of ass's ears in punishment. Midas tries to hide the ears, but a servant soon sees them
and is sworn to secrecy. The servant, overcome with the need to
tell the secret, whispers the story of Midas's ears to a hole in the
ground and then fills in the hole. Unfortunately for Midas, the
reeds growing on the spot then echo the story for all to hear each
time the wind blows. Thus in the context of Heaney's poem, sexual attraction and excitement are linked with guilty *"Secrets, secrets"* for which the command *"Don't tell. Don't tell"* is given (SI
75).

This section also carries a quotation from Horace's *Odes*, specifically III, 21, ln 24. The line from Horace as it appears in
Heaney's poem does not provide any indication as to its context
in the ancient ode. Horace's verse is actually a prayer, not to a god,
but to a bottle of wine, written in the form of an invocation usually used in poems that praise a deity. The invocation to a bottle

of wine in the context of "Station Island" thus mimics the sacrament of the Eucharist. Horace's ode details the various powers of drink and the tempting joys of parties, including sexual joys. Bacchus, Venus, and the Graces will be in attendance, and the party will last the night. It is in this context that "*Till Phoebus returning routs the morning star*" appears. The result is a poem and an attitude toward life that runs contrary both to the ascetic attitude dictated by a religious pilgrimage and to the sublimation of sexual instincts. No wonder the poet finds himself descending stairs the pilgrims ascend.

Section 6 ends with love rather than debauchery, with the sense of renewal and freedom that comes from love. In fact, the section ends with another quotation, this time from Dante's *Inferno*. The context of the quotation is Dante's initial resistance to the pilgrimage with Virgil. Because of Dante's trepidation and because he knows of Dante's love for Beatrice, Virgil tells Dante of Beatrice's visit to him and of her words: "'A man must stand in fear of just those things / that truly have the power to do us harm, / of nothing else, for nothing else is fearsome'" (II, 89–91). To these words, Virgil adds his own reproof:

> "So what is wrong? Why, why do you delay?
>   why are you such a coward in your heart,
>   why aren't you bold and free of all your fear,
> when three such gracious ladies who are blessed
>   watch out for you up there in Heaven's court,
>   and my words, too, bring promise of such good?"
>   (II, 122–27)

After hearing Virgil's story and admonition, Dante proclaims his sense of renewal and empowerment; this is the passage that Heaney uses in his poem. In the context of Heaney's poem, Dante's words carry with them not only the nurturing and restoring power of love that the poet finds with his Beatrice, but also the responsibility of the poet, the current day pilgrim, to take courage and to face the task at hand. Thus, the poet may inhale the "land of kindness" of his own Beatrice and as a result feel "Translated, given, under the oak tree," but the "land of kindness" does not represent the poet's escape from responsibility.

The encounters of sections 7 and 8 resemble one another to the extent that the poet meets people with whom he had a relationship in life. These are the first friends the poet meets in "Station Island." William Strathearn, in section 7, a college mate of Heaney's, was murdered in his home by two off-duty policemen. Tom Delaney, the first figure in section 8, was an archaeologist at the Ulster Museum in Belfast, and Colum McCartney, the second figure in 8, was Heaney's cousin, whom Heaney commemorated in "The Strand at Lough Beg" in *Field Work*. To Strathearn and Delaney, the poet seeks forgiveness for "'circumspect involvement'" (SI 80) and for "'broken / covenants'" (SI 81). However, the poet defends himself against McCartney's charge that he "'whitewashed ugliness and drew / the lovely blinds of the *Purgatorio* / and saccharined my death with morning dew'" (SI 83). The poet has clearly not escaped the massacre. It lives with him, haunts him, and influences his thoughts and feelings, just as the influences of religion and politics persist in his consciousness. Unless Heaney is to apologize for not being dead (which, of course, any survivor would then have to do), then he must concede that hearing of his cousin's murder was in actuality "'encountering what was destined.'" And that destiny is played out in the figure of Francis Hughes in section 9.

Section 9 begins with the starved, tortured, hallucinogenic thoughts of Francis Hughes, an IRA hunger striker who died on May 12, 1981, the second of ten strikers to die. Padraig O'Malley contends that the logic of Bobby Sands, the first of the hunger strikers to die, "was averring the logic of Tone, Emmet and Pearce, the historical continuum as an unchanging point in time."[22] These are a few of the "unquiet founders" whose influence Heaney cites in "After a Killing." O'Malley traces the actions and thoughts of Bobby Sands and the other hunger strikers to an "ennobling tradition," in which the "myth of redemptive sacrifice hardened and held." O'Malley's compelling analysis of this cyclic, mythic perspective is worth quoting at length:

22. Padraig O'Malley, *The Uncivil Wars: Ireland Today* (Boston: Houghton Mifflin, 1983) 266.

In this context the hunger strikes were a metaphysical ritual, a symbol: the blood-stained bond linking the failures of the past to the failures of the present; the confession of defeat transcending the blood-letting of the present, reestablishing the link with the historical past, and reaffirming the legitimacy of the cause and the movement by reaffirming the legitimacy of the means. They were atonement for mutilations, the meaningless maimings, the innumerable futile brutalities, and the hundreds of violent and misdirected deaths sanctioned in the name of holy nationalism. They were expiation, an asking for forgiveness, an abnegation of self, a blind conviction that what could not be achieved by the murder of others could yet be achieved by the murder of self. They were an excuse for the murders of tomorrow, romantic delusion, the sublimation of reality, an aggravated assault on the national psyche, a last desperate attempt to mobilize public opinion by cheating life, an atavistic gesture of impotence to orchestrate a symphony of grief, a callous ploy to infiltrate the hidden recesses of the national consciousness, a reaching back to tribal allegiances, to the myth of martyrdom and redemption.[23]

It is impossible to underestimate the resonance of human starvation upon the Irish psyche. Because the famine has long been a powerful factor in Irish consciousness, the image and the idea of ten men choosing to allow their bodies to consume themselves for lack of food cuts to the very heart of the Irish Catholic identity.

Francis Hughes, the martyr, and William Carleton, the turncoat, are in a sense opposites, in that many Irish citizens in the midnineteenth century, and perhaps even Carleton himself, chose to avoid starvation by converting to Protestantism.[24] Hughes and the other strikers would rather die than submit in any manner. Thus the impasse persists. Furthermore, the veneration of the dead, so clear in O'Malley's analysis, recalls the poet's memories of the dead child and his attachment to the trinket, *qua* relic, in section 3. The tendency to venerate to the point of worship occurs in the final lines of "Sandstone Keepsake" as well, in

23. O'Malley, *The Uncivil Wars* 267.
24. Darcy O'Brien refers to this practice as to "take the soup." O'Brien explores the possibility that such a practice may indeed have motivated Carleton in his decision to convert. See O'Brien, "Piety and Modernism: Seamus Heaney's *Station Island*," *James Joyce Quarterly* 26.1 (1988): 57–60.

which veneration is tied to the need for vengeance and the command to set things right. Therefore, veneration of the dead and
the power of martyrdom, both with pagan and Christian aspects,
work in conjunction with political and religious antagonism and
vengeance in order to forge a race's conscience unified only by its
contradictions.

In the concluding stanza of section 9, the poet repents, not for
sins of commission but for sins of omission: "'I repent / My un-
weaned life that kept me competent / To sleepwalk with conniv-
ance and mistrust.'" The poet then proclaims his hate for "'everything / That made me biddable and unforthcoming'" (SI 85). The
section ends with the undeniable destiny that makes Francis
Hughes's sacrifice inevitable:

> As if the cairnstone could defy the cairn.
> As if the eddy could reform the pool.
> As if a stone swirled under a cascade,
> Eroded and eroding in its bed,
> Could grind itself down to a different core.
> Then I thought of the tribe whose dances never fail
> For they keep dancing till they sight the deer.
>
> (SI 86)

The sentiment here echoes that of Louis McNeice's poem
"Valediction" in which the the "woven figure cannot undo its
thread."[25] The self-fulfilling prophesy of the tribe "whose dance
never fails" because its members keep dancing until the the deer
is sighted recalls the destiny the poet acknowledges in his response to Colum McCartney and the cyclic violence engendered
by the "unquiet founders." If the poet cannot hope to deny or halt
such powerful forces, does he then give in to them, acquiesce to
the inevitable destiny? The answer held out in section 10 is no.

The poet experiences another hiatus in section 10, like those in
sections 3 and 6, when he contemplates an ordinary drinking
mug. The mug, removed from a shelf in Heaney's childhood
home, was temporarily translated as a result of its use in a play:

25. Louis McNeice, *The Collected Poems of Louis MacNeice*, ed. E. R. Dodds (New York:
Oxford UP, 1967) 53.

> Dipped and glamoured from this translation,
> it was restored with all its cornflower haze
>
> still dozing, its parchment glazes fast—
> as the otter surfaced once with Ronan's psalter
> miraculously unharmed, that had been lost
> a day and a night under lough water.
>
> (SI 87)

The translated mug both defamiliarizes and restores the well-known. It is not that the artist transforms reality; rather, it is that art allows the audience temporarily to feel "estranged" from the all too familiar. (The word *Translated* also appears in section 6 regarding the feelings of love the poet experiences in "the land of kindness" (SI 76).) The sense of defamiliarization contrasts with the "ordinary noise" of the curtain shutting. It is as if artistic expression can circumvent, at least temporarily, the audience's normal way of seeing the world—not through an act of transformation, but through an act of translation, revoicing or reinscribing the quotidian: "The dazzle of the impossible suddenly / blazed across the threshold, a sun-glare / to put out the small hearths of constancy" (SI 88).

The translation of the mug as a result of its use in the play is described as analogous to the resurfacing of Ronan's psalter in the Sweeney story. When Sweeney's spear struck Ronan, the book fell in the lough only to be recovered by an otter. The book emerges from the lough waters unharmed, a baptism of sorts, a sign of Ronan's miraculous power and a sanction of his religious duty in Ireland. The thread of translation and emergence are picked up in section 11. In contrast to the emergence of Ronan's psalter from the lough waters, the poet envisions a kaleidoscope pulled from muddy waters that evokes a memory of a monk who had years before spoken of ". . . the need and chance / to salvage everything. . . . // What came to nothing could always be replenished" (SI 89). The monk, admonishing the poet to "Read poems like prayers," assigns the translation of a poem by St. John of the Cross as the poet's penance. This act of translation completes the cycle of renunciation (section 4), contrition and confession (sections 8 and 9), and penance (section 11). But this is not a wholly religious act in that the poet's penance is also an artistic endeavor. Nonetheless, the monk's reference to the "need and chance / to salvage everything, to re-envisage / . . . any gift / mistakenly abased" links the poet's continued sense of obligation with the power of artistic translation.

Most of section 11 entails Heaney's translation of a poem by St. John of the Cross entitled *"Cantar del alma que se huelga de conocer a Dios por fe"* —sometimes entitled *"La fonte"* or "The Fountain." St. John of the Cross is the opposite of William Carleton in that he never deviated from his chosen path, even when imprisoned, beaten, and starved by dissenting members of his own order. As a result, St. John of the Cross developed a spiritual journey in which suffering, the long night of the soul, brings forth the spiritual song of the Christian. Gerald Brenan explains the practices of the Reformed Carmelite Order, in which St. John of the Cross was a motivating force:

[I]t was not a merely intellectual enterprise that these monks and nuns were engaged on: they believed, and in this the authority of the Church supported them, that, if grace were given them, they could carry the whole mind, with its affections as well as its understandings, to union with the source of that mind, which is God. Since love was the motive, Eros the engine in their hull, their course took the form, and is therefore expressed in the language of a love affair. It was the extreme of sublimation—the final point, if one like, of that historic movement of love for the absent, *amor de lonh*, which had inspired the Provençal poets and through them Dante and Petrarch.[26]

Paradoxically, St. John of the Cross has more in common with Francis Hughes, the IRA soldier, than any other figures the poet encounters. Rowan Williams argues that St. John's poetry "is grounded in the practical—and political—struggle to create within his order a style of life authentically reflecting the poverty, the detachment and *disponibilité*, which for him were the central

26. Gerald Brenan, "Studies in Genius II: St. John of the Cross, His Life and Poetry," *Horizon* 15 (May 1947): 259.

characteristics of Christian 'interior' life."[27] This approach clearly places St. John of the Cross on the "contemplation of the motionless point" side of the Milosz equation—as the poem on the Trinity, which is "all sources' source and origin," bears out. In contrast, Francis Hughes obeyed the command to "participate actively in history."

James Joyce appears as the final figure in "Station Island," his voice described as "a prosecutor's or a singer's, / cunning, narcotic, mimic, definite" (SI 92). Joyce is to be the poet's artistic confessor, his "prosecutor," as the monk was the poet's religious confessor. Joyce's influence upon the poet is great, even "narcotic," as the poet addresses him as "'Old father.'" But Joyce is quick to rebut the religious penance the poet sought and performed in section 11:

> "Your obligation
> is not discharged by any common rite.
> ....
> You lose more of yourself than you redeem
> doing the decent thing. Keep at a tangent.
> When they make the circle wide, it's time to swim
>
> out on your own and fill the element
> with signatures on your own frequency,
> echo soundings, searches, probes, allurements,
> elver-gleams in the dark of the whole sea."
>
> (SI 92/93–94)

"Station Island" ends with the poet in a state of artistic limbo because Joyce, the figure who seems most likely to be the poet's Virgil, tells the poet to chart his own course and then, like Chekhov, walks away. The poet does not reach a destination in "Station Island," but finds himself stranded in the rain as his Virgil, having said his peace, proceeds on his own path.

In the course of "Station Island" a number of voices have been heard, various perspectives and experiences shown, and many

27. Rowan Williams, *The Wound of Knowledge: Christian Spirituality from the New Testament to St. John of the Cross* (London: Darton, Longman and Todd, 1979) 161.

contrasts rendered, all of which raises more questions that it answers. "Station Island" seems to say, like the granite chip in "Shelf Life," "*Come to me . . . / all you who labour and are burdened, I / will not not refresh you*" (SI 21). Like Chekhov, who let the horrors of Sakhalin prisoners and the indifferent bureaucracy of the prison officials speak for themselves without any guiding commentary or conclusive judgments, Heaney gives each voice and each perspective its due, most without judgment.

Six years later in *Seeing Things*, Heaney, in "The Journey Back," meets the final "shade," Philip Larkin. Larkin blends Dante's words with his own so that Dante's task "*to face / The ordeal of my journey and my duty*'" becomes Larkin's unsentimental, empirical vision of the drabness and enervation of modern life. The only irony in Larkin's voice is self-directed. This is not a poet returning inspired from an epic journey nor one who has set out like one of the Magi seeking the savior. This is a poet who has ventured into the "'heartland of the ordinary. / Still my old self. Ready to knock one back. / A nine-to-five man who had seen poetry'" (ST 9). The passage from Dante that Larkin quotes comes from the second canto in which Dante contemplates the journey he is about to begin. In Heaney's poem, Larkin has the last word—that is, a post-journey, postvision perspective. However, Larkin's words are less postvisionary—that is, complementing Dante's prevision words—than visionary of the sort that undercuts all epic pretense. The poet is just a man caught up in—even trapped by—daily existence. The poet's duty, then, is to render his nonidealized vision of the lives that surround him.

The poet in section 1 of "Station Island," echoing the *Piers Plowman* poet, envisions a "field [that] was full / of half-remembered faces." The "Station Island" sequence certainly entails a varied procession of folk. The various victims the poet encounters reveal the many different faces of death: Agnes, the tragedy of youthful suffering and death; Strathearn, the terror of sudden violence and the loss of familial relations; Delaney, the valuable life truncated and the valuable relationship squandered; McCartney, the numbing inevitability of violence and suffering; and Hughes, the circular logic of martyrdom. Beyond the victims, three priest figures appear in the sequence: William Carleton in section 2, a failed priest; Terry Keenan in section 4, a doubting priest; and St. John of the Cross in section 11, a devout priest. At various points during the sections of "Station Island," religious rites and rituals occur — some performed in earnest faith, some in doubt, and others in mimicry. Even the speaker's perspective shifts throughout the sequence. Helen Vendler points out that "Heaney is sometimes (as with Joyce) the abashed apprentice, sometimes (as with his murdered cousin) the guilty survivor, sometimes the penitent turning on himself with hallucinatory self-laceration."[28] "Station Island," then, resembles "Singing School" in the sense that it too is a sequence of poems in which a number of different perspectives, points of view, experiences, and influences collectively act as a chorus in the poet's life. However, the poet of "Station Island" has not and does not plan to escape the massacre. He instead sees he must face the massacre.

In section 1, the poet announces himself a "fasted pilgrim, / light-headed, leaving home / to face into my station" (SI 63). Far from the inner émigré of "Exposure," the poet of "Station Island" does face his station. No epiphany occurs at the end of "Station Island" that will place everything in perspective, make all things clear, unify and cohere all dissonance. Though the poet does refer to Joyce's words as a "new epiphany," they are really more an admonition or chastisement. Nonetheless, the realization that an object as simple as a household mug artistically translated might, to use the monk's words, "salvage everything," and that "What came to nothing could always be replenished" holds some promise for the future. The same point is made in "The Settle Bed" from *Seeing Things* where the speaker concludes "that whatever is given / Can always be reimagined, however four-square, / Plank-thick, hull-stupid and out of its time / It happens to be" (ST 31). Here is the "need and chance" of the artist. The artist must avoid being one of the tribe who dances until the deer is sighted. Instead, the artist must tack his or her own course, as Carleton and

28. Helen Vendler, "Echo Soundings, Searches Probes," rev. of *Station Island*, by Seamus Heaney, *New Yorker* 23 Sept. 1985: 108.

Joyce assert, and must walk away from flogging (or "that subject people stuff" as Joyce calls it), for the artist must always remember that to be alive is often also to be violated, that the freedman is often shadowed by the convict. Joyce's voice, "eddying with the vowels of all rivers," has already learned this lesson, and his advice is to "fill the element / with signatures on your own frequency." Heaney's signatures in *Seeing Things* will be translations of common things, everyday existence, like the translation of the mug by the actors who "held it in our gaze." In order to make such translations, though, Heaney finds he must first strip away portions of his old self so that he can recreate himself, reenvision the things around him, and as a result begin seeing things anew.

7 ❧ The Forged Conscience of Race: "Sweeney Redivivus," *The Haw Lantern,* and *Seeing Things*

At the end of "Station Island," before his rather abrupt and solitary exit, Joyce tells the poet to "keep at a tangent," to tack his own course as a writer, and to stop worrying about those questions and topics that concerned him, and other writers, in the past: "When they make the circle wide, it's time to swim / out on your own" (SI 93–94). The ambiguous pronoun *they* in Joyce's words implies that a poet's scope or range is dictated or controlled by others who can, for whatever reason, choose to "make the circle wider" or, by extension, make the circle narrower.

Joyce's advice, it turns out, is more a description of what he did as a writer than an epiphany to direct the poet's next step in that Joyce chose to leave Ireland rather than be held back by the nets of nationality, language, and religion. In the final section of *Station Island*, however, Heaney chooses not to follow Joyce's advice and launch out on an odyssey of his own; he does not attempt to make the circle wider nor to ask who might make it wider for him. Instead, like Sweeney who was stripped of his kingdom, his family, his dignity, his humanity, and his mind, Heaney begins to strip away the burden of "seed, breed and generation" that he has carried for so long. That is, in "Sweeney Redivivus" and *The Haw Lantern*, Heaney begins the process of stripping himself of the cultural dissonance that constitutes the conscience of his race in order to start again (the word *First* appears in the title of three poems) and to see things anew. This practice of unwinding and reenvisioning persists even into his most recent volume, *Seeing Things*.

The first step in this practice leads into the margins, not in order to show that the Irish writer has been marginalized for years by the British literary tradition as Heaney did in the "Open Letter," but to begin unwinding himself, as much as it is possible, from his tradition, perhaps even including texts of his own creation:

> Take hold of the shaft of the pen.
> Subscribe to the first step taken
> from a justified line
> into the margin.
>
> (SI 97)

As a starting point, "The First Gloss" contains no plans to dig, to trace, to discover, to sever, no pretense of creation or anger about violence, simply a gloss or countertext to an existing text. The word *Subscribe* connotes both having an accepted or perpetuated belief or practice as well as being in a subordinate position, an ancient copyist, even though the speaker mentions holding the specifically modern "pen." Rather than digging into (reinscribing) his tradition, this writer plans to step away from the "justified line," or, as he implies elsewhere, to unwind the influences of his tradition: "my head like a ball of wet twine / dense with soakage, but beginning / to unwind" (SI 98). In fact, the text the speaker plans to gloss might even be his own, perhaps "Station Island," or at least the influences that led up to and course through the sequence. Just as mad Sweeney stood in the margin of the newly emergent Christian Ireland, so "Sweeney Redivivus" stands in the margin of "Station Island," the first gloss of a writer questioning and challenging the very conscience of his race, the very conscience that makes him a writer. Throughout "Sweeney Redivivus," in fact, the speaker often finds himself skirting margins — standing along borders, flying out of the reach of others, climbing "the steep-flanked mound" (98), prowling "the rim of his clearing" (SI 109), "climbing down / the unrailed stairs on the wall" (SI 110), recalling the "myopic angers" of scribes who write "In the margins of texts of praise" (SI 111), or perching "on the sill / to gaze at my coffers of absence" (SI 114).

The speaker in "Sweeney Redivivus" begins the process of unraveling because he has become "incredible" to himself. He has become an acknowledged spokesperson "among people far too eager to believe me / and my story, even if it happens to be true" — what might be called the unacknowledged legislator's nightmare (SI 98). The speaker in "Unwinding" continues this practice as he "unravels" and "unwinds" knowledge and influences that have become "unfurtherable" and thus "will have to be unlearned." The word *under* occurs twice by itself and twice embedded in other words, indicating the burden of heritage and responsibility from which the speaker seeks to extricate himself. Even terms that usually suggest progression have a negated quality, resulting in a sense of regressive progression: "So the twine unwinds and loosely widens / backward through areas that forwarded / understandings of all I would undertake" (SI 99).

"In the Beech," "The First Kingdom," "The First Flight," and "Drifting Off" appear in sequence and relate to one another as the speaker unwinds various strands of the past. "In the Beech" uses the metaphor of rings on a tree to account for the advent and advancement of both Christianity and imperialism in Ireland. Thus, the poem's content recalls the title of the section, "Sweeney Redivivus," where the Irish name *Suibhne*, written in its Anglicized form, "Sweeney," is yoked with the Latin *Redivivus*, meaning "restored" or "brought back to life." The words thus distinctively juxtapose points in Irish history before and after Christianity, before and after foreign intrusion. However, the multilingual title problematizes any attempt to restore or revive a purely Celtic past independent of all other influences, for the speaker's heritage — like the words in the section's title and the twine in the poems "Unwinding" and "Sweeney Redivivus" — is composed of many interwoven strands.

The speaker of "In the Beech" is a forgotten lookout, someone whose job it is to warn and advise the people, posted in a "hidebound boundary tree. My tree of knowledge" (SI 100). The word *hidebound* can refer both to trees and humans. Regarding trees, the term refers to a bark so unyielding that it impedes growth;

regarding humans, *hidebound* refers to skin that acts the same as
the bark on a tree but also, figuratively, a restricted view or scope,
bigoted, a mind narrow and obstinately set in an opinion. Of
course, the term also refers to a binding for a text. Consequently,
the tree itself in which the speaker is posted —possessing a Yeatsian "strangeness and a comfort, / as much a column as a bole" —
is both the vantage point from which the speaker reports and the
text the speaker reports. What he has to report, though, is being
ignored, as the speaker in "The First Kingdom" laments:

> They were two-faced and accommodating.
> And seed, breed and generation still
> they are holding on, every bit
> as pious and exacting and demeaned.
>
> (SI 101)

Here is the "they" of whom Joyce speaks, and to whom the forgotten lookout reports, a hidebound people only interested in decrying the injustices of the past, obstinately set in their opinion.

The same sentiment is expressed in "The First Flight," a poem
on the one hand that reads as an allegorical overview of Heaney's
poetic works and life: the Troubles ("the times / were also in
spasm"), the bog poems ("I was mired in attachment / until they
began to pronounce me / a feeder off battlefields"), the move to
the Republic ("my empty place an excuse / for shifts in the camp,
old rehearsals / of debts and betrayal"), the criticism that he was
not sufficiently involved politically ("they came to the tree / with
a stone in each pocket / to whistle me back in"), the poetic rejuvenation Heaney found in Wicklow ("relearning / the acoustic of
frost / and the meaning of woodnote"), the troubling and inescapable awareness of violence in "Oysters" ("my point of repose
knocked askew"). In response, the speaker chooses to evade all
influences and take flight, to fly above the conflicts, and to test
his wings in the jetstream:

> so I mastered new rungs of the air
> to survey out of reach
> their bonfires on hills, their hosting

and fasting, the levies from Scotland
as always, and the people of art
diverting their rhythmical chants

to fend off the onslaught of winds
I would welcome and climb
at the top of my bent.

(SI 103)

"The First Flight," on the other hand, reads as the thoughts of the seventh-century king Sweeney after his metamorphosis at the hands of Ronan. In his note to the section, Heaney states that the "poems in this section are voiced for Sweeney" (SI 123). While this point is easy enough to see in poems such as "The First Flight," "Sweeney's Return," and "Holly," it does not satisfactorily annotate every poem in the section, especially those that have distinctively modern topics, such as "An Artist," "The Old Icons," "In Illo Tempore," and "On the Road." Heaney's footnote to the section is in part a distraction and in part a call for an allegorical reading—both in voice and content—of many of the poems in "Sweeney Redivivus." "Drifting Off," for example, allegorically renders certain political and cultural sensibilities in the form of a beastiary. Words such as "comaraderie," "spiteful vigilance of colonies," "learned to distrust," "kept faith with," "caved in / to pathos" used in reference to Sweeney's relationship with various types of birds apply equally well to nationalist sentiments that Heaney has combated throughout his career.

Furthermore, the reference to "sleepwalk" in "The First Flight" continues in the title of "Drifting Off," both of which echo the word *somnolent* that Heaney has used throughout his career in reference to unquestioned beliefs and practices. Heaney will explore the allegorical method more thoroughly and successfully in *The Haw Lantern*, but in "Sweeney Redivivus" the combination of a voice somewhat distanced from his own and the occasional allegorical mode allows Heaney to unwind various influences that have molded the Irish conscience.

The influence of Christianity, for instance, which began in Ireland with the cleric's "new words" and new "sign," quickly became "History that planted its standards / on his gables and spires / [and] ousted me" (SI 107). The Christian text—both in its physical existence, "the big missal," and its epistemological construct, "the word rubric"—come to dominate the conscience of the speaker's people: "Intransitively we would assist, / confess, receive. The verbs / assumed us. We adored" (SI 118).

So too, political influences, charged with religious intonations, carry a powerful and lasting influence over the speaker's conscience. In "The Old Icons," the speaker, contemplating the unquiet founders' continued influence upon him, looks at an oleograph in which a martyr for the cause beatifically stands "with folded arms in a shaft of light: / the barred cell window and his sentenced face / are the only bright spot in the little etching" (SI 117). The visual text perpetuates the image of the old icons; however, though the impact of these unquiet founders has "grown transparent now," their power over the speaker's cultural conscience remains "inestimable." The word *oleograph* refers both to a form of visual text as well as a pattern formed by oil on water. Likewise, the influence of Ireland's political martyrs continues both in the form of visual texts that mythologize and deify the martyr's actions and as a pattern of thought and belief whose lasting influence is "inestimable."

Another influence is explored in "The Master," most likely a reference to Yeats, who is described as "a rook" dwelling "in an unroofed tower." The speaker braves the narrow, winding steps to reach the master only to discover that the master's words are the same old pap:

> Deliberately he would unclasp
> his book of withholding
> a page at a time and it was nothing
> arcane, just the old rules
> we all had inscribed on our slates.
>
> (SI 110)

Yeats's private mythology or visionary system acts as a veil that flirtatiously conceals and reveals a comprehensible system for understanding history, change, and meaning. The speaker discovers that this "book of withholding"—rather than being a text that transcends and explains history, change, and meaning—is in actuality just the same "old rules." Nonetheless, the master's words have power and resonance because they are inscribed, not in the margins, but squarely on the page, to be read, repeated, and obeyed. Although the speaker perceives the call for "intransigent service" to the master's text, he resists that call. His alternative text, however, can only resist the master's text from the margins, and only after the speaker climbs "down / the unrailed stairs on the wall" (SI 110).

Such encounters are not new in Irish tradition, Robin Flower describes the practice of Irish scribes who, like the speaker in "The First Gloss," fill the margins of the texts they transcribe with their own responses, observations, and complaints: "Irish scribes—and only Irish scribes at that time—had a habit of setting down in the margins and on blank spaces of their manuscripts personal memoranda, invocations of saints, little fragments of verse, and all the flotsam and jetsam of idle fancy. This is a marked characteristic of Irish scribes in all ages."[1]

In like manner, the speaker in "The Master" glosses the canonized text that dominates the page. The dominance of the master can only be challenged at the margins by an alternative voice—a mere scribe—proclaiming that the master's way is not the only way, in fact may not be anything new at all. Like the learning "incubated under lamplight" in "Unwinding" that later has to be "unlearned," defying the master's text "proofed / by intransigent service" is no small feat. Thus, it is not surprising to find the speaker in "On the Road," the final poem of "Sweeney Redivivus," asking the same question the rich young man asked Christ: "*Master, what must I / do to be saved*" (SI 119)? Interestingly, the master does not provide an answer in the poem. Joyce, however, seems to have anticipated the question in "Station Island" when he admonishes the pilgrim, "What you must do must be done on your own" (SI 92). The speaker reaches his own conclusion only after contemplating several alternatives:

1. Robin Flower, *The Irish Tradition* (London: Clarendon, 1947) 36.

For my book of changes
I would meditate
that stone-faced vigil

until the long dumbfounded
spirit broke cover
to raise a dust
in the font of exhaustion.

                    (SI 121)

The speaker plans a "book of changes," in contrast to the master's "book of withholding," that may stir up something new in an otherwise enervated font. The reference to font carries religious and textual implications as the speaker must reinscribe, recharge, or even replace what is now spiritually and textually exhausted. This task begins then with a pen in hand, though not of the adult writer, but in the hand of the child learning his alphabets.

The first poem in *The Haw Lantern* indicates that the speaker must unwind the strands of influence back to the point where they became language—the moment when perception becomes thought inscribed by language, the moment when the speaker's consciousness first encounters those nets of religion, nationality, and language. "Alphabets" traces cultural beliefs and practices from the moment they are identified and named through the molding effects that language has upon the individual's conscience:

A shadow his father makes with joined hands
And thumbs and fingers nibbles on the wall
Like a rabbit's head. He understands
He will understand more when he goes to school.

There he draws smoke with chalk the whole first week,
Then draws the forked stick that they call a Y.
This is writing. A swan's neck and a swan's back
Make the 2 he can see now as well as say.

Two rafters and a cross-tie on the slate
Are the letter some call *ah*, some call *ay*.
There are charts, there are headlines, there is a right
Way to hold the pen and a wrong way.

First it is 'copying out', and then 'English'
Marked correct with a little leaning hoe.
Smells of inkwells rise in the classroom hush.
A globe in the window tilts like a coloured O.

(HL 1)

The poem begins with a child's perception of shadows on a wall, representations of animals made by the father. Like the inside of Plato's cave, this is the realm of perception and representation. The child "understands" from the father that he will "understand" more when he enters school. Although the word *understand* is used twice, its meaning shifts with each instance. The first refers to the child's basic perceptions, the latter to the specific knowledge the child will receive and the changes that will result from his entrance into the social realm of language. "Alphabets" thereby charts not only the transition from personal perception to social integration—or from "pre-reflective" perception to reflective analysis—but also the transition from consciousness to conscience. On this point, though, Heaney parts company with Plato in that the world outside the cave is not the realm of ideal forms, but the realm of social interaction, a public domain of sanctioned knowledge and expected conformity. This reversal of Platonic philosophy recurs as well in "A Daylight Art" where Socrates realizes only at the end of life his true calling of writing poetry.

Once the child exits the cave, which is his realm of personal or private perception and representation, he enters school where he may draw smoke at will for a week—perhaps an ironic reference to or memory of the fire in the cave—but then must learn to control his hand and conform his drawing to the prescribed shapes of the alphabet. The pronoun reference in the line, "the forked stick they call a Y," suggests a group or community into which the child has yet to integrate in that there is still a "they" whose practices the child must imitate. The line "This is writing" could be the child repeating what he has been told he is doing or the voice of a teacher naming the activity the child is learning. In either case, the third stanza, with its series of copulative verbs, names a series of prescribed items and activities the child must

participate in. Various verbs throughout the poem chart the growing influence of language on the conscience of the speaker—from
simple perception and cognition, verbs such as *understand* and
make, in the early stanzas through more advanced interaction and
involvement with the language, verbs such as *learns* or *bends* or
alludes, in the middle stanzas. The poem ends, then, much as it
began, with a series of similes. More sophisticated than the image
of a rabbit's head on a wall, though, these similes acknowledge
various perspectives or methods through which one can perceive,
understand, name, and represent the world.

From the moment the child perceives the analogy between the
configuration of the number "2" and the shape of the swan, he
enters a domain of representation and communication. Once the
child can both "see" and "say," and by extension write, he can
interact with others in that domain. However, that domain is not
homogeneous, but based upon differences—some as simple as
"the letter some call *ah*, some call *ay*," some more complex. Bakhtin makes it clear that entering this domain is a step into a world
that is not only textual, but social:

> The word in language is half someone else's. It becomes "one's own" only
> when the speaker populates it with his own intention, his own accent,
> when he appropriates the word, adapting it to his own semantic and ex-
> pressive intention. Prior to this moment of appropriation, the word does
> not exist in a neutral and impersonal language (it is not, after all, out of
> a dictionary that the speaker gets his words!) but rather it exists in other
> people's mouths, in other people's contexts, serving other people's inten-
> tions: it is from there that one must take the word, and make it one's
> own.[2]

It is not that the child lives in an idyllic, perfect world of presence
before school, only to fall prey to the world of difference and conformity in school. Rather, the differences were always there, but
the child's awareness of them, and their influence upon him, occur as consciousness becomes conscience. For the child, the context of learning the language is school, and the speaker in "Alpha-

---

2. M. M. Bakhtin, *The Dialogic Imagination*, trans. Caryl Emerson and Michael Holquist
(Austin: U of Texas P, 1981) 293–94.

bets" learns first by "'copying out', and then 'English' / Marked correct with a little leaning hoe" (HL 1). Latin is the next language, where "Declensions sang on air like a *hosanna*," followed by Irish, whose calligraphy "felt like home."

The speaker's integration into language is more than simply a matter of learning the sounds of words and the shapes of letters. Language, particularly written language, transforms in the speaker's mind from being something that resembles the world to being a representation of the world. In other words, the speaker's perspective shifts with age and education from one in which an image of the world relates to or represents a letter to one in which letters and written language represent the world. To the child, a forked stick is what others call a "Y," a swan's shape makes the number "2," and a leaning hoe signifies correctly accomplished homework assignments.

For the educated speaker, however, who has learned "this other writing," the letters of the Irish "alphabet were trees. / The capitals were orchards in full bloom, / The lines of script like briars coiled in ditches" (HL 2). This is more than a shift from childhood to adulthood, from grammar school drawings to artistic creations. Language becomes the means of both thought and representation — the way the speaker understands and signifies the world — whether it be the "coloured O" of the schoolroom globe, the "wooden O" of Shakespeare's Globe theater, or the "lucent O" the astronaut perceives from the window of a spacecraft. And as Bakhtin points out, this language was someone else's before it becomes "one's own," thus the young child enters a community whose language and conscience molds his own.

"Alphabets" ends with a series of similes that present alternative methods of perceiving, comprehending, and representing the world — each the product of the "shape-note language" that "Can still command" the speaker. The first relates the story of Constantine the Great, who saw the sign of the cross flaming in the sky before the battle of Mulvian Bridge in A.D. 312. That one sign dictated not only Constantine's actions in battle, but his life, and perhaps the direction of Western civilization thereafter, for

Constantine's conversion to Christianity was a turning point in the life of the young faith.

The sign of the cross that inspired and directed Constantine represents the theological teachings of Christ and the Christian religion, whose impact upon Western conscience is, like the influence upon the Irish of those unquiet founders, "inestimable." The necromancer, interested in signs from the other world, meditates upon a "figure of the world" hanging from his ceiling. This representation of the world reminds him to think "'not just single things,'" but universal things. The "figure of the world," paradoxically, represents things beyond the world to the necromancer and acts as a form of signification that attempts to transcend common perception and consciousness. The astronaut, in contrast, has the unique opportunity to perceive in an entirely different way the place which "he has sprung from." It is not surprising that the world is referred to as a "magnified and buoyant ovum" in this simile because the world is not only the place where the astronaut was physically conceived, but also his perspective of the world that allows him intellectually to conceive of his place of existence and origin. Finally, the speaker as a child looks on as a plasterer writes "our name" on the gable of the house. Each "strange letter" represents not only the name this child will have, but such defining characteristics as family, country, religion, and untold other factors that will influence and alter that "pre-reflective stare." Having charted both the development of language and thought in the young child and the influence of language — including signs, symbols, and representations — upon the conscience of individuals, the poem moves full circle, then, with the return to the child's perceptions and another early encounter with language.

Each of the final similes reveals the value and impact of representation upon the human conscience, a link between percept and concept, but they also segue into the more extensive use of allegory that Heaney uses in *The Haw Lantern* to explore the issue of conscience. Heaney uses allegory and parable as forms of writing that self-consciously acknowledge and explore the power of uage to mold people into what they are. Of course, writing has always been a central topic in Heaney's poetry, as Jay Parini points out: "The metaphorical equation, X is like writing, never seems far away; it is Heaney's readiest and most durable similitude."[3] The allegorical mode thus allows Heaney to unwind various "unfurtherable" influences in order to discern their imprint upon the Irish conscience. Rather than attempting to fly by the nets that threatened Stephen Dedalus, Heaney chooses to unwind them, as he does in "Alphabets," to the point when they began as language.

In "The Spoonbait," for example, the parable or allegorical form, Heaney's "new similitude," is associated with the unwinding motif from "Sweeney Redivivus":

> So a new similitude is given us
> And we may say: The soul may be compared
>
> Unto a spoonbait that a child discovers
> Beneath the sliding lid of a pencil case,
>
> Glimpsed once and imagined for a lifetime
> Risen and free and spooling out of nowhere—
>
> A shooting star going back up the darkness.
> ....
> Reeled through him upstream, snagging on nothing.
>
> (HL 21)

This poem remarkably offers both a backward and forward perspective of Heaney's poetic development while insistently calling attention to itself as trope, as experience understood through and translated by language. This new similitude occurs at both ends of the line. On the one end, the spoonbait itself recalls the "lure," both the tackle and its attraction, from "Relic of Memory" where the relic's primary attraction lies in the "Incarcerate[d] ghosts" that abide in the relic (DD 37). On the other end of the line, the spinning reel spooling out and reeling in recalls the unwinding,

---

3. Jay Parini, "The 'Co-opted and Obliterated Echo': On Heaney's 'Clearances,'" *Salmagundi* 80 (Fall 1988): 73.

in the form of disentangling and unlearning influences from the past, found in such poems as "Sweeney Redivivus" and "Unwinding." References to the spinning reel unwinding during a cast, the feel and tension of the tackle entering the current, and the reel retrieving the line appear in "The Pulse" and "Casting and Gathering" from *Seeing Things*.

The attraction of the spoonbait, "Glimpsed once and imagined for a lifetime," suggests the many personal and historical memories that recur in Heaney's poetry. But unlike encounters in past poems where the speaker finds himself challenged, intimidated, haunted, or displaced by such memories, "Spoonbait" reveals a confidence on the part of the speaker who sees the lure as "a toy of light / Reeled through him upstream, snagging on nothing." That is, the image of the spoonbait, like the other tropes in the poem, becomes for the speaker the means and the end of exploring experiences—even though it retains its configuration, its markings, as language.

The speaker in "Markings" from *Seeing Things* puts it another way: "All these things entered you / As if they were both the door and what came through it. / They marked the spot, marked time and held it open" (ST 11). The spoonbait as a configuration of experience and thought passes through the speaker into the world and back again—free-spooling without apparent limits or restrictions and returning without obstruction or debris. The peaceful confidence of the speaker in "Spoonbait" portends the direction Heaney takes in *Seeing Things*. No longer is language primarily the site of "cultural depth-charges" designed to rupture a verse line, nor is it seen as an inescapable net that impresses indelible linguistic, cultural, or political markings on every soul that encounters it. The speaker in "Spoonbait" recognizes the marvelous human capacity and potential for representation. Such moments of recognition and marvel become central concerns in *Seeing Things*: formal artistic representation, like the pigment in painting that seems beyond "what the reach / Of sense despairs of as it fails to reach it" (ST 26); practical markings, like the impromptu soccer field created by the boys in "Markings"; accounts of the mystical, like the story of the monks of Clonmacnoise and their encounter with an otherworldly ship; personal impressions, like the "near to an imagined perfection" of a pitchfork (ST 25); or even coincidental observations, like the "meaning made of trees" occurring along a stretch of road that is "Not an avenue and not a bower" (ST 85). But even in such recent poems where the speaker "credit[s] marvels," sides are taken, age-old wedges stand in place, and cultural and political factors persist in the subtext: "Years and years ago, these sounds took sides" (ST 15). And the speaker remains content to leave things as they have always been:

> I trust contrariness.
> Years and years go past and I do not move
> For I see that when one man casts, the other gathers
> And then *vice versa*, without changing sides.
>
> (ST 15)

The allegorical mode Heaney employs in *The Haw Lantern* allows him both a distance from and a closeness to his topic. By referring to beliefs and practices in such places as the Canton of Expectation and the Republic of Conscience, Heaney portrays and evaluates certain defining characteristics of Irish conscience without focusing upon any particular person, event, or belief. Furthermore, Heaney uses allegory and parable as devices for imaginatively traveling back to places he knows quite well, places that have stamped their imprint upon him. Several of these poems have the word *From* in the title, as if the speaker is sending a postcard, report, or log back from his visits to these places.[4]

Heaney uses the allegorical mode, for example, in "From the Canton of Expectation," where grammatical terms are used to contrast the conscience of two generations of Irish citizens. The speaker identifies different verb moods as the defining characteristics of each generation. The elder generation—the speaker's people, whose conscience is steeped in the desirable, supposable, conditional, the subjugation of the "optative mood"—has cre-

---

4. Stan Smith explores the ambiguity of prepositions such as *from* and *through* that recur in Heaney's later poetry. See Smith, "The Distance Between: Seamus Heaney," in *The Chosen Ground: Essays of the Contemporary Poetry of Northern Ireland*, ed. Neil Corcoran (Chester Springs, Penn.: Dufour Editions, 1992) 35–61.

ated a world where adults continually enumerate past humilia-
tions and children learn the "old language" by rote. This elder
generation lives in a world of passivity and ceremony while articulating a language of martyrdom and resignation. The poem exposes not only the shortcomings of this generation, but also the
trap of conscience that feeds upon and perpetuates the subjunc-
tive mood. Helen Vendler makes the same point in slightly different terms:

> The cunning and weariness here of the elder generation, their circumlo-
> cutions and defensiveness, their routine bravado and their pious apho-
> risms, mean that although the story of defeated political hopes and easy
> religious evasions may be a universal one, the language in which it is
> couched here is devastatingly particular to Ireland, and gives the parable
> its locality and sting of contempt.[5]

The conscience of the elder generation, then, has been forged in
stories of "defeated political hopes and easy religious evasions"
perpetuated over generations.

The conscience of the younger generation, in contrast, is the
product of a "change of mood." This younger generation will not
repeat the mistakes of its elders: it will not doze "a life away /
against the flanks of milking cows" but will instead scorn the passivity of its antecedents—the elder generation's sense of success
through failure, victory through defeat, power through martyrdom—and actively engage a "grammar / of imperatives":

> They would banish the conditional for ever,
> this generation born impervious to
> the triumph in our cries of *de profundis.*
> Our faith in winning by enduring most
> they made anathema, intelligences
> brightened and unmannerly as crowbars.
>
> (HL 47)

The poem ends as the speaker, looking for "one among us who
never swerved / from all his instincts told him was right action,"

5. Helen Vendler, "On Three Poems by Seamus Heaney," *Salmagundi* 80 (Fall
1988): 68.

longs for the indicative pounding, the "uncompromising report," of Noah's hammer. Such a person would be ready, not only for the cataclysm, but for the profound prospects of change. Repeating the word *stricken* to himself, the speaker realizes that expectation, resignation, and loss have "corroborated us" and, in contrast to the younger generation, made his generation all too susceptible to the would-be "triumph in our cries of *de profundis*." The speaker thus comes to realize Bakhtin's point that words and language begin in the thoughts and mouths of others before his own. As a result, the community built on those words molds the conscience of its members. The speaker's repetition of the word *stricken* suggests the double edge of conscience: he is clearly a member of that elder generation whose conscience is dominated by the optative mood, but his soul, as Stephen Dedalus might say, is also held back, or "stricken," by that dominant mood. The speaker consequently longs for the indicative in the way others might long for the optative, as a sign of hope or a sense of direction.

"The Mud Vision" likewise exposes the recalcitrance of the older "generation who had seen a sign" but who, true to form, nonetheless finds a way to equivocate any lesson or imperative that sign conveys: "We wished it away, and yet we presumed it a test / That would prove us beyond expectation" (HL 49). Thus, rather than becoming a sign of grace, renewal, change, or hope, the mud vision becomes a means of reinforcing the conviction in the minds of the older generation that they are beyond even any of these qualities:

> Our one chance to know the incomparable
> And dive to a future. What might have been origin
> We dissipated in news. The clarified place
> Had retrieved neither us nor itself—except
> You could say we survived.
>
> (HL 49)

Heaney has certainly perceived the shortcomings and anachronistic beliefs of previous generations in his earlier volumes, and even lamented his own complicity in and sense of trepidation regarding such matters, but the poems in *The Haw Lantern* critique a generation that has defined itself by talking its way into a narrow, self-perpetuated, and overwhelmingly limited, or "hidebound," view of itself and the world. For his part, Heaney understands the enervating influence of such views and refuses to perpetuate them. In "Fosterling" from *Seeing Things*, for example, by pointedly negating a well-known line from one of his earlier poems, Heaney laments the loss of simple, unsentimentalized pleasures that should, as much as anything else, be a defining aspect of personal conscience: "And poetry / Sluggish in the doldrums of what happens. / Me waiting until I was nearly fifty / To credit marvels. // . . . So long for air to brighten, / Time to be dazzled and the heart to lighten" (ST 52). In *The Haw Lantern*, though, Heaney is still unwinding the influences of "seed, breed and generation." And in the title poem, the brightening air that in "Fosterling" dazzles and lightens the heart appears instead in the form of light from Diogenes's lantern. Diogenes, like the speaker in "From the Canton of Expectation," is "seeking one just man." The speaker, though, finds himself "scrutinized" in the light from the haw, in response to which he can only flinch. The stricken speaker and his people are easily blinded by such illumination, and can only stand "a small light for small people" (HL 7).

"From the Republic of Conscience" recalls the same optative thinking as well as similar myths and stories found in "From the Canton of Expectation" and "The Mud Vision." The power and draw of conscience almost immediately pervades the speaker upon his arrival in the republic: "You carried your own burden and very soon / your symptoms of creeping privilege disappeared" (HL 12). The speaker—who is now a "dual citizen" and thereby capable of speaking on "their behalf in [his] own tongue"—learns from an old man that his return to the republic, in some form or another, was inevitable because "Their embassies . . . were everywhere / but operated independently / and no ambassador would ever be relieved" (HL 13).

In several of the allegorical poems, Heaney explores the notion of history and heritage as narrative, an ongoing story whose obscure origin is longed after. The speaker in "Parable Island," for instance, charts the development of such a narrative much as the speaker in "Alphabets" charts the development of language in the child. And just as the speaker in "From the Canton of Expectation" repeats the word *stricken*, the citizens of Parable Island continually repeat tales of origin, heritage, and, most importantly, identity: "the forked-tongued natives keep repeating / prophecies they pretend not to believe . . . " (HL 10). Over time, such stories have been told and retold, and the people's allegiance to those stories have solidified, even codified. Finding a point of origin or an original voice poses a challenge because the speaker cannot be sure "that parable is not / at work already retrospectively"—that what is considered truth is not actually trope, that history is not actually narrative glosses of other narrative glosses, and that origin is not actually another optative dream of "boat journeys and havens." Differing schools of archaeology, in their own way, have presented possible scenarios and interpretations of the past while "subversives and collaborators" vie "with a fierce possessiveness / for the right to set 'the island story' straight" (HL 11).

Continually unwinding the story of the island seems a more likely goal than setting the story straight because, as the speaker in "From the Land of the Unspoken" admits, "We are a dispersed people whose history / is a sensation of opaque fidelity" (HL 18) and whose "unspoken assumptions have the force / of revelation" (HL 19). Opaque fidelities, though, need not be submitted to and perpetuated involuntarily; they may instead be accepted, rejected, deferred, or revised—what the speaker in the dedication poem to "Clearances" calls the "co-opted and obliterated echo" (HL 24). To that extent, the poignant and powerful sonnet sequence is primarily a memoriam for Margaret Heaney but a farewell to certain opaque fidelities as well.

The first sonnet in "Clearances," for instance, recounts the interfaith marriage of Heaney's maternal great-grandmother. While the octave sets the wedding scene "a hundred years ago," the sestet describes and analyzes this piece of personal heritage in terms of a film or fictional story:

Call her "The Convert". "The Exogamous Bride".
Anyhow, it is a genre piece
Inherited on my mother's side
And mine to dispose with now she's gone.
Instead of silver and Victorian lace,
The exonerating, exonerated stone.

(HL 25)

The forked root or dual heritage that has played such an important part in Heaney's poetry in the past recurs here with a twist.
This heritage exists as a mere story, "a genre piece," that, like any
other trope or literary device, can be accepted or discarded as the
writer sees fit. The great-grandmother's union that once had the
power to incite a riot —as well as the separation and difference
that act of union violated—exists now as a formalized text from
another era. So too the stone once cast in anger, signifying the
violation of the great-grandmother's tribal fidelity, liberates the
speaker because, now hollowed of its symbolic potency, it no
longer carries the recurrent burden of "seed, breed and generation." Thus, "Clearances" at once mourns the death of Heaney's
mother but also sweeps clean ties to the past, certain fidelities that
are no longer viable. In the fourth sonnet, for instance, the son
recognizes and temporarily compensates for the difference between his own tongue and his inherited mother-tongue:

So I governed my tongue
In front of her, a genuinely well-
adjusted adequate betrayal
Of what I knew better.

(HL 28)

The subtle give and take between mother and son conveys the
complex relationship with tradition that has been the hallmark
of Heaney's poetry from the beginning. The son, aware both of
the language of his elders as well as the language of a tradition
not entirely his own, governs his tongue to a register compatible
with his mother's. The speaker's "well- / adjusted adequate betrayal" indicates neither a return to lost origins nor a rejection of
anachronistic practices. Rather, his governed tongue is part of an

inheritance that, like the "genre piece" of "'The Convert,'" the speaker is free "to dispose with now she's gone" (HL 25). In contrast, the speaker in "The Settle Bed" from *Seeing Things* describes a different kind of inheritance, an old settle bed, which, despite its physicality and links to the past, can be reimagined continually for use in the present, rather than merely discarded as a valueless vestige of the past: ".. . . whatever is given / Can always be reimagined, however four-square, / Plank-thick, hull-stupid and out of its time / It happens to be" (ST 31).

The idea of heritage as a "genre piece" recurs in "Shooting Script," where a slowly fading heritage, reminiscent of that of the elder generation in "From the Canton of Expectation," is recorded on film. The filmic techniques used to document the vestiges of this heritage capture not only its glory, but its futility as well:

> They are riding away from whatever might have been
> Towards what will never be, in a held shot:
> Teachers on bicycles, saluting native speakers,
> Treading the nineteenth-twenties like the future.

> (HL 45)

The goal of the shooting script and the film is to capture the essential Ireland and its language.[6] But the film, while recording the past forever "in a held shot," also documents movement without progress, and the "soundless sequence" segues to a fade out. The script, however, ends not with a fade out, but continues into a tracking shot up the strand until it reaches a stick that marks the beach with "Words in the old script in running sand" (HL 45).

"Shooting Script" possesses a facetious quality in that the very serious issues of heritage and language are reduced to a series of

---

6. The experience of the poem may have been derived from Heaney's involvement with the documentary *The Story of English*, in which the issue of heritage and language recurs throughout the episode on "The Irish Question": "In 1986, there are only a handful of monoglot Irish speakers, and fewer than 100,000 Irish citizens have a good knowledge of Irish. In fact, some pessimistic commentators predict that by the year 2000 Irish Gaelic will have become a dead language, remaining, in Seamus Heaney's words, only 'mythically alive'" (182). See Robert McCrum et al., eds., *The Story of English* (New York: Elisabeth Sifton/Viking, 1986).

shots in a documentary that presumes to, but cannot possibly, capture the complexity and diversity of its subject matter. Within that playfulness, though, lingers an indictment of a generation as potent as that in "From the Canton of Expectation," for the subjects in the shots ride their bicycles "from whatever might have been / Towards what will never be." And while their language and practices persist into the present day, they are as anachronistic, as frozen in a held shot, as the "nineteenth-century milestone in grass verges." Implied too in the contrast of the "names like R. M. Ballantyne" and in the "cape of a soutane, / Biretta, Roman collar" is another shooting script that has resulted in much violence and bloodshed.

The final tracking shot of a stick writing a text in the "running sand" that is only to be washed away by an oncoming wave captures both Heaney's view of his heritage and his role as a writer. An inheritance may be something as intangible as the story of a stone hurled at an ancestor who violated her tribal affiliation one hundred years ago or as tangible as a "plank-thick" settle bed. But both, like the text written in the wet sand, are reimaginable and reinscribable—an inheritance and a heritage waiting to be reinvented. In like manner, the final sonnet of "Clearances," whose opening lines repeat lines from section 3 of "Station Island," articulates this view through the dual images of the felled chestnut tree and the departed soul of his mother, Margaret Heaney:

> I thought of walking round and round a space
> Utterly empty, utterly a source
> Where the decked chestnut tree had lost its place
> In our front hedge above the wallflowers.
> ....
> Its heft and hush become a bright nowhere,
> A soul ramifying and forever
> Silent, beyond silence listened for.

(HL 32)

Memory has always played an important role in Heaney's poetic imagination—from the recurrent memory of his father and grandfather in "Digging" whose actions metaphorically forecast his own poetic work, to his physically absent but spiritually present mother whose ramifying soul directs her son's imagination toward otherworldly things. In Heaney's most recent work, *Seeing Things*, memory—often sparked by or linked to powerful sensory perceptions—is perhaps the most potent poetic stimulus. In past volumes, memory has almost always directed Heaney's attention back to very real and very significant matters of tradition, language, and myth, but in *Seeing Things* Heaney takes the liberty of stepping onto old ground that he sees with new eyes. This is a confident Heaney who conceives of a poetry "Refined beyond the dross into sheer image" (ST 29). This is a poet who wishes to speculate about the "phenomenal instant when the spirit flares / With pure exhilaration before death" (ST 66), a poet who recognizes "The virtue of an art that knows its mind" (ST 91).

Contemporary (postdeconstructive) critical theory that focuses upon the social text or minor literature emphasizes several key elements: an exploration of the way people position themselves (and by extension one an-*other*) within and through language; an examination of the way language is internalized, displaced, deferred, decentered, or destabilized; and conversely, an exposition of the power of some people to name, define, represent, and position other people through apparently stabilized or hegemonic discourses. All of these elements, at some time or another, are to be found at work in Heaney's poetry up to *Seeing Things*. At times, particularly in the early texts, such issues of language are presented in the form of an I/They or We/They dualism, in which the speaker positions himself in relation to tradition(s) or in which the speaker identifies himself with a group that has been controlled or exploited by another. However, a reading of Heaney's poetry as a series of texts in dialogue with one another subverts simple dualisms in favor of a more complex interplay of texts, voices, and perspectives. In contrast with or, more accurately, in conjunction with I/They or We/They dualisms, Heaney exposes the plurality of identification that constitutes the individual and collective conscience. This is the most intriguing aspect of Heaney's poetry, and its significance in Heaney's poetic imagination can be seen most clearly in "From the Frontier of Writing."

The poem's eight stanzas, divided into two complementing sections, explore the connection between the real and the written, experience and its representation. The first four stanzas of the poem recount an experience at a checkpoint where a driver, held at gun point, is interrogated and checked before being allowed to continue his journey. The latter four stanzas reflect upon the necessity of recounting and representing such an experience in writing. The opening line of the poem captures the sense of oppression at the roadblock: "The tightness and the nilness round that space / when the car stops in the road" (HL 6). Although the experience is one of subjugation, the sense of empty space recalls the darkness the speaker in "Personal Helicon" conceives as the space in which his poetic utterance must resound: "I rhyme / To see myself, to set the darkness echoing" (DN 57).

In contrast to "Personal Helicon," however, in which the space is identified but the utterance never heard, the second half of "From the Frontier of Writing" creates a space that resounds with an echo, "where it happens again." Passing through the checkpoint, the speaker acknowledges that he is "through, arraigned yet freed" to travel beyond the frontier and into new territory where things can be seen anew. On the one hand, the speaker passes "through," that is survived, the physical roadblock so that he is now free to explore, reenact, or reimagine the experience in writing. On the other hand, the speaker is "through," that is finished, with such tyranny, choosing to accept his freedom and move "past armour-plated vehicles, out between / the posted soldiers flowing and receding / like trees into the polished windscreen" (HL 6). This new frontier of writing that is "past" the violent oppression exerted by an occupying army begins as the images of those soldiers and their weapons recede from direct sight and become instead distorted shadows cast upon a windscreen — gradually clearing and opening the way, the reader is left to imagine, for a new horizon, a new frontier of writing before the speaker.

Seeing Things represents this very transition for Heaney as he passes through the frontier of his own writing — the social and political issues, the conflicts of dialect and tribe, he explored for years—in favor of a poetry that focuses upon the often-over-looked beauty in the quotidian, what in the opening lines of "Squarings" he calls "Shifting brilliancies" (ST 55).[7] Of course, it would be excessive to suggest that Heaney has abandoned the Irish question or his heritage in favor of a transcendent or neo-romantic aesthetic. Such was not the case in the early years, and such will more than likely not prove true in the future. The final poem in the lengthy and meandering sequence entitled "Squarings"—which often suggests or encourages juxtapositions and comparison but no clear, linear prosaic gloss—looks upon this new frontier of perception and writing for Heaney. These sensations certainly are not pristine and insulated from social and political influences, but invariably carry with them vestiges of the past. The question is what will be emphasized, the sensations or the influences that course through them:

> Strange how things in the offing, once they're sensed,
> Convert to things foreknown;
> And how what's come upon is manifest

> Only in light of what has been gone through.
> Seventh heaven may be
> The whole truth of a sixth sense come to pass.
>
> (ST 102)

Joyce's advice to the poet in "Station Island" was to "Let go, let fly, forget" (SI 93). While Heaney is not likely to forget or abandon the issues of tradition, language, and myth that have played such an important role in his poetry in the past, he has since "Station Island" taken flight, as the speakers in various poems find themselves floating, flying, or gliding above the ground or observing objects that do so. And *Seeing Things* seems to be Heaney's mature attempt, again at Joyce's behest, to "fill the element / with signatures on your own frequency, / echo sounding, searches,

7. At the time this book was written, little had appeared in print about *Seeing Things* other than book reviews. In the recent volume of essays edited by Elmer Andrews, though, both Andrews and Alan Peacock offer interesting readings of poems from *Seeing Things*. See *Seamus Heaney: A Collection of Critical Essays*, New York: St. Martin's Press, 1992, chaps. 11 and 12.

probes, allurements, / elver-gleams" (SI 94). Heaney's frequency in his most recent volume is such where much of the cultural dissonance that reverberated throughout his earlier poetry is attenuated, and that fine-tuned frequency, at least for now, represents the frontier of writing. And while the speaker in "Markings" concentrates on such things as the jackets that mark the goals on a soccer field where boys play beyond their physical means, the furrows in a garden, on the angles of a foundation, and the markings made from mowing corn, hauling water, or cutting grain—other markings invariably come to mind.

Markings and marks signify differences, such as the mark of Cain, or a wound. A mark can be a point of reference or even a moment of synchronization (on my mark). And of course Heaney constantly returns to language and writing, his markings on the page. This new frontier of writing as it appears in *Seeing Things* entails passageways, doorways, and other points of transition or departure where new similitudes allow Heaney to mark the spot and mark time in his translation of the ordinary into the marvelous and his search of the marvelous for momentary glimpses of and insights into the ordinary. Questioning and self-reflection continue as key activities in Heaney's poetry—though the questioning is less a cross-examination, the self-reflection less a challenge to accepted personal beliefs and cultural practices than they were in earlier volumes. In the final poem of "Clearances," the speaker thinks of "walking round and round a space / utterly empty, utterly a source" (HL 32). This empty space is all that remains of a great chestnut tree—identified as "my coeval / chestnut from a jam jar in a hole"—that has now been felled, chipped, cut, cracked, and collapsed into a "bright nowhere." (The echoes and variations of digging are significant.) In this empty space, this source, a soul ramifies "forever / Silent, silent beyond the silence listened for" (HL 32). Once vestiges of and links with the past have been cleared, passed through and passed away, they clear a space where the commonplace can be experienced anew, a space where the "music of the arbitrary" needs no justification other than its own sounds, a space too where in moments of acute silence the soul can be heard and its continued influences felt.

In earlier volumes, such empty spaces were areas of darkness filled with the reverberating voice of the poet excavating and reinscribing an ever-present and influential past, grappling with an often threatening present, and acknowledging responsibility for actions past and present. Seeing things does not acquit the poet of such matters, though neither does it indict. Seeing things involves the realization that whatever is real must invariably be imagined and that whatever is imagined is then quite real. In "Bogland," the speaker proclaims that the Irish "have no prairies / To slice a big sun at evening" (DD 55). While that geographical fact has certainly not changed, a horizon has presented itself where none was seen before. In "Bogland," historical necessity draws the speaker's vision invariably downward and inward, truncating in the process the possibilities disclosed in the vast spatial regions of an open horizon. The speaker can only dig. But Heaney has cleared such necessities in *Seeing Things* and chooses instead to explore horizons—spatial regions of memory, sensation, and speculation closed to him in the past.

Heaney's preoccupation with passages, transitions, movements, and positions indicates a breaking away from digging—a metaphor that served him well over the years—in favor of what might be called mysticism, but what is more likely a form of meditative open-endedness. Heaney affords himself at this stage in his career the freedom to "trust contrariness." While he certainly continues his interest in the "music of what happens," in *Seeing Things* Heaney also allows himself the freedom to listen for the music of what happened, the music of happening itself, the music of what might have happened, and even—and here is a new frontier of writing for Seamus Heaney—the music of what might yet happen.

🌿 References and Readings

By Seamus Heaney

"A Chester Pageant." *Use of English* 17.1 (1965): 58–60.
Death of a Naturalist. London: Faber, 1966.
"Out of London: Ulster's Troubles." *New Statesman* 1 July 1966: 23–24.
"Frogman." *The Listener* 4 July 1968: 11.
"Old Derry's Walls." *The Listener* 24 Oct. 1968: 521–23.
Door into the Dark. London: Faber, 1969.
"Seven Poems by Seamus Heaney: 'Serenades,' 'Midnight,' 'Navvy,' 'First Calf,' 'Medallion,' 'Icon,' 'Idyll.' " *The Listener* 4 Sept. 1969: 311.
"A Winter's Tale." *The Listener* 30 Oct. 1969: 592.
"Offerings (In Memoriam Patrick Rooney): 'Turnip Man,' 'High Street, 1786,' 'Cave Hill,' and 'September Song.' " *The Honest Ulsterman* 19 Nov. 1969: 4–6.
"Delirium of the Brave—Seamus Heaney Writes about the Ireland of Wolfe Tone and the Persistence of Anachronistic Passions." *The Listener* 27 Nov. 1969: 757+.
"Poems: 'High Street, Belfast, 1786,' 'Tweed,' and 'Dawn.' " *Critical Quarterly* 11 (Winter 1969): 293–95.
"Three Poems: 'Their Brother,' 'Crowing Man,' and 'Lictor.' " *The Listener* 18 Dec. 1969: 864.
"Two Poems: 'Limbo' and 'Elegy for a Postman.' " *The Listener* 5 Feb. 1970: 182.
"The Last Mummer." *The Honest Ulsterman* (March/April 1970): 15.
"King Conchobor and his Knights." *The Listener* 26 March 1970: 416–17.
"Third Degree." *New Statesman* 10 April 1970: 515.
"Dream of the Trenches." *New Statesman* 17 April 1970: 557.
"Tinder." *New Statesman* 15 May 1970: 704.
"The Tollund Man." *Threshold* (Summer 1970): 5–6.
"Last Camp." *New Statesman* 12 June 1970: 840.
"Poems: 'Retort,' 'The Last Mummer,' and 'Icon.' " *The Michigan Quarterly Review* 9 (Summer 1970): 165–67.
Munro (transcript of a radio play). *Everyman* 3 (1970): 58–65.
"Views." *The Listener* 31 Dec. 1970: 903.
"Four Poems by Seamus Heaney: 'As We Roved Out,' 'Intimidation,' 'Nocturne,' 'Rubric.' " *Malahat Review* 17 (Jan. 1971): 33–36.
"Seamus Heaney Praises Lough Erne." *The Listener* 4 Feb. 1971: 142–43.

"Whatever You Say, Say Nothing—Seamus Heaney Gives his Views on the Irish Thing." *The Listener* 14 Oct. 1971: 496–97.

"A Poet's Childhood." *The Listener* 11 Nov. 1971: 660+.

"Servant Boy" and "The Last Mummer," "Letter to the Editor." *The Honest Ulsterman* (Nov./Dec. 1971): 5–7.

"A Northern Hoard." *Hibernia* 17 Dec. 1971.

Wintering Out. London: Faber, 1972.

"After the Synge-song—Seamus Heaney on the Writings of Patrick Kavanagh." *The Listener* 13 Jan. 1972: 55–56.

"Five Poems by Seamus Heaney: 'Oracle,' 'Traditions,' 'Bog Oak,' 'Cairn-Maker,' 'Nerthus.' " *The Listener* 23 March 1972: 372.

"Watermarks: 'Anahorish,' 'Toome,' 'Broagh.' " *Stand* 13.3 (July 1972): 4–5.

"Bog Queen." *The Listener* 23 Nov. 1972: 713.

"Now and in England." *Spectator* 4 May 1974: 547.

Stations. Belfast: Ulsterman Publications, 1975.

North. London: Faber, 1975.

". . . English and Irish." *Times Literary Supplement* 24 October 1980: 1199.

"Now and in England." *Critical Inquiry* 3 (1977): 471–88.

"The Interesting Case of John Alphonsus Mulrennan." *Planet* (Jan. 1978): 34–40.

Field Work. New York: Farrar, 1979.

Poems: 1965–1975. New York: Farrar, 1980.

Preoccupations: Selected Prose, 1968–1978. New York: Farrar, 1980.

Robert Lowell: A Memorial Address and Elegy. London: Faber, 1978. Rpt. in *Agenda* 18.3 (1980): 23–28.

"A Tale of Two Islands: Reflections on the Irish Literary Revival." *Irish Studies 1.* Ed. P. J. Drudy. London: Cambridge UP, 1980. 1–20.

"Current Unstated Assumptions about Poetry." *Critical Inquiry* 7 (1981): 645–51.

"Bennett Award Acceptance Speech." *Hudson Review* 35 (1982/83): 518–520.

"Leaving the Island." *James Joyce and Modern Literature.* Ed. W. J. McCormack and Alistair Stead. London: Routledge, 1982.

An Open Letter. Belfast: Field Day, 1983.

"Forked Tongues, Ceilís and Incubators." *Fortnight* 197 (1983): 18–21.

Sweeney Astray: A Version from the Irish. New York: Farrar, 1984.

"Envies and Identifications: Dante and the Modern Poet." *Irish University Review* 15 (1985): 5–19.

"Place, Pastness, Poems: A Triptych." *Salmagundi* 68–69 (1985/86): 30–47.

Station Island. New York: Farrar, 1985.

" 'Place and Displacement': Recent Irish Poetry from Northern Ireland." *The Wordsworth Circle* 16 (Spring 1985): 48–56.

The Haw Lantern. New York: Farrar, 1987.

The Government of the Tongue: Selected Prose 1978–1987. New York: Farrar, 1988.

"Earning a Rhyme: Notes on Translating *Buile Suibhne.*" *The Art of Translation: Voices from the Field.* Ed. Rosanna Warren. Boston: Northeastern UP, 1989. 13–20.

"Fosterling." *Hill Field: Poems and Memoirs for John Montague on His Sixtieth Birthday, 28 February 1989*. Ed. Thomas Dillon Redshaw. Minneapolis, Minn.: Coffee House Press, 1989.

"Learning from Eliot." *Agenda* 27.1 (Spring 1989): 17–31.

The Place of Writing. Emory University: Scholars Press, 1989.

The Cure at Troy. London: Faber, 1990.

Seeing Things. New York: Farrar, 1991.

"Keeping Going." *New Yorker* 12 Oct. 1992: 76–77.

"To a Dutch Potter in Ireland." *The Threepenny Review* (Spring 1993): 15.

"The Flight Path." *The Threepenny Review* (Winter 1993): 5.

By Other Writers

Allen, Michael. "Provincialism and Recent Irish Poetry: The Importance of Patrick Kavanaugh." Dunn, *Two Decades* 23–36.

Allison, Jonathan. "Imagining the Community: Seamus Heaney in 1966." *Notes on Modern Irish Literature* 4 (1992): 27–34.

Allum, Percy. "The Irish Question." Hederman and Kearney 643–51.

Andrews, Elmer. *The Poetry of Seamus Heaney: All the Realms of a Whisper*. Basingstoke: Macmillan, 1988.

———. *Seamus Heaney: A Collection of Critical Essays*. New York: St. Martin's Press, 1992.

Annwn, David. *Inhabited Voices: Myth and History in the Poetry of Geoffrey Hill, Seamus Heaney, and George Mackay Brown*. Fromme, Somerset: Bran's Head Books, 1984.

Arkins, Brian, and Patrick F. Sheeran. "Coloniser and Colonised: The Myth of Hercules and Antaeus in Seamus Heaney's *North*." *Classical and Modern Literature* 10.2 (Winter 1990): 127–34.

Armstrong, David. *Horace*. New Haven: Yale UP, 1989.

Arthur, Paul, and Keith Jeffery. *Northern Ireland Since 1968*. London: Blackwell, 1988.

Atfield, J. R. "Creative Tensions in the Poetry of Seamus Heaney." *Critical Survey* 3.1 (1991): 80–87.

Attridge, Derek, Geoff Bennington, and Robert Young, eds. *Post-Structuralism and the Question of History*. Cambridge: Cambridge UP, 1987.

Auden, W. H. *Selected Poems*. Ed. Edward Mendelson. New York: Vintage, 1979.

Bailey, Anthony. *Acts of Union*. New York: Random House, 1977.

———. "A Walk along the Boyne." *New Yorker* 2 June 1980: 92–122.

Bakhtin, M. M. *The Dialogic Imagination*. Trans. Caryle Emerson and Michael Holquist. Austin: U of Texas P, 1981.

Bauman, Zygmunt. *Freedom*. Minneapolis: U of Minnesota P, 1988.

Bayley, John. "Living In and Living Out: The Poet's Location for the Poetry." *Agenda* 27.1 (Spring 1989): 32–36.

Beckett, Samuel. "Recent Irish Poetry." *Disjecta*. Ed. Ruby Cohn. London: John Calder, 1983.

Begley, Monie. *Rambles in Ireland*. New York: Methuen, 1977.

Beisch, June. "An Interview with Seamus Heaney." *Literary Review* 29 (1986): 161–69.

Bhabha, Homi K. "The Other Question: Difference, Discrimination and the Discourse of Colonialism." *Out There: Marginalization and Contemporary Cultures*. Ed. Russell Ferguson. New York: New Museum of Contemporay Art, 1990. 71–88.

———. " 'Race', Time and the Revision of Modernity." *Oxford Literary Review* 13.1–2 (1991): 193–219.

Blake, James J. "Mad Sweeney: Madness in Irish Literature." *The Nassau Review* 5.3 (1987): 40–47.

Bloom, Harold, ed. and intro. *Seamus Heaney*. New Haven: Chelsea House, 1986.

Boland, John. "Winter of Discontent." Rev. of *Wintering Out*, by Seamus Heaney. *Hibernia* 1 Dec. 1972: 11.

Bottigheimer, Karl S. *Ireland and the Irish: A Short History*. New York: Columbia UP, 1982.

Bradbrook, Muriel. "Doing Literature on Dover Beach." *The Humanist Citizen*. Ed. Peter Riesenberg and Walter Allan Tuttle. Chapel Hill: Nat. Humanities Center, 1981. 117–32.

Bradley, Anthony, ed. *Contemporary Irish Poetry*. Berkeley: U of California P, 1980.

———. "Landscape as Culture: The Poetry of Seamus Heaney." Brophy and Porter 1–14.

———. "Literature and Culture in the North of Ireland." Kenneally 36–72.

———. "The Irishness of Irish Poetry after Yeats." *New Irish Writing*. Ed. James D. Brophy and Eamon Grennan. Boston: Iona College Press, 1989. 1–12.

Braidwood, John. *The Ulster Dialect Lexicon*. Belfast: Queens UP, 1969.

Brandes, Rand. "Seamus Heaney: An Interview." *Salmagundi* 80 (Fall 1988): 4–21.

Brenan, Gerald. "Studies in Genius II: St. John of the Cross, His Life and Poetry." *Horizon* 15 (May 1947): 256–81.

Brinton, George A. "A Note on Seamus Heaney's *Door into the Dark*." *Contemporary Poetry* 1.2 (1973): 30–34.

Broadbridge, Edward, ed. *Seamus Heaney*. Copenhagen: Radio Danmark, 1977.

Brophy, James D., and Raymond J. Porter, eds. *Contemporary Irish Writing*. Boston: Twayne for Iona College, 1983.

Brown, Duncan. "Seamus Heaney's 'Book of Changes': *The Haw Lantern*." *Theoria* 74 (Oct. 1989): 79–96.

Brown, Mary. "Seamus Heaney and *North*." *Studies* 70 (1981): 289–98.

Brown, Richard. "Bog Poems and Book Poems: Doubleness, Self-translation and Pun in Seamus Heaney and Paul Muldoon." *The Chosen Ground: Essays of the Contemporary Poetry of Northern Ireland*. Ed. Neil Corcoran. Chester Springs, Pa.: Dufour Editions, 1992. 153–67.

Brown, Terence. *Northern Voices: Poets from Ulster*. Dublin: Gill and Macmillan, 1975.

————. *Ireland: A Social and Cultural History, 1922–79*. Glasgow: William Collins, Fontana, 1981.

————. "Poets and Culture: Seamus Heaney, Derek Mahon, and Tom Paulin." *Northern Ireland: Living in Crisis*. Ed. Alan J. Ward. New York: Praeger, 1984. 141–54.

————. *The Whole Protestant Community: The Making of a Historical Myth*. Derry: Field Day, 1985.

————. "Irish Ideology." *The Crane Bag* 9.1 (1985): 92–93.

————. *Ireland's Literature: Selected Essays*. Totowa, N.J.: Barnes and Noble, 1988.

Browne, Joseph. "Violent Prophesies: The Writer and Northern Ireland." *Éire-Ireland* 10.2 (1975): 109–19.

————. "'Words at Once Both Gaff and Bait': The Writer's Response to Northern Ireland." *Northern Ireland: Living in Crisis*. Ed. Alan J. Ward. New York: Praeger, 1984. 155–71.

Brownjohn, Alan. "A View of English Poetry in the Early 'Seventies." *British Poetry Since 1960: A Critical Survey*. Ed. Michael Schmidt and Grevel Lindop. Oxford: Carcanet, 1972. 240–49.

Bruns, Gerald L. "What is Tradition?" *New Literary History* 22 (Winter 1991): 1–21.

Buckley, Vincent. "Poetry and the Avoidance of Nationalism." *Irish Culture and Nationalism, 1750–1950*. Ed. Oliver MacDonagh, W. F. Mandle and Pauric Travers. New York: St. Martin's Press, 1983. 258–79.

Burris, Sidney. *The Poetry of Resistance: Seamus Heaney and the Pastoral Tradition*. Athens: Ohio UP, 1990.

Butler, Alban, Rev. *The Lives of the Saints*. Vol. 1. Baltimore: John Murphy, 1884.

Buttle, Robert. *Seamus Heaney*. Lewisberg, Pa.: Bucknell UP, 1975.

————. "Hopkins and Heaney: Debt and Difference." In *Hopkins Among the Poets: Studies in Modern Responses to Gerard Manley Hopkins*. Ed. Richard F. Giles. Monograph #3. Hamilton, Ont.: Hopkins Assn., 1985. 110–13.

————. "Seamus Heaney." *Poets of Great Britain and Ireland Since 1960*. Part 1: A-L. Ed. Vincent B. Sherry, Jr. *Dictionary of Literary Biography*. Vol. 40. Detroit: Gale, 1985. 179–201.

Cahalan, James M. *The Irish Novel*. Boston: Twayne, 1988.

Cahill, Eileen. "A Silent Voice: Seamus Heaney and Ulster Politics." *Critical Quarterly* 29.3 (1987): 54–70.

Carleton, William. *Traits and Stories of the Irish Peasantry*. Ed. D. J. O'Donoghue. London: J. M. Dent, 1896.

Carpenter, Andrew. *Place, Personality and the Irish Writer*. Irish Literary Studies 1. Gerrards Cross, Bucks: Colin Smythe, 1977.

Carson, Ciarán. "Escaped from the Massacre?" Rev. of *North*, by Seamus Heaney. *The Honest Ulsterman* 50 (1975): 183–86.

Chekhov, Anton. *The Island: A Journey to Sakhalin*. Trans. Luba and Michael Trepak. Intro. Robert Payne. New York: Washington Square, 1967.

Clifton, Harry. "Real and Synthetic Whiskey: A Generation of Irish Poets, 1975–85." *New Irish Writing*. Ed. James D. Brophy and Eamon Grennan. Boston: Iona College Press, 1989. 232–47.

Cluysenaar, Anne. "Formal Meaning in Three Modern Poems." *Dutch Quarterly Review* 12 (1982): 302–20.

Clarke, Aidan. "Ireland and the General Crisis." *Past and Present* 48 (Aug. 1970): 79–99.

Connolly, Peter, ed. *Literature and the Changing Ireland*. Irish Literary Studies 9. Gerrards Cross, Bucks: Colin Smythe, 1982.

Conroy, John. *Belfast Diary: War as a Way of Life*. Boston: Beacon, 1987.

Coogan, Tim Pat. *Disillusioned Decades: Ireland 1966–87*. Dublin: Gill and Macmillan, 1987.

Corcoran, Neil. *Seamus Heaney*. London: Faber, 1986.

———. "Seamus Heaney and the Art of Exemplary." *Yearbook of English Studies* 17 (1987): 117–27.

———. "Heaney's Joyce, Eliot's Yeats." *Agenda* 27.1 (Spring 1989): 37–47.

Crozier, Andrew. "Thrills and Frills: Poetry as Figures of Empirical Lyricism." *Society and Literature 1945–1970*. Ed. Alan Sinfield. London: Methuen, 1983. 199–233.

Crowder, Ashby. "Heaney's 'Elegy for a Still-Born Child.' " *Explicator* 47.2 (Winter 1989): 51–52.

Cullingford, Elizabeth. " 'Thinking of Her . . . as . . . Ireland': Yeats, Pearse and Heaney." *Textual Practice* 4.1 (1990): 1–21.

Curtis, Simon. "Seamus Heaney's *North*." Rev. of *North*, by Seamus Heaney. *Critical Quarterly* 18.1 (1976): 81–83.

Curtis, Tony, ed. *The Art of Seamus Heaney*. Bridgend: Poetry Wales, 1982. Rpt. and rev. 1985.

———. "The Permanent City: The Younger Irish Poets." Harmon, *Irish Writer* 180–96.

Davie, Donald. "Poet: Patriot: Interpreter." *Critical Inquiry* 9 (Sept. 1982): 27–43.

———. "Responsibilities of *Station Island*." *Salmagundi* 80 (Fall 1988): 58–65.

———. *Under Briggflatts: A History of Poetry in Great Britain 1960–1988*. Chicago: U of Chicago P, 1989.

Dawe, Gerald. "A Question of Covenants: Modern Irish Poetry." Hederman and Kearney 508–11.

———. "Checkpoints: The Younger Irish Poets." *The Crane Bag* 6.1 (1982): 85–89.

———. "The Permanent City: The Younger Irish Poets." Harmon, *Irish Writer* 180–96.

———. "Poetry and the Public: Solitude and Participation." *The Crane Bag* 8.2 (1984): 104–8.

———. "Getting Through: A Brief Look at the Fifth Province." *The Crane Bag* 9.1 (1985): 107–9.

———. "A Question of Imagination—Poetry in Ireland Today." Kenneally 186–96.

Deane, Seamus. "The Appetites of Gravity: Contemporary Irish Poetry." *Sewanee Review* 82 (1976): 199–208.

———. "The Literary Myths of the Revival: A Case for Their Abandonment." *Myth and Reality in Irish Literature.* Ed. Joseph Ronsley. Ontario: Wilfrid Laurier UP, 1977. 317–29.

———. "Talk With Seamus Heaney." *New York Times Book Review* 2 Dec. 1979: 47+.

———. "Unhappy and at Home." Hederman and Kearney 66–72.

———. "Yeats, Ireland and Revolution." Hederman and Kearney 139–47.

———. "An Example of Tradition." Hederman and Kearney 373–79.

———. "Remembering the Irish Future." *The Crane Bag* 8.1 (1984): 81–92.

———. *Celtic Revivals: Essays in Modern Irish Literature.* London: Faber, 1985.

———. "A Noble, Startling Achievement." Rev. of *Station Island*, by Seamus Heaney. *Irish Literary Supplement* Spring 1985: 1+.

———. "National Character and National Audience: Races, Crowds and Readers." *Critical Approaches to Anglo-Irish Literature.* Ed. Michael Allen and Angela Wilcox. Gerrards Cross: Colin Smythe, 1989.

Deane, Seamus, et al. *Ireland's Field Day.* Notre Dame, Ind.: U of Notre Dame P, 1986.

Deane, Seamus, et al., eds. *Field Day Anthology of Irish Writing.* New York: Faber, 1991.

Deleuze, Gilles, and Félix Guattari. "What Is a Minor Literature?" *Mississippi Review* 11 (Spring 1983): 13–33.

de Man, Paul. *Blindness and Insight: Essays in the Rhetoric of Contemporary Criticism.* New York: Oxford UP, 1971.

de Paor, Liam. *Divided Ulster.* Hammondsworth, Middlesex: Penguin, 1970.

———. "Colour Schemes." Hederman and Kearney 120–23.

———. "Ireland's Identity." Hederman and Kearney 354–61.

———. "The Rebel Mind: Republican and Loyalist." *The Irish Mind.* Ed. Richard Kearney. Dublin: Wolfhound, 1985.

Derrida, Jacques. *Writing and Difference.* Chicago: U of Chicago P, 1978.

———. "Racism's Last Word." *Critical Inquiry* 12 (Autumn 1985): 290–99.

———. "But, beyond . . ." *Critical Inquiry* 13 (Autumn 1986): 155–70.

Dillon, John. "Reflections on the Irish Classical Tradition." Hederman and Kearney 448–52.

Donoghue, Denis. "Being Irish Together." *Sewanee Review* 84.1 (Winter 1976): 125–33.

———. *We Irish.* Berkeley: U of California P, 1986.

Druce, Robert. "A Raindrop on a Thorn: An Interview with Seamus Heaney." *Dutch Quarterly Review* 9 (1978): 24–37.

Duffy, Charles. "Heaney's 'Digging.' " *Explicator* 46.4 (Summer 1988): 44–45.

Dunn, Douglas, ed. and intro. *Two Decades of Irish Writing: A Critical Study.* Chester Springs, Pa.: Dufour, 1975.

Durkan, Michael J. "Seamus Heaney: A Checklist for a Bibliography." *Irish University Review* 16 (1986): 48–76.

Eagleton, Terry. "Myth and History in Recent Poetry." *British Poetry Since 1960:*

A Critical Survey. Ed. Michael Schmidt and Grevel Lindop. Oxford: Carcanet, 1972. 233–39.

Eagleton, Terry, Fredric Jameson, and Edward Said. *Nationalism, Colonialism, and Literature.* Intro. Seamus Deane. Minneapolis: U of Minnesota P, 1990.

Edwards, Ruth Dudley. *An Atlas of Irish History.* 2d ed. London: Routledge, 1989.

Elliott, Marianne. *Watchmen in Sion: The Protestant Idea of Liberty.* Derry: Field Day, 1985.

Ellmann, Richard. *James Joyce.* Oxford: Oxford UP, 1983.

———. "Heaney Agonistes." Rev. of *Station Island*, by Seamus Heaney. *New York Review of Books* 14 Mar. 1985: 19–20. Rpt. in Bloom 159–66.

Emerson, Caryl. "The Outer Word and Inner Speech: Bakhtin, Vygotsky, and the Internalization of Language." *Critical Inquiry* 10 (1983): 245–64.

Engle, John. "That Always Raised Voice: Seán Ó Riada and Irish Poetry." Brophy and Porter 33–47.

Fahey, William A. "Heaney's 'Fieldwork.' " *Explicator* 46.2 (Winter 1988): 47–49.

Farrell, Michael. *Northern Ireland: The Orange State.* London: Pluto, 1976.

———. "Emergency Legislation: The Apparatus of Repression." Derry: Field Day, 1986.

Fennell, Desmond. *Whatever You Say, Say Nothing: Why Seamus Heaney is No. 1.* Dublin: ELO, 1991.

Finneran, Richard J., ed. *Recent Research on Anglo-Irish Writers.* New York: MLA, 1983.

Fitzgerald, Jennifer, et al. "The Arts and Ideology." *The Crane Bag* 9.2 (1985): 60–69.

Fitzgerald, Robert. "Seamus Heaney: An Appreciation." *New Republic* 27 March 1976: 27–29. Rpt. in Bloom 39–44.

Flanagan, Thomas. *The Irish Novelists: 1800–1850.* New York: Columbia UP, 1959.

Flower, Robin. *The Irish Tradition.* London: Clarendon, 1947.

Foster, John Wilson. "Seamus Heaney's 'A Lough Neagh Sequence': Sources and Motifs." *Éire-Ireland* 12.2 (1972): 138–42. Rpt. in Bloom 45–50.

———. "The Poetry of Seamus Heaney." *Critical Quarterly* 16.1 (1974): 35–48.

———. "The Landscape of the Planter and the Gael in the Poetry of John Hewitt and John Montague." *Canadian Journal of Irish Studies* 1.2 (1975): 23–36.

———. "The Artifice of Eternity: Medieval Aspects of Modern Irish Literature." *Medieval and Modern Ireland.* Ed. Richard Wall. Totowa, N.J.: Barnes and Noble, 1988. 123–34.

———. "Culture and Colonisation: View from the North." *The Irish Review* 5 (Autumn 1988): 17–26.

———. "Post-war Ulster Poetry: A Chapter in Anglo-Irish Relations." Kenneally 154–71.

Foster, R. F. *Modern Ireland: 1600–1972.* New York: Penguin, 1988.

Foster, Thomas C. *Seamus Heaney.* Boston: Twayne, 1989.

Foucault, Michel. *Language, Counter-Memory, and Practice.* Ithaca: Cornell UP, 1977.

———. *Power/Knowledge: Selected Interviews and Other Writings, 1972–1977.* Ed. Colin Gordon. Trans. Colin Gordon et al. New York: Pantheon, 1980.

———. "The Order of Discourse." *Untying the Text: A Post-Structuralist Reader.* Ed. Robert Young. Boston: Routledge and Kegan Paul, 1981.

Frazier, Adrian. "Irish Poetry after Yeats." *Literary Review* 22 (1979): 133–44.

Freeman, T. W. *Ireland: Its Physical, Historical, Social, and Economic Geography.* London: Methuen, 1950.

Friel, Brian. *Selected Plays.* London: Faber, 1984.

Fry, August J. "Confronting Seamus Heaney: A Personal Reading of His Early Poems." *Dutch Quarterly Review* 18 (1988): 242–55.

Gallet, René. "Le Sacré: Le Centre et les marges (S. Heaney; C. H. Sission; G. Hill)." *Études Anglaises* 38 (1985): 180–92.

Garratt, Robert F. *Modern Irish Poetry: Traditions and Continuity from Yeats to Heaney.* Berkeley: U of California P, 1986.

Gibbons, Luke. "Race Against Time: Racial Discourse and Irish History." *Oxford Literary Review* 13.1–2 (1991): 95–117.

Gifford, Terry, and Neil Roberts. "Hughes and Two Contemporaries: Peter Redgrove and Seamus Heaney." *The Achievement of Ted Hughes.* Ed. Keith Sagar. Manchester: Manchester UP, 1983. 90–106.

Gitzen, Julian. "British Nature Poetry Now." *Midwest Quarterly* 15 (1974): 323–37.

———. "An Irish Imagist." *Studies in the Humanities* 4.2 (1975): 10–13.

Golden, Sean V. "Traditional Irish Music in Contemporary Irish Literature." *Mosaic* 12.3 (1979): 1–23.

———. "Post-Traditional English Literature." Hederman and Kearney 427–38.

Goldensohn, Barry. "The Recantation of Beauty." *Salmagundi* 80 (Fall 1988): 76–82.

Grant, Damian. "Verbal Events." *Critical Quarterly* 16.1 (1974): 81–86.

———. "The Voice of History in British Poetry, 1970–1984." *Études Anglaises* 38 (1985): 158–79.

Gravil, Richard. "Wordsworth's Second Selves?" *The Wordsworth Circle* 14 (Autumn 1983): 191–201.

Green, Carlanda. "The Feminine Principle in Seamus Heaney's Poetry." *Ariel* 14.3 (1983): 3–13. Rpt. in Bloom 143–52.

Greene, David. "Language and Nationalism." Hederman and Kearney 331–35.

Haberer, Adolphe. "Les Émigrés de l'intérieur: Seamus Heaney, Derek Mahon et Tom Paulin, Poètes d'Ulster." *Études Anglaises* 38 (1985): 193–207.

Haberstroh, Patricia Boyle. "Poet and Artist in Seamus Heaney's *North.*" *Colby Library Quarterly* 23.4 (1987): 206–15.

Haffenden, John. *Viewpoints: Poets in Conversation.* London: Faber, 1981.

———. "Seamus Heaney and the Feminine Sensibility." *Yearbook of English Studies* 17 (1987): 90–116.

Halpin, Eamon. "Seamus Heaney and the Politics of Imagination." *Canadian Journal of Irish Studies* 17 (Dec. 1991): 64–71.

Harmon, Maurice, ed. *Image and Illusion: Anglo Irish Literature and its Contexts.* Dublin: Wolfhound Press, 1979.

———, ed. *Irish Poetry after Yeats.* Boston: Little Brown, 1979.

———, ed. *Irish Writers and the City.* Irish Literary Studies 18. Gerrards Cross, Bucks: Colin Smythe, 1984.

Hart, Henry. *Seamus Heaney: Poet of Contrary Progressions.* Syracuse, N.Y.: Syracuse UP, 1992.

Hartnett, Michael. *Collected Poems*, Vol. 1. Dublin: Raven Arts Press, 1985.

Hassan, Ihab. *The Postmodern Turn: Essays in Postmodern Theory and Culture.* Columbus: Ohio State UP, 1987.

Hawlin, Stefan. "Seamus Heaney's 'Station Island': The Shaping of a Modern Purgatory." *English Studies* 73.1 (1992): 35–50

He, Gongjie. "A Poet in the Fine Tradition." *Foreign Literatures* 1 (1988): 57–58.

Hederman, Mark Patrick. "*The Crane Bag* and Northern Ireland." Hederman and Kearney 731–40.

———. "A Hidden Tradition." Hederman and Kearney 403–7.

———. "Seamus Heaney: The Reluctant Poet." Hederman and Kearney 481–90.

———. "Poetry and the Fifth Province." *The Crane Bag* 9.1 (1985): 110–19.

Hederman, Mark Patrick, and Richard Kearney, eds. *The Crane Bag Book of Irish Studies (1977–1981).* Dublin: Blackwater, 1982.

Henigan, Robert H. "The Tollund Man on Bogside: Seamus Heaney's Objective Correlative." *Publications of the Arkansas Philological Association* 7 (1981): 48–60.

Hickey, D. J., and J. E. Doherty. *A Dictionary of Irish History 1800–1980.* Dublin: Gill and Macmillan, 1987.

Higgins, Michael D. "The Tyranny of Images." *The Crane Bag* 8.2 (1984): 132–42.

Hildebidle, John. "A Decade of Seamus Heaney's Poetry." *Massachusetts Review* 28 (1987): 393–409.

Hill, John. "An Archetype of the Irish Soul." Hederman and Kearney 136–38.

———. "An Archetype of the Irish Soul II." Hederman and Kearney 253–59.

Hillis Miller, J. "Tradition and Difference." *Diacritics* 2.4 (Winter 1972): 6–13.

Hobsbawm, Eric, and Terence Ranger, eds. *The Invention of Tradition.* Cambridge, Mass.: Cambridge UP, 1983.

Hogan, Robert, et al., eds. *Dictionary of Irish Literature.* Westport, Conn.: Greenwood, 1979.

Holub, Miroslav. *Saggital Section: Poems New and Selected.* Trans. Stuart Friebert and Dana Habova. Oberlin, Ohio: Oberlin College, 1980.

Hooker, Jeremy. *Poetry of Place: Essays and Reviews 1970–1981.* Manchester: Carcanet, 1982.

———. *The Presence of the Past: Essays on Modern British and American Poetry.* Brigend, Mid-Glamorgan: Poetry Wales, 1987.

Hughes, Brian. "Myth and History in the Poetry of Seamus Heaney." *Revista Canaria de Estudios Ingleses* 13/14 (1987): 109–23.

Hulse, Michael. "Sweeney Heaney: Seamus Heaney's *Station Island.*" *Quadrant* 30.5 (1986): 72–75.

JanMohamed, Abdul R. "Humanism and Minority Literature: Toward a Definition of Counter-hegemonic Discourse." *Boundary 2* 12.3/13.1 (1984): 281–99.

———. "The Economy of Manichean Allegory: The Function of Racial Difference in Colonialist Literature." *Critical Inquiry* 12 (Autumn 1985): 59–87.

JanMohamed, Abdul R., and David Lloyd, eds. *The Nature and Context of Minority Discourse.* New York: Oxford UP, 1990.

Jeffares, A. Norman. "Place, Space, and Personality and the Irish Writer." Carpenter 11–40.

John, Brian. "Contemporary Irish Poetry and the Matter of Ireland: Thomas Kinsella, John Montague, and Seamus Heaney." *Medieval and Modern Ireland.* Ed. Richard Wall. Totowa, N.J.: Barnes and Noble, 1988. 34–59.

———. "Irelands of the Mind: The Poetry of Thomas Kinsella and Seamus Heaney." *Canadian Journal of Irish Studies* 15.2 (Dec. 1989): 68–92.

Johnston, Conor. "Poetry and Politics: Responses to the Northern Ireland Crisis in the Poetry of John Montague, Derek Mahon, and Seamus Heaney." *Poesis* 5.4 (1984): 13–35.

Johnston, Dillon. "'The Enabling Ritual': Irish Poetry in the Seventies." *Shenandoah* 25.4 (1974): 3–24.

———. *Irish Poetry after Joyce.* Notre Dame, Ind.: Notre Dame UP, 1985.

———. "The Go-Between of Recent Irish Poetry." Kennelly 172–85.

———. "Next to Nothing: Uses of the Otherworld in Modern Irish Literature." *New Irish Writing.* Ed. James D. Brophy and Eamon Grennan. Boston: Iona College Press, 1989. 121–40.

Jolly, Roslyn. "Transformations of Caliban and Ariel: Imagination and Language in David Malouf, Margaret Atwood and Seamus Heaney." *World Literature Written in English* 26 (Autumn 1986): 295–330.

Joyce, James. *A Portrait of the Artist as a Young Man.* New York: Viking, 1964.

———. *Ulysses.* New York: Vintage, 1986.

Kavanagh, Patrick. *The Green Fool.* New York: Harper, 1939.

———. *Collected Pruse.* London: MacGibbon, 1967.

Keane, Patrick K. *Yeats, Joyce, Ireland, and the Myth of the Devouring Mother.* Columbia: U of Missouri P, 1988.

Kearney, Colbert. "The Treasure of Hungry Hill: The Irish Writer and the Irish Language." Kennelly 124–37.

Kearney, J. A. "Heaney: Poetry and the Irish Cause." *Theoria* 63 (Oct. 1984): 37–53.

Kearney, Richard. "Myth and Terror." Hederman and Kearney 273–87.

———. "The Repossession of Poetry." Hederman and Kearney 897–901.

———. "Those Masterful Images." Hederman and Kearney 491–501.

———. "Between Politics and Literature: The Irish Cultural Journal." *The Crane Bag* 7.2 (1983): 160–71.

———. "Between Conflict and Consensus." *The Crane Bag* 9.1 (1985): 87–89.

———, ed. *The Irish Mind: Exploring Intellectual Traditions.* Dublin: Wolfhound Press, 1985.

————. *Transitions: Narratives in Modern Irish Culture.* Manchester: Manchester UP, 1987.

————. "Postmodernity and Nationalism: A European Perspective." *Modern Fiction Studies* 38 (1992): 581–93.

Kearney, Timothy. "The Poetry of the North: A Post-Modern Perspective." Hederman and Kearney 465–73.

Kelly, H. A. "Heaney's Sweeney: The Poet as Version-Maker." *Philological Quarterly* 65 (1986): 293–310.

Kenneally, Michael, ed. *Cultural Contexts and Literary Idioms in Contemporary Irish Literature.* Gerrards Cross: Colin Smythe, 1988.

Kennelly, Brendan. "Poetry and Violence." *History and Violence in Anglo-Irish Literature.* Ed. Joris Duytschaever and Geert Lernout. Amsterdam: Rodopi, 1988.

Kenner, Hugh. *Joyce's Voices.* Berkeley: U of California P, 1978.

————. *A Colder Eye.* New York: Knopf, 1983.

Kersnowski, Frank. *The Outsiders: Poets of Contemporary Ireland.* Ft. Worth, Tex.: TCU Press, 1975.

Kiberd, Declan. "Writers in Quarantine? The Case of Irish Studies." Hederman and Kearney 341–53.

————. "Inventing Irelands." *The Crane Bag* 8.1 (1984): 11–25.

Kiely, Benedict. "A Raid into Dark Corners." *Hollins Critic* 7.4 (1970): 1–12.

Kilroy, Thomas. "The Irish Writer: Self and Society, 1950–1980." Connolly 175–88.

Kinahan, Frank. "An Interview with Seamus Heaney." *Critical Inquiry* 8 (1982): 405–14.

"King of the Dark." (synopsis of Heaney interview on BBC) *The Listener* 5 Feb. 1970: 181–82.

King, P. R. *Nine Contemporary Poets.* London: Methuen, 1979. 190–210. Rpt. "'I Step through Origins.' " Bloom 97–120.

Kinsella, Thomas. "The Irish Writer." *Davis, Mangan, Ferguson: Tradition and the Irish Writer.* Ed. Roger McHugh. Dublin: Dolmen Press, 1970.

————. "The Divided Mind." *Irish Poets in English.* Ed. Sean Lucy. Cork: Mercier, 1973.

Kinzie, Mary. "Deeper than Declared: On Seamus Heaney." *Salmagundi* 80 (Fall 1988): 22–57.

Laffan, Michael. "Two Irish States." *The Crane Bag* 8.1 (1984): 26–40.

Lane, Denis, and Carol McCrory Lane, eds. *Modern Irish Literature: A Library of Literary Criticism.* New York: Ungar, 1988.

Law, Pamela. "Seamus Heaney." *Sydney Studies in English* 12 (1986–87): 92–100.

Leerssen, Joseph Th. *Mere Irish and Fior-Ghael: Studies in the Idea of Nationality, Its Development and Literary Expression Prior to the Nineteenth Century.* Amsterdam: Denjamins, 1986.

Lentricchia, Frank. *After the New Criticism.* Chicago: U of Chicago P, 1980.

Lernout, Geert. "The Dantean Paradigm: Thomas Kinsella and Seamus

Heaney." *The Clash of Ireland: Literary Contrasts and Connections*. Ed. C. C. Barfoot and Theo D'haen. Amsterdam: Rodopi, 1989. 248–64.

Levin, Harry. *Contexts of Criticism*. Cambridge: Harvard UP, 1957.

Liddy, James. "Ulster Poets and the Catholic Muse." *Éire-Ireland* 13.4 (1978): 126–37.

Lloyd, David. "'Pap for the Dispossessed': Seamus Heaney and the Poetics of Identity." *Boundary 2* 13 (1985): 319–42.

———. "Race under Representation." *Oxford Literary Review* 13.1–2 (1991): 62–94.

———. *Anomalous States: Irish Writing and the Post-Colonial Moment*. Durham, N.C.: Duke UP, 1993.

Longley, Edna. "Heaney's Hidden Ireland." *Phoenix* (July 1973): 88–89.

———. "Searching the Darkness: Richard Murphy, Thomas Kinsella, John Montague, and James Simmons." Dunn, *Two Decades* 118–53.

———. "Stars and Horses, Pigs and Trees." Hederman and Kearney 481–90.

———. "The Writer and Belfast." Harmon, Irish Writer 65–89.

———. "Poetry and Politics in Northern Ireland." *The Crane Bag* 9.1 (1985): 26–40.

———. "Poetic Form and Social Malformations." *Tradition and Influence in Anglo-Irish Poetry*. Ed. Terence Brown and Nicholas Grene. London: Macmillan, 1989. 153–80.

———. " 'When Did You Last See Your Father?': Perceptions of the Past in Northern Irish Writing 1965–1985." Kenneally 88–112.

———. *From Cathleen to Anorexia*. Attic, 1990.

———. "Hospitable Meta-Narrative or Hegemonic Bid?" Rev. of *The Field Day Anthology of Irish Writing*. Ed. Seamus Deane. *The Canadian Journal of Irish Studies* 18.2 (Dec. 1992): 119–21.

Lucy, Sean. "Metre and Movement in Anglo-Irish Verse." *Irish University Review* 8 (1978): 151–77.

MacCana, Proinsias. "Notes on the Early Irish Concept of Unity." Hederman and Kearney 205–19.

McCartney, Donal. "The Quest for Irish Political Identity: the Image and the Illusion." Harmon, *Image and Illusion* 13–22.

McCartney, R. L. *Liberty and Authority in Ireland*. Derry: Field Day, 1985.

McCormack, W. J. "Yeats and a New Tradition." Hederman and Kearney 362–72.

———. *The Battle of the Books: Two Decades of Irish Cultural Debate*. Westmeath, Ire.: Lilliput, 1986.

McCracken, Kathleen. "Madness or Inspiration? The Poet and Poetry in Seamus Heaney's *Sweeney Astray*." *Notes on Modern Irish Literature* 2 (1990): 42–51.

McCrum, Robert, et al., eds. *The Story of English*. New York: Elisabeth Sifton/Viking, 1986.

McDiarmid, Lucy. "Joyce, Heaney, and 'That Subject People Stuff.' " *James Joyce and His Contemporaries*. Ed. Diana Ben-Merre and Maureen Murphy. Westport, Conn.: Greenwood, 1989. 131–42.

McElroy, James. "Poems That Explode in Silence: A Meditation on the Work of Seamus Heaney." *Studia Mystica* 7.2 (1984): 40–44.

———. "Seamus Heaney: Skull Handler and Parablist." *Greenfield Review* 12.1–2 (1984): 200–213.

McGrory, Patrick J. "Emergency Legislation: Law and the Constitution: Present Discontents." Derry: Field Day, 1986.

McGuinness, Arthur E. "'Hoarder of the Common Ground': Tradition and Ritual in Seamus Heaney's Poetry." *Éire-Ireland* 13.2 (1978): 71–92.

———. "The Craft of Diction: Revision in Seamus Heaney's Poems." *Irish University Review* 9 (1979): 62–91. Rpt. Harmon, *Image and Illusion* 62–91.

———. "Seamus Heaney: The Forging Pilgrim." *Essays in Literature* 18 (Spring 1991): 46–67.

McHugh, Roger, and Maurice Harmon. *Short History of Anglo-Irish Literature*. Dublin: Wolfhound Press, 1982.

McLoughlin, Deborah. " 'An ear to the line': Mode of Receptivity in Seamus Heaney's 'Glanmore Sonnets.' " *Papers on Language and Literature* 25 (Spring 1989): 201–15.

MacMenamin, John. "Irish Politics: Ideologies and Realities." *The Crane Bag* 9.2 (1985): 43–51.

MacNamara, John. "The Irish Language and Nationalism." Hederman and Kearney 124–28.

MacNeice, Louis. *The Collected Poems of Louis MacNeice*. Ed. E. R. Dodds. New York: Oxford UP, 1967.

Macrae, Alastair. "Seamus Heaney's New Voice in *Station Island*." Sekine 122–38.

Mahaffey, Vicki. "The Case against Art: Wunderlich on Joyce." *Critical Inquiry* 17 (Summer 1991): 667–92.

Mahon, Derek. "Poetry in Northern Ireland." *Twentieth Century Studies* 3 (1970): 89–93.

Mahony, Phillip. "Seamus Heaney and the Violence in Northern Ireland." *Journal of Irish Literature* 11. 3 (1982): 20–30.

Malloy, Catharine. "Seamus Heaney's *Station Island*: Questioning Orthodoxy and Commitment." *Notes on Modern Irish Literature* 4 (1992): 22–26.

Marten, Harry. "'Singing the darkness into the light': Reflections on Recent Irish Poetry." *New England Review* 3 (1980): 141–49.

Martins, Graham. "John Montague, Seamus Heaney and the Irish Past." *New Pelican Guide to English Literature*. Vol. 8. *The Present*. Ed. Boris Ford. Harmondsworth, Middlesex: Penguin, 1983. 380–95.

Mason, David. "Seamus Heaney's Gutteral Muse." *Mid-American Review* 4.2 (1984): 101–5.

Mathews, Aidan Carl. "A God in Ruins Part I, Notes on the Fall of the Artist." Hederman and Kearney 777–82.

———. "Modern Irish Poetry: A Question of Covenants." Hederman and Kearney 380–89.

Maxwell, D. E. S. "Imagining the North: Violence and the Writers." *Éire-Ireland* 8.2 (1973): 91–107.

————. "Contemporary Poetry in the North of Ireland." Dunn, *Two Decades* 166–85.

————. "Semantic Scruples: A Rhetoric for Politics in the North." Connolly 157–74.

————. "Heaney's Poetic Landscape." Bloom 19–24.

Mays, J. C. C. "Mythológized Presences: *Murphy* in Its Time." *Myth and Reality in Irish Literature.* Ed. Joseph Ronsley. Ontario: Wilfrid Laurier UP, 1977, 197–218.

Meyer, Carolyn. "Orthodoxy, Independence and Influence in Seamus Heaney's *Station Island.*" *Agenda* 27.1 (Spring 1989): 48–61.

Miller, Karl. "Opinion." *The Review* 27/28 (Autumn/Winter 71/72): 41–52.

Milosz, Czeslaw. *Native Realm.* New York: Doubleday, 1968.

Montague, John. *The Rough Field.* Dublin: Dolmen Press, 1972.

Morgan, George. "Seamus Heaney and the Alchemy of Earth." *Études Irlandaises* 14.1 n.s. (June 1989): 127–36.

Morrison, Blake. "Out from the Shoal." Rev. of *Field Work,* by Seamus Heaney. *New Statesman* 9 Nov. 1979: 722–23.

————. "Speech and Reticence: Seamus Heaney's *North.*" *British Poetry Since 1970: A Critical Survey.* Ed. Peter Jones and Michael Schmidt. Manchester: Carcanet, 1980. 103–11.

————. "Young Poets in the 1970s." *British Poetry Since 1970: A Critical Survey.* Ed. Peter Jones and Michael Schmidt. Manchester: Carcanet, 1980. 141–56.

————. *Seamus Heaney.* London: Methuen, 1982.

Mullan, Fiona. "Seamus Heaney—The Poetry of Opinion." *Verse* 1 (1984): 15–21.

Mulloy, Eanna. *Emergency Legislation: Dynasties of Coercion.* Derry: Field Day, 1986.

Murphy, John A. "Further Reflections on Irish Nationalism." Hederman and Kearney 304–11.

O'Brien, Conor Cruise. "Nationalism and the Reconquest of Ireland." Hederman and Kearney 95–100.

O'Brien, Darcy. "In Ireland After *A Portrait.*" *Approaches to Joyce's "Portrait."* Ed. Thomas F. Staley and Bernard Benstock. Pittsburgh: U of Pittsburgh P, 1976. 213–37.

————. "Seamus Heaney and Wordsworth: A Correspondent Breeze." *The Nature of Identity: Essays Presented to Donald E. Haydon by the Graduate Faculty of Modern Letters, the University of Tulsa.* Ed. William Weathers. Tulsa: U of Tulsa P, 1981. 37–46.

————. "Piety and Modernism: Seamus Heaney's *Station Island.*" *James Joyce Quarterly* 26.1 (1988): 51–66.

O'Driscoll, Denis. "Remembering the Past." Hederman and Kearney 420–23.

O'Grady, Thomas B. " 'At a Potato Digging': Seamus Heaney's Great Hunger." *Canadian Journal of Irish Studies* 16 (1990): 48–58.

O'Malley, Padraig. *The Uncivil Wars: Ireland Today.* Boston: Houghton Mifflin, 1983.

Ó'Murchu, Máirtin. "Whorf and Irish Language Politics." Hederman and Kearney 326–30.

Parini, Jay. "Seamus Heaney: The Ground Possessed." *Southern Review* 16 (1980): 100–123. Rpt. Bloom 97–120.

———. "Poet of Ireland: The Poetry of Seamus Heaney Is about Ireland but Speaks to Us All." *Horizon* June 1984: 26–27.

———. "The 'Co-opted and Obliterated Echo': On Heaney's 'Clearances.' " *Salmagundi* 80 (Fall 1988): 71–75.

Parkin, Andrew T. L. "Public and Private Voices in the Poetry of Yeats, Montague and Heaney." *Arbeiten aus Anglistik und Amerikanistik* 13.1 (1988): 29–38.

Paulin, Tom. *Ireland and the English Crisis.* Newcastle upon Tyne: Bloodaxe, 1984.

———. *The Riot Act: A Version of Sophocles' "Antigone."* London: Faber, 1985.

Pearson, Henry. "Seamus Heaney: A Bibliographical Checklist." *American Book Collector* 3.2 (1982): 31–42.

Porter, Carolyn. "History and Literature: 'After the New Historicism.' " *New Literary History* 21 (Winter 1990): 253–72.

Press, John. "Ted Walker, Seamus Heaney, and Kenneth White: Three New Poets." *Southern Review* 5 (1969): 673–88.

Quinlan, Kieran. "Forsaking the Norse Mythologies: Seamus Heaney's Conversion to Dante." *Studies in Medievalism* 2.3 (1983): 19–28.

———. "Unearthing a Terrible Beauty: Seamus Heaney's Victims of Violence." *World Literature Today* 57 (1983): 365–69.

Rabate, Jean-Michel. "Bogland: Quelques Tours de Tourbe, de James Joyce a Seamus Heaney." *Critique* 38 (1982): 513–36.

Randall, James. "An Interview with Seamus Heaney." *Ploughshares* 5.3 (1979): 7–22.

Redshaw, Thomas Dillon "RÍ, as in Regional: The Ulster Poets." *Éire-Ireland* 9.2 (1974): 41–64.

Rees, Alwyn, and Brinley Rees. *Celtic Heritage: Ancient Tradition in Ireland and Wales.* New York: Grove, 1961.

Reilly, Kevin P. "Remembering: Irish Poetry after Yeats." *Éire-Ireland* 15.1 (1980): 120–26.

Ricks, Christopher. *The Force of Poetry.* Oxford: Clarendon, 1984.

Riordan, Maurice. "Eros and History: On Contemporary Irish Poetry." *The Crane Bag* 9.1 (1985): 49–55.

Schirmer, G. A. "Seamus Heaney: Salvation in Surrender." *Éire-Ireland* 15.4 (1980): 139–46.

Schmidt, A. V. C. "'Darkness Echoing': Reflections on the Return of Mythopoeia in Some Recent Poems of Geoffrey Hill and Seamus Heaney." *Review of English Studies* n.s. 36.142 (1985): 199–225.

Sealy, Douglas. "The End of Tribalism, Irish Poetry in the Last Decade." *The Crane Bag* 6.1 (1982): 74–84.

Sekine, Masura, ed. *Irish Writers and Society at Large.* Gerrards Cross: Colin Smythe, 1985.

Shapiro, Alan. "Crossed Pieties." Rev. of *Poems: 1965–1975* and *Preoccupations:*

Selected Prose 1968–1978, by Seamus Heaney. *Parnassus* 11.2 (1983/84): 336–48.

Sharratt, Bernard. "Memories of the Dying: The Poetry of Seamus Heaney." *New Blackfriars* 57 (July/Aug. 1976): 313+.

Smith, J. C., and E. De Selincourt, eds. *Spenser: Poetical Works.* Oxford: Oxford UP, 1970.

Smith, Stan. *Inviolable Voice: History and Twentieth Century Poetry.* Dublin: Gill and Macmillan, 1982.

————. "The Distance Between: Seamus Heaney." *The Chosen Ground: Essays of the Contemporary Poetry of Northern Ireland.* Ed. Neil Corcoran. Chester Springs, Penn.: Dufour Editions, 1992. 35–61.

Stallworthy, John. "The Poet as Archaeologist: W. B. Yeats and Seamus Heaney." *Review of English Studies* n.s. 33.130 (1982): 158–74.

Stetler, Russell. *The Battle of Bogside.* London: Sheed and Ward, 1970.

Stevenson, Anne. "The Recognition of the Savage God: Poetry in Britain Today." *New England Review* 2 (1979): 315–26.

Stewart, A. T. Q. *The Narrow Ground: Aspects of Ulster, 1609–1969.* London: Faber, 1977.

Stewart, James. "Sweeney among the Fighting Gaels: Aspects of the Matter of Ireland in the Work of Seamus Heaney." *Angles on the English Speaking World* 1 (Autumn 1986): 7–37.

Stuart, Francis. "Literature and Politics." Hederman and Kearney 77–80.

Swann, Joseph. "The Poet as Critic: Seamus Heaney's Reading of Wordsworth, Hopkins, and Yeats." *Comparison and Impact.* Vol. 2. *Literary Interrelations: Ireland, England and the World.* Ed. Wolfgang Zach and Heinz Kosok. 3 vols. Tübingen: Narr, 1987. 361–70.

Tamplin, Ronald. *Seamus Heaney.* Philadelphia: Open UP, 1989.

Thwaite, Anthony. *Poetry Today: A Critical Guide to British Poetry 1960–1984.* London: Longman, 1985.

Titley, Alan. "Contemporary Irish Literature." Hederman and Kearney 890–96.

Todd, Loreto. *The Language of Irish Literature.* London: Macmillan, 1989.

Toolan, Michael. "Language and Affective Communication in Some Contemporary Irish Writers." Kenneally 138–53.

Tracy, Robert. "An Ireland/The Poets Have Imagined." Hederman and Kearney 502–7.

Ua Clerigh, Arthur. *The History of Ireland To the Coming of Henry II.* Port Washington, N.Y.: Kennikat, 1970.

"Ulster's Differences." *Times Literary Supplement* 15 Dec. 1972: 1524.

Vance, Norman. *Irish Literature: A Social History.* Oxford: Blackwell, 1990.

Vendler, Helen. "The Music of What Happens." *New Yorker* 28 Sept. 1981: 146+.

————. "Echo Soundings, Searches Probes." Rev. of *Station Island,* by Seamus Heaney. *New Yorker* 23 Sept. 1985. 108+. Rpt. Bloom 167–80.

————. "On Three Poems by Seamus Heaney." *Salmagundi* 80 (Fall 1988): 66–70.

Wade, Stephen. "Creating the Nubbed Treasure: *Station Island.*" *Agenda* 27.1 (Spring 1989): 62–71.

Warner, Alan. *A Guide to Anglo-Irish Literature.* New York: St. Martin's Press, 1981.

Water, Donna A. van de, and Daniel C. O'Connell. "In and about the Poetic Line." *Bulletin of the Psychonomic Society* 23 (1985): 397–400.

Waterman, Andrew. "Ulsterectomy." Best Poetry of the Year Selected by Dannie Abse. *Poetry Dimension Annual 6.* London: Robson, 1979. 42–57.

————. "Irish Stew and Flummery." *PN Review* 14.1 (1987): 23–26.

Waters, Maureen. "Heaney, Carleton and Joyce on the Road to Lough Derg." *Canadian Journal of Irish Studies* 14.1 (July 1988): 55–65.

Watson, George. "The Narrow Ground: Northern Poets and the Northern Ireland Crisis." Sekine 207–24.

Watson, Michael, ed. *Contemporary Minority Nationalism.* London: Routledge, 1990.

Welch, Robert. "Some Thoughts on Writing a Companion to Irish Literature." Sekine 224–36.

Westendorp, Tjebbe A. "Songs of Battle: Some Contemporary Irish Poems and the Troubles." *The Clash of Ireland: Literary Contrasts and Connections.* Ed. C. C. Barfoot and Theo D'haen. Amsterdam: Rodopi, 1989. 234–47.

Westlake, John H. J. "Seamus Heaney's 'Punishment': An Interpretation." *Literatur in Wissenschaft und Unterricht* 18.1 (1985): 49–58.

Wicht, Wolfgang. "Seamus Heaney's *Field Work*: The Politics of Poetics." *Zeitschrift fur Anglistik und Amerikanistik* 35.4 (1987): 299–309.

Williams, Rowan. *The Wound of Knowledge: Christian Spirituality from the New Testament to St. John of the Cross.* London: Darton, Longman and Todd, 1979.

Williamson, Alan. "The Values of Contemporary European Poetry." *American Poetry Review* 13.1 (1984): 28–36.

Wills, Clair. "Language Politics, Narrative, Political Violence." *Oxford Literary Review* 13.1–2 (1991): 20–60.

Witoszek, Nina, and Pat Sheeran. "Giving Culture a Kick—Modern Irish Culture Forum." *The Crane Bag* 9.1 (1985): 94–95.

Yeats, William Butler. *The Collected Poems of W. B. Yeats.* New York: Macmillan, 1956.

Zach, Wolfgang. "Brian Friel's *Translations*: National and Universal Dimensions." *Medieval and Modern Ireland.* Ed. Richard Wall. Totowa, N.J.: Barnes and Noble, 1988. 74–90.

Zoutenbier, Rita. "The Matter of Ireland and the Poetry of Seamus Heaney." *Dutch Quarterly Review* 9 (1979): 4–23. Rpt. Bloom 51–68.

❦ Index

Questioning Tradition, Language, and Myth: The Poetry of Seamus Heaney was composed in Stone Serif by World Composition Services, Sterling, Virginia; printed and bound by Thomson-Shore, Inc., Dexter, Michigan; and designed and produced by Kachergis Book Design, Pittsboro, North Carolina.